Conversations with John Banville

Literary Conversations Series
Monika Gehlawat
General Editor

Conversations with John Banville

Edited by Earl G. Ingersoll and John Cusatis

University Press of Mississippi / Jackson

The University Press of Mississippi is the scholarly publishing agency of
the Mississippi Institutions of Higher Learning: Alcorn State University,
Delta State University, Jackson State University, Mississippi State University,
Mississippi University for Women, Mississippi Valley State University,
University of Mississippi, and University of Southern Mississippi.

www.upress.state.ms.us

The University Press of Mississippi is a member
of the Association of University Presses.

First printing 2020
∞

Library of Congress Cataloging-in-Publication Data available

Hardback ISBN 978-1-4968-2875-0
Trade paperback ISBN 978-1-4968-2876-7
Epub single ISBN 978-1-4968-2877-4
Epub institutional ISBN 978-1-4968-2878-1
PDF single ISBN 978-1-4968-2879-8
PDF institutional ISBN 978-1-4968-2880-4

British Library Cataloging-in-Publication Data available

Books by John Banville

Long Lankin. London: Secker & Warburg, 1970; New York: Vintage International, 2013.
Nightspawn. London: Secker & Warburg, 1971; New York: Norton, 1971.
Birchwood. London: Secker & Warburg, 1973; New York: Norton, 1973.
Doctor Copernicus. London: Secker & Warburg, 1976; New York: Norton, 1976.
Kepler. London: Secker & Warburg, 1981; Boston: Godine, 1983.
The Newton Letter: An Interlude. London: Secker & Warburg, 1982; Boston: Godine, 1987.
Mefisto. London: Secker & Warburg, 1986; Boston: Godine, 1989.
The Book of Evidence. London: Secker & Warburg, 1989; New York: Scribners, 1989.
Ghosts. London: Secker & Warburg, 1993; New York: Knopf, 1993.
Athena. London: Secker & Warburg, 1995; New York: Knopf, 1995.
The Untouchable. London: Picador, 1997; New York: Knopf, 1997.
Eclipse. London: Bridgewater, 2000; New York: Knopf, 2001.
Shroud. London: Picador, 2002; New York: Knopf, 2003.
Prague Pictures: Portraits of a City. London: Bloomsbury, 2003; New York: Bloomsbury, 2003.
The Sea. London: Picador, 2005; New York: Knopf, 2005.
The Infinities. London: Picador, 2010; New York: Knopf, 2010.
Ancient Light. London: Penguin, 2012; New York: Knopf, 2012.
Possessed of a Past: A John Banville Reader. London: Picador, 2012.
The Blue Guitar. London: Penguin, 2015; New York: Knopf, 2015.
Mrs. Osmond: A Novel. London: Penguin, 2017; New York: Knopf, 2017.
Time Pieces: A Dublin Memoir. Dublin: Hatchett, 2016; New York: Knopf, 2018.

Books by Benjamin Black

Christine Falls: A Novel. London: Picador, 2006; New York: Holt, 2006.
The Silver Swan: A Novel. London: Picador, 2007; New York: Holt, 2008.
The Lemur: A Novel. London: Picador, 2008; New York: Holt, 2008.
Elegy for April: A Novel. London: Macmillan, 2010; New York: Holt, 2010.
A Death in Summer: A Novel. Macmillan, 2011; New York: Holt, 2011.
Vengeance: A Novel. London: Macmillan, 2012; New York: Holt, 2012.
Holy Orders: A Quirke Novel. London: Macmillan, 2013; New York: Holt, 2013.

The Black-Eyed Blonde: A Philip Marlowe Novel. London: Macmillan, 2014; New York: Holt, 2014.

Even the Dead: A Quirke Novel. London: Viking, 2015; New York: Holt, 2015.

Prague Nights. London: Viking, 2017. Published in America under the title *Wolf on a String: A Novel.* New York: Holt, 2017.

Contents

Introduction

John Banville has been publishing his fiction for over a half-century. In 2005 he won the Man Booker Prize, the most prestigious literary award given in the Commonwealth. His readership has become global, and he continues to be identified as a candidate for the Nobel Prize in Literature. Granted, Banville has not enjoyed the celebrity of, say, 2016 Nobel Laureate, Bob Dylan, but he certainly deserves to be better known than he is in North America. When he eventually is tapped for the Nobel, American readers may not know Banville's many novels, just as many Americans had never read William Faulkner, whose selection was more strongly supported by the French than Americans, before he became a Nobel Laureate. The analogy is not groundless since Banville's novels, like Faulkner's, aspire to be works of art, written for the ages, within an old tradition valuing works with resonance for future generations.

As Banville notes, this aspiration to art carries with it an enormous challenge to achieve perfection, even though perfection is not humanly possible. Unlike Picasso who could create a work of art in less than an hour, art for Banville has been a long labor of love: indeed, he tells us that occasionally he spends a morning crafting one sentence that he finds satisfactory, but even then, he may not be happy with what he has produced. (He often identifies the sentence as the most important human invention.) Similarly, he can spend months with the opening paragraphs of a novel because the function of a novel's opening is to inform his readers how they are to read this novel. Once the novel is finished, he wants nothing to do with it again: were he to reread it—as he never does—he would be even more appalled by its shortcomings. In fact, he tells us that when he walks past a bookstore window displaying copies of his novels, he wishes for magical powers to make the words disappear and give him the opportunity to start over again to get closer to perfection. And when asked which of his novels he likes best, he is likely to choose one, such as *The Infinities*, which he hates least.

Central to Banville's art is the representation of what it means to be alive, to be a human being, to be conscious. Banville strives to achieve that representation of consciousness through frequent appeals to the five senses, often within a single paragraph and occasionally within a single sentence. The fiction to which he aspires is a poetry in prose. More than once in the conversations, he refers to his notion of poetry, as expressed by another writer: "My good friend the late John McGahern, the Irish novelist, used to make a wonderful distinction. He said there is verse and there is prose, and then there is poetry. Since he was a novelist, he said it happens more often in prose than it does in verse."

Banville's style is certainly inappropriate for the speed reader, or those who skim, because, as he reminds us, his readers must focus upon this poetry masquerading as prose. He adds that we cannot read poetry and crochet or plan what we are going to have for dinner, as we might while listening to a piano concerto or looking at a painting. Readers with the honesty and courage to give themselves over to Banville's writing often feel that they have been somewhere for a few hours—*where*, they are not certain—but it felt like Life. It is, incidentally, also the experience of the author himself, whose wife occasionally tells him she is going out shopping and when he hears her return, he says, "I thought you were going out to shop."

Banville's novels could not be more different from the fiction written by his alter ego Benjamin Black. Two decades ago, Banville discovered Georges Simenon's fiction, which most of us would call "detective stories," until Banville tells us, "I hate genre." Genre is for Banville a marketing plan that would consign his novels to the recent ghetto of "literary fiction," as though readers need to be warned off. He would prefer a bookstore in which books were shelved in alphabetical order by the author's last name so that occasionally readers could accidentally encounter a book they might otherwise never have considered, were it in one ghetto or another. To explain why he hates genre, Banville points to Simenon's *romans durs*, or "hard novels," as so exquisitely written that Simenon deserved a Nobel Prize in Literature more than most who have received that Prize in the century or more since it was first awarded. Unlike the British novelist Graham Greene, who wrote not only novels but what he called "entertainments," in part perhaps to excuse these novels whose royalties supported him, Banville emphasizes the difference between his novels and Black's in not only the category of who is likely to read them but the whole range of what we mean when we say "how they are written."

The way the Banville and the Black novels are written is strikingly different. Banville's deep immersion in representing consciousness is understandably slow. He tells his interviewer Chris Morash, "When I write my Banville books, I have to write in longhand because I need the resistance of the page to the nib . . . Handwriting is about the same pace at which I think. When I do the Benjamin Black books, I have to do them straight onto the computer because they need that speed, and they need that fluidity and spontaneity that a word processor gives." This division, Banville conjectures, came out of his evening/night work on a newspaper and his "day job" as a novelist. Black's work and Banville's work both end as novels, without value assessments. Banville recalls a passage in Darwin's journal in which the scientist cautions himself: "no upper," "no lower," to resist the temptations of making value judgments.

As the interviews clearly demonstrate, John Banville is an "Irish" writer of a different sort. He points out that no one "emigrated" from Ireland; they saw themselves, instead, as "exiled" or "self-exiled." The classic "Irish writer" is James Joyce, who exiled himself to Europe to write only about Ireland. Joyce sensed that if he attempted to write his conception of Ireland, without leaving, the actuality of the country would get in the way of his conception of Ireland. Banville has seen himself as "self-exiled," not from Ireland but *in* the country of his birth. He would not live anywhere but Ireland—except perhaps Italy—because he loves the Irish climate and weather with which his spirits are compatible.

In what he considers his first real novel, *Birchwood*, Banville set out to write an "Irish novel," set in Ireland—where else?—and jammed full of every stock character in "Irish" fiction from A to Z to satirize popular notions of "Irishness." Gabriel Godkin, the narrator and main character, with definite features of the author himself, ends with a declaration Banville claims to be the only statement he has ever made in a character who is transparently Banville himself. Gabriel says, "I will stay here, but I will be different from the rest." Banville's strategy backfired, however, when he discovered he had written himself out of a profession and faced a "second-novel" challenge of such dimensions that he would have had to find a replacement for his career as author, just as he turned to writing after deciding as an adolescent that he had no talent as a painter.

Banville's failed efforts as a painter were by no means a waste of his time because painting would continue to play a major role in his own art as a novelist. Countless readers and several interviewers have focused attention upon the frequent appearance of painters in Banville's novels. More importantly, he has risked accusations of arrogance in frequently drawing attention to his novels as "works of art," as he did when he received his Man Booker Prize. In this regard, *Conversations with John Banville* is particularly valuable in the insights the author provides into what he means by that "arrogant" claim.

As a literary artist, Banville reveals that he is somewhat embarrassed to admit he dislikes the novel as a genre. He explains that he has no interest in the elements usually associated with fiction—although he points out that his novels do have plots. In his earlier of two conversations with Hedwig Schwall, Banville celebrates the end of modernism, which he equates with experimentation, in the past century. His argument with that experimentation is that it became a dead end—experimentation for experimentation's sake in Joyce, but *not* in Beckett, whom he sees as on the right track. The early Modernists of a century ago, he feels, would have been better off if they had continued the work of the novelist that Banville identifies as *the* greatest exponent of that form—Henry James—exemplified in Banville's recent novel *Mrs. Osmond*, his sequel to James's *The Portrait of a Lady*. Banville sees James as opening the potential for other fiction, while he feels Joyce's *Ulysses* and *Finnegans Wake* are unlikely to grant a similar legacy to novelists following Joyce.

Unlike some writers, Banville welcomes interviews as an opportunity to talk about his work and offer some strategies for reading his novels. He can seem daunting to some, as we note in the conversations to follow, but less often to those who are less easily daunted. Belinda McKeon, the interviewer for the *Paris Review*—often considered the gold standard of literary interviews—admitted that she got off to a rough start, but the interchange improved measurably. Readers may note the shifting here between "interview" and "conversation." We think of interviews as rather mechanical strategies of confronting an author with a string of set questions the interviewer imposes upon the interviewee to gather information, while the conversation has more give and take, allowing the interchange to open out into what the author might want to talk about, rather than being confronted with stock questions such as, "Who were the writers that influenced your early work?"

The choice between "interview" or "conversation" obviously depends upon the circumstances of whether the interview can take place in the same venue, or will have to be conducted by telephone, Skype, or email exchange. The face-to-face conversation, especially in the presence of an audience, can obviously be livelier, but also more like a performance in which authors feel they must acquit themselves well enough to escape embarrassment or the feeling they are offering "canned" responses. One suspects that an author such as Banville might prefer to provide written responses through email exchange, offering opportunities for more thoughtful answers than the occasionally glib responses of interviewees while performing on stage. Indeed, when a member of his audience asked why there are so many theater people in his novels, Banville responded at length. He stressed how much of our day is spent in varieties of performance and, in particular, how aware *he* is in performing as interviewed author, reminding his audience that he is *not* the writer of the novels back in his literary workshop but the public "author," who knows little more than his readers about how and why he writes as he does. Just as Faulkner, tongue in cheek, told students at the University of Virginia that he had learned he was using symbols he hadn't been aware of but would remember to use them when he returned to his writing in Oxford, Mississippi, Banville is surprised by questions about elements in his writing of which he had not been aware. Seasoned interviewers often become sensitive to the potential damage they might do by making the author self-conscious by bringing the "public" author into awareness of what she or he is doing in that inner sanctum of the writing session itself.

The conversations that follow are arranged in chronological order. Additionally, there has been an attempt to select interviews from throughout John Banville's career, in part, to provide his commentary on the whole continuum of his oeuvre. Not surprisingly, his receiving the Man Booker Prize for *The Sea* brought a measure of celebrity as well as more requests for interviews. An effort has also been made to balance longer conversations with shorter ones, and to provide a mix of published conversations and edited transcriptions.

Additionally, readers need to be aware of two schools of thought on repetition in collections of conversations such as this one. Some editors of these collections are urged to eliminate repetitions that inevitably appear when interviewees forget what they may have said in earlier interviews or feel a point deserves to be repeated. Removing repetitions assumes that all the conversations in a collection will be read from first to last, as though it were a novel. Obviously, that is a faulty assumption. A collection of conversations is inevitably a selection—in this case, from something close to one hundred interviews in which Banville participated. Two volumes, however, were clearly not an option. Furthermore, some very good conversations were simply not available for reprinting.

In the end, these conversations offer a variety of "biography," not of an author's public life, but a sense of what the writer is trying to do, what is important or not, why he or she writes.

EGI
JC

Chronology

1945   John Banville is born on 8 December in Wexford, Ireland, to
        Martin Banville, a garage clerk, and Agnes Banville (née Doran),
        a homemaker. JB attends Christian Brothers Schools for his pri-
        mary and secondary education.

1963   JB graduates from the Christian Brothers secondary school, St.
        Peter's College, in Wexford and begins working as a clerk for the
        Irish airline Aer Lingus.

1966   JB publishes his first short story, "The Party," which he wrote at
        the age of seventeen, in *The Kilkenny Magazine*.

1968   JB travels to America in the spring, courtesy of Aer Lingus, and
        visits Berkeley, California, during the height of the countercul-
        ture revolution.

1969   JB joins *The Irish Press* as a subeditor, a position he holds until 1983.

1970   British publisher Secker and Warburg publishes JB's first book,
        Long Lankin, a collection of eight short stories and a novella.
        Reviewing the book in the *New Statesman*, Stanley Reynolds her-
        alds JB as "a ray of hope for the future of fiction."

1971   Secker & Warburg publishes JB's second book, the novel *Night-
        spawn*, which also appears in America from W.W. Norton.

1973   JB's second novel, *Birchwood*, is published and is awarded the
        Allied Irish Banks Prize from the Irish Academy of Letters. JB
        also receives an Irish Arts Council Macaulay Fellowship.

1976   JB publishes the first of his science tetralogy, *Doctor Copernicus*,
        which wins the Whitbread Prize, the James Tait Black Memorial
        Prize, and the American-Irish Foundation Literary Award.

1981   JB publishes *Kepler*, which wins the *Guardian* Prize for Fiction.

1982   JB publishes *The Newton Letter: An Interlude*.

1983   JB publishes *Reflections*, a film adaptation of *The Newton Letter*,
        directed by Kevin Billington for Channel 4 Television and RTÉ.
        JB leaves his position at the *Irish Press* but frequently contributes

	reviews and other literary articles to such publications as the *Sunday Tribune, Irish Times,* and the *New York Times Book Review.*
1984	JB's first book, *Long Lankin,* is reissued and published for the first time in the United States. The new edition omits the novella *The Possessed* and the short story "Persons," which appeared in the 1970 edition, and adds "De Rerum Natura," a short story which appeared in the *Transatlantic Review* in 1975. JB becomes a member of Aosdána, established in 1981 by the Irish Arts Council "to honor artists whose work has made an outstanding contribution to the creative arts in Ireland."
1986	JB publishes *Mefisto,* the final novel of his science tetralogy. He joins the *Irish Times* as a subeditor.
1988	JB is named Literary Editor at the *Irish Times* and holds this position until 1999.
1989	JB publishes *The Book of Evidence,* which is awarded the Guinness Peat Aviation Book Award and the Marten Toonder Award, and is shortlisted for the Man Booker Prize for Fiction.
1990	JB becomes a regular contributor of essays and book reviews to the *New York Review of Books.*
1991	*La Spiegazione dei Fatti,* the Italian translation of *The Book of Evidence,* is awarded Italy's Premio Ennio Flaiano.
1993	JB publishes *Ghosts,* which, like its predecessor, revolves around the character Freddie Montgomery. The novel is shortlisted for the Whitbread Fiction Prize.
1994	The script of JB's first adaptation of a drama by Heinrich von Kleist, the comedy *The Broken Jug,* is published by Gallery Press in Ireland and is staged at the Abbey Theater in Dublin in June, directed by Ben Barnes. RTÉ television airs *Seachange,* JB's film adaptation of his uncollected short story "Rondo," published in 1977 in the *Transatlantic Review.* The film is directed by Thaddeus O'Sullivan.
1995	JB publishes *Athena,* which forms what he has called a "triptych" with his two earlier novels about Freddie Montgomery, who has changed his name to Morrow in *Athena.*
1996	JB publishes *The Ark,* a limited-edition children's book illustrated by Conor Fallon.
1997	JB publishes *The Untouchable.* His protagonist Victor Maskell is based on the British art historian Anthony Blunt, who confessed to having been a Soviet spy during World War II. The novel

earns JB the Lannan Literary Award and is shortlisted for the Whitbread Fiction Prize.

1999   JB's film adaptation of Elizabeth Bowen's 1929 novel, *The Last September*, is released, directed by Deborah Warner and featuring Jane Birkin, Michael Gambon, Fiona Shaw, and Maggie Smith; Yvonne Thunder produced the film and Neil Jordan and Steven Woolley served as executive producers.

2000   JB publishes *Eclipse*. Gallery Press publishes *God's Gift: A Version of Amphitryon by Heinrich von Kleist*, JB's second adaptation of Kleist, which premieres at the O'Reilly Theatre during the Dublin Theatre Festival on 12 October, directed by Veronica Coburn. RTÉ television airs *Undercover Portrait: John Banville* produced by Orpheus Productions and directed by Michael Garvey. JB publishes *The Revolutions Trilogy*, which collects the first three books of his science tetralogy: *Doctor Copernicus*, *Kepler*, and *The Newton Letter*.

2001   JB resigns from Aosdána, wishing to create a spot for an artist who might make better use of the position. JB publishes *Frames*, which collects his three Freddie Montgomery books, *The Book of Evidence*, *Ghosts*, and *Athena*, in one volume.

2002   JB publishes *Shroud*, which is longlisted for the Man Booker Prize. The Kilkenny Theatre Festival features a one-man adaptation of *The Book of Evidence*. The Ark in Dublin stages JB's children's play *Dublin 1742* on 5 June. BBC Radio's The Verb airs *Stardust: Three Monologues of the Dead*.

2003   JB publishes *Prague Pictures: Portraits of a City*, his first book of nonfiction, for Bloomsbury's "Writer and the City" series. The one-man theater adaptation of *The Book of Evidence* has an extended run at Dublin's Gate Theatre.

2004   BBC Radio 4 airs JB's radio play *Kepler* on 11 August.

2005   JB publishes *The Sea*, which wins the Man Booker Prize for Fiction and is named the Irish Book Awards "Novel of the Year." Gallery Press publishes JB's third Kleist adaptation, *Love in the Wars: After Kleist's Penthesilea*. RTÉ television airs JB's *A World Too Wide*, a radio play based on the sixth of William Shakespeare's "Seven Ages of Man" from the comedy *As You Like It*.

2006   JB follows his Man Booker Prize–winning novel, *The Sea*, with *Christine Falls: A Novel*, the first of a series of crime novels written under the pseudonym Benjamin Black. In her laudatory review in the *New York Times* Janet Maslin described the novel as "crossover fiction of a very high order." BBC4 airs JB's radio play *Todtnauberg*, a fictional conversation between the poet and Holocaust survivor Paul Celan and the philosopher Martin Heidegger, who had been a member of the Nazi party. JB receives the Premio Grinzane-Francesco Biamonti Prize.

2007   JB is awarded a Royal Society of Literature Fellowship and the Prix Madeleine Zepter. He is also named a Foreign Honorary Member of the American Academy of Arts and Sciences. JB publishes *The Silver Swan: A Novel*, as Benjamin Black. RTÉ television airs *Being John Banville* produced by Ice Box Films and directed by Charlie McCarthy.

2008   JB publishes *The Lemur: A Novel* as Benjamin Black. Gallery Press publishes a limited edition of the script from *Todtnauberg* titled *Conversation in the Mountains*.

2009   JB publishes *The Infinities*.

2010   JB publishes *Elegy for April: A Novel* as Benjamin Black. *The Sea* is shortlisted for the Irish Book of the Decade by the Bord Gáis Energy Irish Book Awards.

2011   JB is awarded the Franz Kafka Award and publishes *A Death in Summer: A Novel* as Benjamin Black. A film adaptation of George Moore's 1927 novella, *Albert Nobbs*, which JB wrote with Glenn Close and Gabriella Prekop is released, starring Close and Janet McTeer, who were nominated for Academy Awards for Best Actress and Best Supporting Actress, respectively.

2012   JB publishes *Ancient Light*, his fifteenth novel writing as John Banville and *Vengeance: A Novel*, his sixth as Benjamin Black. Picador publishes the voluminous *Possessed of a Past: A John Banville Reader*, edited by Raymond Bell, which includes excerpts from Banville's fiction (but not Black's), as well as radio and stage scripts, essays, reviews, lectures, and works in progress.

2013   JB is awarded the Irish PEN Award for Outstanding Achievement in Irish Literature, the Austrian State Prize for European Literature, and the Bob Hughes Lifetime Achievement Award from the Irish Book Awards. He publishes *Holy Orders: A Quirke Novel* as Benjamin Black.

2014   JB publishes *The Black-Eyed Blonde: A Philip Marlowe Novel* as Benjamin Black. He wins the Prince of Asturias Award for Literature.

2015   JB publishes *The Blue Guitar* as John Banville and *Even the Dead: A Quirke Novel* as Benjamin Black. JB's film adaptation of his 2005 novel, *The Sea*, is released featuring Sinead Cusack, Ciaran Hinds, and Charlotte Rampling.

2017   JB publishes *Mrs. Osmond: A Novel*, as a sequel to Henry James's *The Portrait of a Lady*. JB publishes *Prague Nights* as Benjamin Black; the American edition is titled *Wolf on a String: A Novel*.

2018   JB publishes his second nonfiction book, *Time Pieces: A Dublin Memoir*.

Conversations with John Banville

John Banville:
A Bio-Bibliographical Guide

Contemporary Authors / 1988

From *Contemporary Authors*. © 1990 Gale, a part of Cengage, Inc. Reproduced by permission. www.cengage.com/permissions. *CA* interviewed John Banville by telephone on 9 February 1988, at his home in Dublin, Ireland.

Contemporary Authors: The first thing that strikes me about your fiction is its poetic texture and sound. And it abounds in quotations from and allusions to poetry. Has poetry played a major part in your desire to write and your development as a writer?

John Banville: I read more poetry than I do prose. I suppose I regard poets as being more of an influence than prose writers, yes.

CA: Were you reading poetry early?

Banville: Yes. Adolescent reading—Keats, Dylan Thomas, that kind of thing. I don't mean that they are just for adolescents, but that's the kind of poetry that adolescents read. I like the dense texture that poetry has, and I'd like prose to have that kind of density. I'd like prose to make the same demands on the reader that poetry does.

CA: A concern with the possibilities and limits of order runs throughout your fiction, not only in its themes but also in the way you shape the writing. How early in your formal education or your own reading did you begin consciously to examine the idea of order?

Banville: *Consciously* is a very difficult word. I think that, as Wallace Stevens says, we have a rage for order, and I think that must have been very deeply built into me from the start. But it's not a kind of conscious artistic motivation or methodology that one uses. These are very deep desires that one has, and I don't know that I've ever examined them very closely. I think an artist really delves into these areas at his peril.

CA: You do like testing the limits of the novel form, as you've said before this interview.

Banville: I've never liked the novel as a form. I read very few novels, and most of them that I read, I don't like. I don't like what Henry James called the "loose baggy monster," the novel as a form into which everything can be thrown as into a portmanteau. I don't say that such things shouldn't be written; some of the great masterpieces have been written in that form. But it's not something I would do. I don't even like the kind of length that a novel normally has to be in order to be published and to be accepted by the public. This may seem a somewhat trivial way to look at it, but people's expectations of what an art form should look like and feel like are very important.

So, from the start I didn't particularly like or trust the novel form, and I fought against it for a long time. I still do, I think, although lately I find, I suppose with encroaching age, I begin to accept it a little more. But I think that an artist has to keep pushing against the form and not just sink back into it as into a kind of maternally comforting catch-all for his ideas.

CA: Perhaps some of the restrictions put on the novel form are arbitrary anyway.

Banville: Curiously enough, I don't know that I agree. There is a peculiar internal mechanism in works of art, in the same way that an elephant is really about the biggest that living creatures can get to be—otherwise, the animal would simply fall over because of the force of gravity. I think that works of art are the same way. They have their absolute limits. I'm inclined to think that a novel like [Leo Tolstoy's] *War and Peace* is probably the biggest elephant there has been! In our time, or near our time, Thomas Mann began to play with the form of the great epic nineteenth-century novel. I liked the way that Mann treated the form, and for a while I was interested in doing that, certainly when I was doing *Doctor Copernicus*—even the title is a direct reference to Mann's *Doktor Faustus*.

At the moment, I don't quite know where I am. I suppose I've reached a watershed. I was doing a series of four books—*Copernicus, Kepler, The Newton Letter,* and *Mefisto*. When I finished *Mefisto*, in April of 1986, I suddenly realized that I was free to do whatever I wanted to do, which for an artist is the worst possible position to be in. It's absolutely terrifying. As long as you have a scheme, a program, you know what you're doing, but when suddenly you're free, it's a terrifying prospect.

CA: How were you attracted to the scientific figures as subjects for fiction?
Banville: I began in the early seventies. When I finished *Birchwood*, which was my third book and my second novel, I couldn't see any way to go forward. For a while I was going to give up fiction. At the time I was reading people like Hermann Broch, and in a way *Doctor Copernicus* was, not influenced by, but certainly got some of its motivation from Broch's *Death of Virgil*—and, as I said, Mann's *Doktor Faustus*.

But the scientific aspect is probably for the most part taken too seriously. I don't really care all that much for science per se, but as a mode of thought and as a way of dealing with the world, it attracts me very much because it seems to me very like art. Scientists seem to think in the same way that artists do. You asked me earlier about the notion of order. Copernicus and Kepler certainly were obsessed with the notion that they could find the secret order of the universe, and it seems to me that this is what artists try to do all the time. It's an absolutely impossible task. It can't be done because I don't really believe that there is any order. But it's the pathos of that quest that fascinates me, the pathos of highly intelligent human beings who know that the world is built on chance but are still going ahead, saying, "I will not accept this: I'm going to manufacture order, if necessary, and impose it on the chaos." That attracts me very much. So, in a way you could say that talking about science was a way of talking about art, without actually going through the boring thing of talking about a man who's writing a book about a man who's writing a book about a man who's writing a book. . . .

CA: I'm interested still in the fact that those were real people whom you dealt with in fictional form. Did they have to be separated somehow, in your mind, from their factual existence to work in the fictional treatment?
Banville: Yes, I suppose they did. I had to find out something about them as they existed in history, and then I had to invent them. Copernicus was difficult because there's not very much known about his adult life. I mean, he was difficult from the point of view of doing the research, but he was quite easy because one could invent anything. With Kepler it was the opposite problem. There is so much known about him that I had to suppress a lot of what I knew. His life was so extraordinary and fraught with so much grotesque comedy that fiction simply wouldn't be able to sustain it; only life could sustain that kind of fictional invention. For instance, in my Kepler

book, the time that he spends defending his mother against the charge of witchcraft is quite short. In fact, Kepler gave something like eight years of his life to that. And then the old lady upped and died about six months after he got her off anyway. His life was so fraught with tragedy.

Apart from anything else, it's very difficult to write about someone so far away from us in the past. My touchstone always was to say to myself, "Imagine what a toothache was like in that period." They had different expectations from ours. For instance, infant mortality was so high that the death of children, while it was awful, wasn't the absolute tragedy then that it is now. It didn't destroy your life the way it would destroy your life nowadays. So, it was very difficult to try to make him acceptable to readers in the 1980s, and, therefore, one necessarily had to invent the man himself.

CA: Obviously you did a great deal of research to create the social and political settings of the books about Copernicus and Kepler.
Banville: Not half so much as it may seem.

CA: Was there a point with each book when you knew unequivocally that you had the setting right in your head so that you could convey it to the reader?
Banville: I was never very interested in getting the period right. I was halfway through writing *Copernicus* before I realized that I was writing a historical novel and that I had to give some attention to the historical details. It never interested me. Really, all novels are historical. Any novel that's in the past tense is historical. You have to create a time and a place. Creating the fifteenth century is really not any more difficult than creating 1983 because it's a specific world. If I write about Dublin in 1988, it's a specific world, and I have to make it universal. It has to be possible for someone in Japan to read about Dublin in 1988 and know exactly what it feels like, what it tastes like, what it smells like. It's just the same task as writing about the fifteenth century. This is something that's hard for people to understand, I think, but it is the case. You really only need a few facts. I had to read a few things; I had to get the history right; I had to look at a few paintings by [Hans] Holbein; I had to read up about what people wore and what the houses were like. But these are really trivial details which never interested me very much.

CA: *Mefisto*, your 1986 book, has in common with the earlier book *Birchwood* a hero named Gabriel, and other parallels can be drawn between the two stories and the two main characters. Was the second Gabriel an offspring of the first, in your mind?

Banville: I wanted to signal the fact that I was finished with a particular series of books, which went from *Kepler* to *Copernicus* to *The Newton Letter* to *Mefisto*, and that I was now, I suppose, in a way coming back to Ireland, that I was going back to something that I was doing before. I don't really know what the significance of that is. *Mefisto* was an odd book for me because it was the most instinctual book that I had done. I let things happen in *Mefisto* even when I didn't know why they were happening or what I was doing; I just said, "Well, it seems right, so I'll do it." I had never done that in any previous book—except, I think, in *Birchwood*, where things did happen because they just sounded right. It was a kind of personal return, a personal revisionism almost. So, I consciously gave the second Gabriel the same name. But one shouldn't read too much into it. It's simply a personal touchstone.

CA: In the *Irish University Review* for spring 1981, a special John Banville issue, there's the text of a talk you delivered at the University of Iowa. Do you have extensive contact with other writers and with writers' workshops?
Banville: Oh no, practically none. That was a particular thing, which I did essentially because I was offered it, and I got some free time from the newspaper where I was working to go off to the States for a while. I enjoyed it and it was interesting, but it's by no means part of a pattern. I've chosen to stay in Ireland, which means inevitably that one is isolated, certainly from the European mainstream, which is what I would look towards.

Most Irish writers have either to emulate or fight against the tradition of the English novel, the novel as written in England. I've always tried to go beyond that and look towards Europe and towards America—not because of any nationalism or anti-British feeling, but simply because I feel that, artistically, my roots are in Europe—and I suppose the future is in America.

But I have not very much contact with other writers. There has always been a tradition of the great literary social life in this country, of going to pubs and talking the night away and so on, which I think is terribly dangerous. It's certainly helped to destroy a lot of people here. *That* world has ended, I think, that world of Brendan Behan and Flann O'Brien and so on.

CA: Does being an Irish writer put one automatically at risk of being treated in a narrowly national context by reviewers and critics?
Banville: Frequently I wish that I were a real Irish writer, because then I would be reviewed and treated as such. As it is, I am regarded as a kind of hybrid. This is a very small country. We have pretensions to internationalism, but it really is still a very provincial little place. If you don't write about

the Ireland of today directly, you're not regarded as being a real writer. But, of course, abroad one is regarded as an Irish writer because one comes from Ireland, and therefore as being provincial. I find myself caught between the two extremes, which makes it difficult.

A couple of my books, *Birchwood* and *Kepler*, have done very well in America, which is gratifying. And for a while I think I was selling more books in Germany in English than I was selling in Ireland. It's very difficult for a writer to talk about his own position. I don't know how to comment on how people regard me, if they regard me at all. But I think that eventually, perhaps not in my time, the books will have some kind of life.

CA: Are you doing any newspaper work now?
Banville: I used to work for the *Irish Press*, and I left there in 1983. Then I had about four years when I didn't work. But I couldn't make enough money to live, so I've gone back and I'm working at the *Irish Times* now as a subeditor. It's a four-day week, which allows me a lot of free time. It's a good way to earn a living, and it means I don't have to make a huge effort to sell books to publishers. It allows me a lot more freedom. This is essentially what one does if one works: one is just buying freedom.

CA: Your work has won honors, including the Allied Irish Banks Prize, an Irish Arts Council Macaulay Fellowship, the Irish-American Foundation Literary Award, the James Tait Black Memorial Prize, and the *Guardian* (London) Fiction Prize. How well do literary awards in Ireland serve to support the country's writers and direct attention to their work?
Banville: Most of the awards that I've won have been in England, certainly the ones that people take any notice of, the James Tait Black Memorial Prize and the *Guardian* prize. Literary awards usually don't do anything for writers. They do something for publishers, I think; they sell books. But you'd need to win at least one large one a year for them to do anything for you. And people forget very, very quickly. It's Andy Warhol's saying everybody's famous for fifteen minutes. You win a prize and you get your fifteen minutes, and that's it. In a way it's bad because that is your fifteen minutes; people think, Oh, yes, he's the guy that won the such-and-such prize, and therefore they know you—you're placed. It's then not necessary to read you. It's really different in the States. There you get these extraordinary prizes like the MacArthur Fellowship. But I would be very fearful of something like that. I think I would probably never write a word again. It could be crippling. Still, I'd like to try it—for a while, anyway!

CA: You told Rudiger Imhof at the end of an interview published in the previously mentioned issue of *Irish University Review* that "if we can keep our nerve, the novel is only beginning to explore its own possibilities." Do you see the novel's possibilities as capable of continuous evolution?

Banville: Curiously enough, I think that depends more on readers than on writers. The business end of that statement is "if we can keep our nerve." If one is content to look beyond one's own time and say, "The work that I'm doing now, if it can survive—even in a few libraries, in a few paperback editions— eventually will have its life," then yes, I think the novel is capable of all kinds of things. But I don't see many people whose nerve is holding at the moment. And this is not to put myself up as a paragon, because my nerve frequently cracks.

I think that certainly the novel is an extraordinary form. It's got everything: poetry, prose, music, the visual. You can put all the arts into the novel form. But it requires a huge amount of discipline and a huge amount of artistry to make art rather than a huge baggy monster. If enough artists are willing to give the time and the effort to press on the form hard enough to make it produce works of art, then yes, it can do it. But in a way that phrase in the interview was whistling in the dark. I don't think it's actually going to happen. I think the novel probably is finished. It's the youngest art form of all, and I think it's going to be the first to die.

I think the novel was invented for a specific time, invented for the eighteenth and nineteenth centuries, when a whole middle class was trying to invent itself, the mercantile class in England and on the continent. The handover of power from the aristocracy to a middle class was such a huge and slow change, and the art form created by that particular historical shift was the novel. Well, that shift has been completed. The middle class is now triumphant, and all kinds of other things are happening.

The novel really doesn't have an audience. The audience for novels hasn't increased since the beginning. In Britain there have always been about two or three thousand people who would read novels consistently, and that audience is still there; it goes on from generation to generation. Any decent novel that is not hyped by publishers and the radio will sell about two or three thousand copies to that audience. In Jane Austen's time, if she sold two or three thousand copies of a novel, she knew that she was speaking to the people who ran the country. Nowadays it's not like that; it's quite the opposite. It's the odd, marginal people who are reading novels—still very good people, but not the people with the political power.

So there just isn't a function for the novel anymore—that kind of nineteenth-century novel—and it has to change into either a poetic form or a documentary form or something else; it can't continue to pretend that the nineteenth century is still going on. What was invented and what was achieved can still be used, can be pushed into new directions. The way that I'm trying to go is to turn the novel into something that would have the density and force of poetry without being poetic—in the sense of being about moons and Junes and so forth—simply by the force and concentration of the work. I don't know if it's possible; it may not be. It's a continuing experiment that I'll be going on with until I drop.

There are encouragements. Certainly, Samuel Beckett in his trilogy [*Molloy*, *Malone Dies*, and *The Unnamable*] achieved an extraordinary poetry that had never been done before, and I think he's a continuing and great example of what it's possible to do with the form. He took the novel and threw out all the ballast, all the accretions that had gone up around it in the nineteenth century, and just kept a few props—a bicycle, a bowler hat—and made extraordinary poetry out of them. We don't get many Becketts, but he is a living example of what it's possible to do.

The Beauty and the Tenderness of the World

Douglas Glover / 1995

Printed with the permission of Joseph Donahue, WAMC/Northeast Public Radio; Suzanne Lance, NYS Writers Institute; and Douglas Glover, who has published four novels, five story collections, and three works of nonfiction. In 2003 Glover won the Governor-General's Award for Fiction, and in 2005 his novel *Elle* was a finalist for the International IMPAC Dublin Literary Award. His most recent book is *Strange Love* (short stories, 2013). He edited the annual *Best Canadian Stories* from 1996 to 2006. He published the literary magazine *Numéro Cinq* from 2010 to 2017.

The following interview was produced and aired by WAMC Public Radio in cooperation with the Writers Institute at the State University of New York. The telephone interview was conducted on 23 August 1995, and aired on 29 August 1995, with a radio audience.

Glover: Welcome to *The Book Show*. I am your host, Douglas Glover, of the New York State Writers Institute, University at Albany, State University of New York. My guest is the Irish novelist John Banville, speaking to me from his home in Howth, just outside Dublin.

John Banville is an author singularly unafraid of the stigma of hyperbole and baroque excess; his novels are littered with flamboyant pathologies, decaying families, waifish women inviting the whip or the hammer, drunken, ineffectual males, and orphans, real or figurative, that move through an atmospheric fog of drift, and dread worthy of the great Gothic masters. Known best in North America for his historical novels *Kepler* and *Doctor Copernicus*, Banville has lately returned to the Irish setting of his earlier books—for example, *Birchwood* and *Long Lankin*—a fantastically sterile, degenerate place of crumbling aristocracy, mythically dysfunctional families, murder, incest, drunkenness, and mega-alienation, a land of such hyperbolic scabrousness that it becomes a kind of comic, Beckettian endgame of metaphysical loss.

Banville's last two novels have centered on a character called Freddie Montgomery; in *The Book of Evidence*, published in 1989, Freddie, drinking too much and down on his luck, tries to steal a painting from a squire's country house and ends up murdering the maid with a hammer. In *Ghosts*, published in 1993, free after serving ten years in prison—a life sentence in Ireland— Freddie turns up on a sparsely populated island where he has been hired as a secretary to an aging professor whose specialty is a little-known Parisian painter named Vaublin. The plot—if it can be said there is a conventional plot in *Ghosts*—turns on Freddie's abortive love affair with a waifish young woman dropped ashore by a drunken ferryboat captain. Now, Freddie's back, in a new Banville novel called *Athena*, just published by Alfred A. Knopf. This time Freddie surfaces in Dublin under an assumed name—Morrow—hired by a man called Morden, who works in a street called Rue, to authenticate a cache of seventeenth-century paintings on classical themes. *Athena* is knee deep in conventional plots: there is an art fraud plot—something out of *The Rockford Files* with a cop called Hackett and a sinister transvestite gangster called Da; there is a plot of sexual obsession and sadomasochistic love between Freddie/ Morrow and a girl called A; and there's a tender, astringently touching plot involving Freddie's elderly Aunt Corky, though not a blood aunt—the connection is vague and largely syntactical—who moves into his dingy two-room flat to die. In the background lurks a mysterious serial killer who drains his victims' blood. And yet for all this plottish hyperbole, *Athena* is a kind of echo chamber of comic despair, in which everything seems fated or written by another hand, where gods toy with humans and turn them into beasts, where a miasma of solipsism hangs in a world of dreams, where reality and dream haunt each other, and mysterious lost children, doubles, and putative parents hover just out of focus (though one is constantly aware of them as force fields, as emanations, magnetic, incestuous, and invisible).

John Banville, welcome to the *Book Show*.
Banville: Thank you.

Glover: Thank you. Did you like that?
Banville: Well, I hardly recognized myself—hardly recognized my work from your description.

Glover: Really?
Banville: Oh yes. I mean, people do say that my work is full of hyperbole

and grotesqueries and exaggeration, but, to me, my work is completely realistic. This is the world I see when I look about me. If the reader were to look closely enough, and carefully enough at their own world, they would see it largely in my terms. We do live in a ferocious world; we live in a kind of civilized jungle. I see my books as a true reflection of that world.

Glover: Now, that actually makes sense to me, but the books themselves are very complex constructions full of complex thematics: there are the art theme, the crime theme, the sex theme, and the truth/fraudulence theme, plus the comic plotting, the manic despair, the seediness, and the gothic romanticism. A teeming hyperreality with a humorous twist. And then— and I hate to say this because it seems reductive—there's also a thoroughgoing critique of modernity itself.
Banville: Yes, there is a critique; there is humor; of course, I think that . . .

Glover: When you're sitting there are you being serious, or do you chuckle to yourself as you're writing these . . .
Banville: Well, of course, nobody chuckles to themselves when they write—it's such a horrible business anyway that you just grind your teeth—but it would be fatal to enjoy one's own work. That would be the beginning of the end. But I do see the books, certainly *The Book of Evidence*, as comedy, which surprises and even angers quite a few people. But I do see it as a comedy in the sense that the narrator, Freddie, who is a killer and a thief and generally a bad lot . . .

Glover: That has one of the great murder scenes in literature, when he . . .
Banville: Yes, I do quite like that scene, but it is comic, as well. Comic in a ghastly sort of way. But I do see it as a comedy because comedy to me is a form in which a character erects a vast panoply of what he thinks of as reality, which is in fact a self-delusion. And the comedy comes from the fact that he doesn't see that it's a self-delusion. In a way, *The Book of Evidence* has to be read twice: once just to read it and a second time to find out what it's about. But every work of art deserves at least two looks.

Glover: Oh yes. Just as an aside, is Morden, the character in *Athena*—that's not an anagram for "modern," is it?
Banville: No, no. There's trouble when you read a book, which is full of anagrams and games and tricks, that you do begin to get paranoid, and you think everything is a game and trick, but sometimes, as Freud said, a cigar is just a cigar.

Glover: In all three books, there's a nexus of motifs—a collection of paintings, a woman who is very sexual in her vulnerability and waifishness, and Freddie, in this last book, *Athena*, called Morrow—and I haven't completely penetrated what is going on here, but the paintings are all on classical themes; they're paintings that date roughly from the beginning of modernity, and in *Ghosts* and in *Athena*, especially, you hint that some of the characters are people who have walked out of the paintings. Is that true?

Banville: Yes, all three books deal with painting because—*The Book of Evidence* says it in its title—this is evidence. This is what we look at, it's what we see, and it's the surfaces of things. In *The Book of Evidence*, Freddie says, "On the surface—that's where there's real depth." And it is taking art as essentially superficial but in a very complex usage of the word *superficial*. All three books are first-person narratives. They are what the first-person narrator sees; he makes no pretense to knowing what is behind the surface of what he looks at, essentially the state that art is in. In terms of art, when I hear the word *psychology* I reach for my revolver. I don't believe that art is a psychological weapon. It is a matter of surfaces, but in that surface, there is extraordinary depth. All the books are, at one level—and I emphasize at one level and not a terribly important level—sort of essays or excursions on the nature of art itself. And the medium I chose is one that is as far away from the novel as it is possible to get—painting.

Glover: And you play constantly with the rereading of the paintings and the idea that some of them might be fraudulent. Vaublin is a painter whose biography is given in *Ghosts*, and he is haunted, late in life, by someone who is imitating him.

Banville: Yes, and in *Athena*, the narrative is punctuated by two-page descriptions of specific paintings. And these descriptions are written as if they were catalog entries: the style is very dry, academic. But there are lots of jokes lurking in there as well.

Glover: Jokes and foreshadowings and reinterpretations of the actual plot that's going on.

Banville: And there are eight paintings but seven descriptions. And at the end he realizes, I think—at least I realized when I came to the end—that there couldn't be a description of the eighth painting because the book itself is the eighth painting.

Glover: Which is *The Birth of Athena*?

Banville: And the eighth painting is the only one—I think, again, I'm not quite sure of this—that the eighth painting is the only one that is authentic. Of course, *authentic* is a difficult word.

Glover: Right. Because it could have been painted by the false Vaublin. That's not mentioned in the book, but of course it's always a possibility.

Banville: Yes, that is one of the questions about doing three linked books: How much does each depend on the other two?

Glover: I don't think they do depend on each other in a strict sense, but there are so many jokes and inside references that it's fun to read the books back and forth.

Banville: Yes, certainly I've talked to a few people who have read only *Athena*, and they say, "Yes, it's self-contained," and they don't feel that there are two missing links. If they were to go back and read the other two, they would get a lot of the jokes and a lot of the references, and there would be, I hope, an increase in the aesthetic pleasure, which, after all, is what one sets out to provide.

Glover: In that catalog listing, some of the paintings, even the titles of the paintings, are suggestive: "The Pursuit of Daphne," "The Rape of Proserpina," and this brings me to the woman in the novel. In every novel, the maid from *The Book of Evidence* appears; in some ways, it's the same woman showing up again and again. Only in *Athena*, she has a very large role, and she's a kind of mysterious, waifish, very contemporary kind of woman in a black dress, with almost perpetually bruised lips, and she and Morro—Freddie—embark on this strange and mysterious relationship, almost a parody of a Victorian sex book, where they go deeper and deeper into a kind of sadomasochistic performance. And yet, she is also, in some way, tied up very much with his sense of who he is. She's also apparently come out of the painting. When the paintings disappear, she disappears. It's a very strange relationship.

Banville: Yes, there are two things to be said about A, the woman character in *Athena*, one of them quite simple at least, it's simply said, I don't know if the implications of it are simple—but it's only that I noticed when I'd finished the books she is never there, really, when there are other people about. If she's in a room with him and someone else appears, she's suddenly gone. As you read the book, you don't quite notice she's simply vanishing into thin air, so one begins to wonder if she does exist at all. The second thing to be said about her is much more important in terms of the three books taken as a whole, and I *do* think of them as one book, really. In *The Book of Evidence*, he kills a woman and practically everything he encounters is described in minute detail, except one thing, the woman he kills. The only thing we ever find out about her is her blue eyes. And she is simply something that gets in his way, and he swats it out of his way. And, as he himself says, he killed her because he could, because of the failure of his imagination; he failed to imagine her into reality, he failed to create her for himself, as we all have to do with other people; we have to create a version of them. If we fall in love, it's a version pretty close to what the other person thinks he or she is. But we do have to invent our own versions of people to find any kind of compact with them. And this is what he doesn't do in *The Book of Evidence*, and he's therefore able to kill this woman. In *Ghosts*, the second book, he is in a kind of hell, or, as there used to be in Catholicism, in a kind of purgatory. And he's there. He's an old-fashioned Catholic, and he's spending time, an incoherent time. This is one of the things that made *Ghosts* difficult for people to read, because they couldn't quite figure out what was going on, because the fact is that nothing is going on. This is a man in freefall, and he's just turning on the spit of his own guilt, punishing himself. In *Athena*, he realizes that he has to re-create a life, fill the space he emptied by killing the woman in the first book. And he fills this space by imagining this woman, to such a degree, that she begins to exist, even if she doesn't exist in reality, by that extraordinary act of the imagination, describing her, looking at her. As he says, she'd never been looked at in this way before, and he brings her into a kind of reality. Of course, the only reality that she can have is the reality of art. She exists as an artistic object in the same way that the pictures exist as artistic objects. The pictures, all of them, except one, turn out to be frauds. Or at least, fakes, there is a difference. And it's a question at the end of the book—and, of course, art never provides answers, only rephrases questions—whether she does exist, or what kind of reality she exists in. Certainly, the reader will have an extraordinarily vivid sense of her physicality but no sense of her as a human being because, of course, as we discover at the end, she's been telling him a pack of lies throughout the book—which he has willingly fallen for.

Glover: And even suspected.
Banville: That's the artistic process. It sounds more complex than it is; it's really quite simple.

Glover: I understand that. The simplicity is not exactly concealed, but there is a surface complexity and beauty to this. I'm sure people have said this to you: you're so at ease with this material there's a danger of appearing to be *only* playing games. But what you're doing *is* a critique of modernity, and you're creating a sense of the individual, the great invention of modern times, who, when he looks at himself very closely, turns out to be nothing—to be evanescent, to be empty. And there's a line in the book, when Freddie's talking about A: "No, it is not the anima lost in me that I am after, but the ineffable mystery of the other," and then parenthetically I can hear your ribald snigger. And there is this sense of doubling and then finding emptiness there that turns into a kind of melancholy, which suffuses these books.

Banville: Yes. His effort from the start of *The Book of Evidence*, through *Ghosts*, to *Athena*, is to find some sense of authenticity, some authentic self, some version of himself . . .

Glover: Which is the effort of the modern.

Banville: Yes. Yes, it is. At the end of the three books, it is in question whether he has found anything of himself. Certainly, he mellows as the books go on—he's not quite as violent a creature in *Athena* as he was in *The Book of Evidence*. But the curious thing about the reception of *Athena* is that people take Aunt Corky—this aged aunt that he takes care of—as a merely Dickensian decoration on the book. Actually, after finishing the book, the more I thought it's not about A, the woman he has an affair with, at all, but it's about Aunt Corky. Because while he is busily trying to make A come alive, artistically, physically, sexually, he's helping Aunt Corky to leave the world, to die. And by some curious, paradoxical ethics, the effort of helping Aunt Corky to die is infinitely more important and more rewarding to him than his love affair with A. The old woman dies, and she proves to be a bit of a fake, as well. But she has more reality, and certainly more authenticity, than A, and that reality, and that authenticity, reflects on the narrator and gives him a tiny possibility of redemption at the end. It may be an artistic flaw in the book that she is not emphasized enough. Now, I'm hoping that she's lying there like a kind of landmine, and that, eventually, in time, if the book is given time, if it lives, I hope that Aunt Corky will be seen as much more important than she's been seen.

Glover: There is a melancholy tone coupled with a sense that Freddie/Morrow is a sad clown; there's this Keatonish or Chaplinesque quality to him. Since you're Irish, it feels that this characteristic comes down to you from Beckett. Is that true, or is that being reductive?

Banville: Yes. I think that all Irish writing is at a certain level—again, I would emphasize "at a certain level"—comic. And the Irish vision, insofar as one can ever speak of a national vision, is essentially comic, in a very melancholy, sometimes self-destructive way. When I set out to write a scene, which inevitably will have to be tragic or sad or pathetic, comedy will creep in. But this is not something that I impose on the books. It's what I get from life. To me, the tragic and the appalling are always attended by the most grotesque comedy. All you have to do is look in the right corner of the room and something grotesque and comic will be going on. It's a matter of choosing. All art is a matter of choosing what to say, which aspect of a scene to emphasize. And, of course, this is where the artist shows his hand. But life to me seems comic in a melancholy and a very beautiful way. I have to emphasize that one of the main things I'm after in the books, in art, is a sense of the beauty and the tenderness of the world. Freddie himself has a part in *The Book of Evidence*—and this is about the only piece of fiction that I've ever written that is absolutely my own view—where he says the world wasn't meant for us, that we're here by some kind of cosmic blunder, because the world is too tender and too gentle to contain people like us. And he asks, "What about the people who were meant for here? These gentle Earthlings over there on the other side of the galaxy?" And he says, "No, they would have been extinct long ago." Because how could they have survived in a world that was meant to contain us? And I do believe that. One only has to look at the newspapers or the television news, especially these days, when a new miniholocaust is happening in the midst of Europe. This is bathos to bring in vast tragedies to illustrate an artistic point, but it's more than an artistic point that I'm making. It's a point that life itself seems to me a hellish thing, and the world seems a hellish place and, yet, a place vibrating with beauty and tenderness as well. It's just a strange paradox that we're caught in. It's what makes life interesting, precious. And that's one of the main things I want to communicate in the book. As I said of your description of my "gothic imagination" at the start, I don't see it that way. I see it merely as trying to present the world—the world that I know—to present it in all its vividness.

Glover: With that, I'm afraid we have to close. And thank you very much for being on the show.

Banville: Thank you.

An Interview with John Banville

Hedwig Schwall / 1997

The interview appeared in the *European English Messenger* 6.1 (Spring 1997): 13–19.
Reprinted by permission.

Hedwig Schwall interviewed John Banville 28 December 1996, in the Shelbourne Hotel, Dublin. Banville had just finished his latest novel, *The Untouchable,* to be published by Picador/Macmillan in May 1997.

Hedwig Schwall: The protagonist of your new novel is a spy, I'm told, but also dealing in art?
John Banville: Yes. It is loosely based on the figure of Anthony Blunt, one of the Cambridge spies.

HS: Loosely based on a given life, as with your other protagonists?
JB: Oh, very loosely, indeed, because I gave Blunt the poet Louis MacNeice's life. They were good friends at school, Blunt and MacNeice. Blunt was an expert on the painting of Poussin, and when I was doing research, I opened up Louis MacNeice's *Selected Poems* and the first poem was called "Poussin," so I thought this was a good omen.

HS: So, the next novel is again dealing with paintings?
JB: Yes, but not as much as the previous ones. It's a straightforward book, really; I'm surprised.

HS: So, with a real plot?
JB: A real plot, *yes*!

HS: But one taken from some biographies.
JB: Yes. I couldn't resist the story. This man was leading a double life, and

he was fascinated by art and fascinated by betrayal. It seemed to me I had to follow this path.

HS: The previous books, constituting the trilogy, also deal with these themes, but each novel had more poetry than plot, it seemed to me. When you write these trilogies, do you conceive them as such from the very start?
JB: No, not quite. I planned to do a tetralogy with the science books; I planned that from the start. I didn't think there would be two more books after *The Book of Evidence*, and, in fact, when I began to write *Ghosts*, I didn't realize the voice of Freddie Montgomery from *The Book of Evidence* was going to come back into it. I had a lot of trouble. I couldn't get past that first chapter. And then that voice just began to speak again. And when I finished the book, I realized there had to be a third one. It had to be an arch shape, with *Ghosts* as a kind of central stone. But I'm not sure I was right; maybe *Athena* was one book too many.

HS: I wouldn't say so; it's the one I prefer. But which of the three do you like most yourself?
JB: *Ghosts*, I think.

HS: Why?
JB: Because it is such a failure.

HS: Why should it be a failure?
JB: Because it had to be. Because the narrator, Freddie Montgomery, is trying to construct a world, and, naturally, he can't. Therefore, the book has to fail. It couldn't be as neatly rounded as *The Book of Evidence* or *Athena*. It had to be open-ended. There is no reason for the book to start where it starts, and there is no reason for it to end where it ends. It could just go on forever, so it's kind of a bleeding chunk. The character of Flora faded out because he could not construct her. That's why there had to be *Athena*. He had to set a woman in the place of the one that he killed.

HS: In discussing this book with friends and colleagues, we came to the conclusion that A was not a real woman but an invention of the narrator, like Flora.
JB: I think so. A disappears every time other people appear. She literally disappears, and she disappears from a room that has only one door. So, yes, I think she doesn't really exist.

HS: On the other hand, it is a very physical relationship?

JB: *The Book of Evidence* is a very physical book. It *is* a book of evidence; everything he comes across he describes in great detail. Except for the woman he kills. There is no description of her. All we know about her is that she has blue eyes. And when she speaks, she speaks in a very stilted, unidiomatic way. So, he has destroyed her virtually by the fact that he hasn't imagined her sufficiently enough to exist. In *Ghosts* he is trying to find ground to stand on. He's in purgatory, and he's trying to find a solid corner in it. And he can't. In *Athena* he has to imagine a creature into existence. You know Rilke's poem about the unicorn? [not the poem from the *Neue Gedichte*, but poem IV of *Die Sonnette an Orpheus*, Part 2] "This is the creature that there never was." It is a beautiful poem. In the end, because of the maiden's concentration on him, the unicorn begins to be. This is the way of *Athena*. It was quite difficult to do, because A has to be physically palpable—but not present. She's even less present than the unicorn in the poem, for all the precise description. In a way, all three books are about images in Freddie's imagination.

HS: Talking about Rilke, I had the impression *The Book of Evidence* is a kind of translation, a prose version of "Archaischer Torso Apollos." The brooch is looking at the onlooker, parts of the Dutch woman are looking at him, as the parts of the "Archaischer Torso" are looking at the observer.

JB: Yes, Rilke goes throughout the books. There are direct quotations from Rilke. [laughs]

HS: Very often you start a novel with some famous quote and then you stop. Like opening *Ghosts* with the setting for *The Tempest* or starting *Mefisto* with Yeats's "Leda and the Swan," but then you don't sustain the references. Is that just a game, or is there some system in it?

JB: It's a game. *Mefisto* has Yeats, Joyce, Beckett—everybody is there on page one. I always think of the first paragraph of a book as like one of those decorated initials in the *Book of Kells*.

HS: Apart from the Irish masters, you seem to have a predilection for German literature? One finds Hofmannsthal in your work, Thomas Mann, and the Licht-figure in *Ghosts*.

JB: I took the name from Kleist's *The Broken Jug*. Kleist is one of the very great artists of the modern era. It's a shame that especially in the English-speaking world he is hardly known at all. That's why I did my version of *The Broken Jar*, to get him on the stage here.

HS: Kleist was a writer who was a profound thinker, well-read in philosophy. Your books, too, seem to owe much to philosophers, like Nietzsche and the poststructuralists. Do you also read Lacan?
JB: I haven't read Lacan. I should.

HS: I ask because in *The Book of Evidence* you seemed to insist on a difference between "meaning" and "significance," which is a difference that is rather prominent in Lacan's first seminar. How do you see that difference?
JB: I would see "meaning" in the sense of an explicable, translatable content. You cannot translate a "life" into another medium. I cannot translate my life into "story," "image." I can only *live* my life. So, it has no meaning; there is no meaning you can extract from it. But it has "significance." Do you see what I mean? This is why art is always artifice, because the work of art has a beginning, a middle, and ending. Lives don't. We don't know much: we don't remember our birth, we don't experience our death. All we have is this stuff in the middle, whereas a work of art is closed. Even the most "chaotic" work of art is closed, simply by virtue of the fact that there is a start and an end. Nothing is translatable, really. I don't think anything has meaning, in the sense that I define it. One of Nietzsche's most profound observations is that the notion of "the identical" is completely spurious because nothing is identical, really. Everything is absolutely unique. That's an extraordinary statement to make at the end of the nineteenth century.

HS: As with meaning and significance (respectively, deception and promise of understanding), you always try to differ between knowing and understanding. You do it in *Kepler*, in *The Book of Evidence*.
JB: We know everything; we've been given all the information, but nothing is *explained* to us. It can't be. This is the only reason for doing art: to show the absolute mystery of things. Knowing is having information; understanding is absorbing it, internalizing the world. This is one of the reasons why I'm fascinated by Rilke, who says the task of the human being is to "destroy" the world—you internalize and thereby transform it.

HS: So, it is with reading Lacan: you do not understand it but it works, and you do something with it. Or one is like an alchemist—Rilke's Alchimist, who is a "Laborant," a worker—who has to put the world into himself through some kind of distillation?
JB: Yes.

HS: You always talk about truth in your last trilogy, truth being always, of course, a highly problematical thing. How would you try to define it?

JB: I am becoming very, very interested in American pragmatism, beginning seriously to read Emerson. There is a line from Emerson through Nietzsche to modern pragmatism. Defining truth within pragmatism is very attractive to me because it says that truth is what works, is what's useful. There is no absolute truth. And if there is, it is of no interest or no use to us. And, even though I have been *very* interested in European philosophy since I was a teenager, I was always troubled about the way in which philosophers try to build systems. Even philosophers I love, for instance, Schopenhauer, are obsessed with building systems. It always seemed ridiculous because, if you build a system, you have to make things fit into it. This is very much the case with *Kepler*; there is a deep influence of European philosophy on the Kepler of my book, because he devises a system, then tries to put all cosmology into it and it won't fit, though the system is fine, and it works. Kepler's intellectual journey is to recognize that the system is manmade, that *he* made it, and it sustains *him*. And it sustains many things; it "saves the phenomena," as the scientists say. A philosophy like Nietzsche's *fits the world*. With most philosophers and scientists, the world has to fit their system, rather than the other way round. Nietzsche has very great admiration for people like Emerson. He was one of the few philosophers he did admire. Emerson is strange. I think he is a poet in prose. And I think Nietzsche is a poet as well. I don't really know if even he is a philosopher. . . . So, I suppose I believe in the poetic philosophers.

HS: So, you would agree with Derrida that real philosophers are literary?

JB: Oh, yes.

HS: And vice versa. Would the opposite be true too, really good writers being philosophical?

JB: I think a writer like me is infected with "the idea." It's a kind of sickness. It would be better just to be an artist and not to be bothered about ideas. Beckett was fascinated by philosophy, by ideas, but artistically he weaned himself away from it and took all the ideas out of his art. And that way he got very close to a kind of "pure art," which in a way is philosophy by virtue of being antiphilosophical. Some of his late work is just pure statement of "being." It's the kind of thing Heidegger tried to get at in his involuted, weighty style, whereas Beckett in these marvelously simple, light works at the end

of his life actually lets "being" "free" and actually makes "a house for being."
I think that's the ideal of what the artist should be. That is the reason I have
written this relatively straightforward novel. It was a watershed for me; I
could go in a completely different direction. I've always been fascinated by
the possibility of taking the form of the popular novel and turning it into an
art form. That's what I have been trying to do since the start, with more or
less success—maybe less. A book like *Athena* has a plot and characters and
so on, but also poetry.

HS: It is very straightforward, but there is also that fascination with "reality."
JB: Yes. It's doing things beneath the surface of the plot.

HS: That seems the ideal way of writing. But that's what Joyce does in his
early work: *Dubliners* and *The Portrait* give a story, but the symbols abound.
Yet, in the talk you once gave on a Joyce Colloquium you call *Portrait* a
problematical book. Why?
JB: Because I don't believe in it, I think it's a pose.

HS: I'm sure it is, but it is a well-staged pose.
JB: Yes, it is, but I think it's dishonest. I think Joyce is putting forward things
he does not actually believe in artistically. He is setting up an aesthetic. But
an artist's aesthetic is something he sets up but in the end throws away. I do
have great difficulty with Joyce. I find him very uncanny; and very . . . (very
long pause) I find him dishonest, in a strange, complicated way.

HS: Why dishonest? Why should a writer not experiment with language to
see what comes out? Or do you think he made up too much of a system, out
of other systems, as in *Ulysses* and *Finnegans Wake*?
JB: His books are much too systematized. But that was his way of working;
I wouldn't blame him for that. But I think he was damaged by modernism.
When I look at *Ulysses*, I think of that novel that could have been, instead
of the one he wrote. If he'd continued to write that book the way he wrote
the first chapters . . . but he just destroyed it. There is something in him that
wants to destroy his own systems. But not in the Beckettian way. Beckett
sets out to fail. But Joyce's ego is such that he has to succeed, and he has to
spoil what he has done. You can see it in *Ulysses*; you can see it going wrong.
The stylistic experiments for me don't work. I can admire it; I think it is a
very great achievement, but I feel that there is an even greater achievement
lost, an even greater book lost, by his fascination with experiment. He was

surrounded by a lot of very stupid, fashionable people, especially in Paris. People like Gertrude Stein and the Crosbys and a lot of little people who ran little presses and who were in love with modernism. Joyce was lionized; he became the god of modernism. And I think now, at the end of the century when modernism has died, we see that it was a real shift in art; it was just a blip on the screen. Now the novel has gone back to traditional narrative. Whether that's good or bad, I don't know, but I think modernism has come to an end; it has run its course. I am fascinated by the question of what would have happened if there had been no modernist movement. Let's say if there had been no Ezra Pound, no Freud, no T. S. Eliot, none of the theorists, no T. E. Hulme, and if the novel (let's leave music and painting aside), if the novel had followed the Jamesian route, what would have happened? Because James was doing what modernism attempted to do and failed. James was writing before Freud, and he was writing extremely perceptive psychological studies, which were also extraordinarily finished, closed works of art. To me, the work of art is always closed. It doesn't invite the reader, or listener, in. It is spectacular. It stands. It says, I'm here. James managed to make novels that were psychologically profound but which were also closed works of art. There is a profound mystery about the best of Henry James's books, even though they are perfectly comprehensible. The object itself stands in its own mystery. And I suppose I have been following that Jamesian line rather than the Joycean line. Because I think Joyce is a dead end. *Finnegans Wake* is a dead end.

HS: Once you said that James and Catullus are the people from whom an apprentice can really learn a lot; whereas Virgil and Joyce are the ones you stand in awe of.

JB: Yes. An artist has a duty to make art that may help people coming after; I'm not attacking Joyce on this level. *Ulysses* seems a completely closed work, one that is trying to be open. Take the Molly Bloom monologue at the end. I hate it. It is completely fraudulent. Technically, it's . . . miraculous. But it is a fraud as well. It is . . . spurious in its affirmations. It just sets my teeth on edge. Give me Beckett any day. Because Beckett is saying something that I consider closer to how things are. The Molly Bloom monologue is very cunning—well, all of Joyce's work is cunning. But I don't love it; I don't like it. Whereas Beckett was a mystery. These differences are complicated, but important. Because every Irish writer has to take one of these two directions: you have to go into the Joycean direction or the Beckettian direction. And I go in the Beckettian direction.

HS: And in that of James?

JB: And James. The book I am finishing at the moment owes more to Henry James than it does to Beckett or Joyce. You see . . . the first people I began to read when I was an adolescent were P. G. Wodehouse, Evelyn Waugh, Graham Greene . . . more traditional storytellers. That is the direction I am taking now.

HS: You started delving into literature from very early on. Did you see a literary future then, from early on?

JB: Certainly, an artistic future. I began to write when I was about twelve. First, I wrote short stories, imitations of *Dubliners*. And then I got frustrated with that and I tried to paint—when I was about fourteen, fifteen. I had no gift. I made rubbish—but it was good to do. Very good exercise. Makes you look at things in a particular way. They were efforts to get away from the world in which I lived. I was very, very solitary. I had very little contact with my family, even though I lived amongst them. They couldn't understand my concerns, and they had no interest. There were no books in the house I grew up in—no real books. I may at some stage write a kind of autobiography. I might use the biography to write a novel. [laughs] But at the moment, I can't see any use for that world. It was very disturbing, really. There was no present, and now there is no past. Everything was future for me, and an artistic future. I saw from very early on that I was much more interested in *expressing* life than living life. Things only became real for me when they are felt through art, when they are *expressed*. And that's a very Irish thing. The Irish are obsessed with language. All our public scandals have to do with language. If a politician does something dreadful, the scandal will be about how he explains himself, not about what he did, but about how he accounts for what he did. It always goes back to language. When Mary Robinson was running for president, her opponent did something awful. I forget what it was. He said that "on mature recollection" he realized he had done this thing. Everybody remembers this phrase "on mature recollection." Few can remember what it was he did. But we can all remember his performance on television when he made a fool of himself and lost the election. It didn't matter what he had done; what mattered was that he had failed to explain himself well enough for us to forgive him. Look at the talks in Northern Ireland at the moment. It's all about how it is going to be expressed, what is going to be said. Everybody wants to know what is going to be said before it is said. And then they'll agree to it . . . say it.

HS: So, it's all politics of the word?

JB: Absolutely. This is why we're not good in painting, in music . . . It's language we are obsessed with.

HS: Your novels, it seems to me, are composed around characters, or say *figures,* because they are no real characters, rather carriers of ideas?

JB: I never had any interest in character (that is, in fiction). Freddie Montgomery is a mere voice, no character. These figures carry the pattern of the books. When Graham Greene was judging some prize *The Book of Evidence* won, he complained that there is nobody in the book he would remember. And I thought, Absolutely right. This is what I wanted. When I did *Birchwood,* my first real novel, I deliberately chose stock characters, caricatures, the beautiful, suffering mother, the hard-drinking, cruel father, the sensitive son, the ghastly grandparents, the comic servants, and I put them all in a big house, the most clichéd thing in Irish fiction. And then I tried to subvert the type, to make something else out of it. The only direct statement I've *ever* made in any book that I have written is at the end of *Birchwood,* where the protagonist says, "I'll stay in the house, and I'll live a life different from any the house has ever known." And that is my statement. I stay in this country, but I'm not going to be an Irish writer. I'm not going to do the Irish thing.

Interviewing John Banville

Laura P. Z. Izarra / 2002

From *Kaleidoscopic Views of Ireland*, ed. M. H. Mutran & L. P. Z. Izarra. São Paulo: Humanities, 2003. 227–47.

Laura P. Z. Izarra conducted the following interview in Sao Paulo, Brazil, 31 July 2002. John Banville had been invited to the University of Sao Paulo by organizers of the International Conference for the Study of Irish Literatures to speak about his work not only to an audience of 150 scholars of Irish literatures from various countries, but also to his Brazilian readers. Translations of his novels into Portuguese have established him as one of the most important contemporary world novelists.

Laura Izarra: John, do you consider yourself an international writer? Has this influenced you in any way? Would you say that the value of writing lies in its globalicity as well as its locality?

John Banville: When I wrote *Birchwood* back in the early 70s, I considered that to be my Irish novel, and I didn't know where to go after that. In fact, I was going to give up writing fiction and do a variation on historical writing; then I remembered I had read Koestler's *The Sleepwalkers* when I was a teenager, and I found a renewed interest in Copernicus and Kepler. I conceived this grand idea, a tetralogy of three tragedies and a satire on classical grounds. I saw myself very much in the tradition of the great European novelists; I didn't want to keep writing the Irish novel over and over again. I was in my twenties and saw myself very much in the heroic mode. My wife keeps reminding me I didn't actually leave Ireland; I didn't go into exile. But then, no Irishman has ever emigrated; he has always gone into exile. I decided, like the great Ruskin, to go into internal exile. I find the only way to get really away from Ireland is to live there. I suppose I see myself in some kind of international way. But it sounds so pretentious to say this kind of thing. Mostly, people ask me with deep frowns on their faces, how I deal with the criticism that I'm not an Irish writer. And I say I wouldn't regard this as criticism unless I could see how it works. Because if you write in Hibernal English and you're an Irish writer, what's the subject?

LI: How would you describe your way of seeing literature? Would you say that the novel is a great intellectual synthesis with a hybrid form (echoing Bakhtin's definition of polyphonic narrative)? If we take *Kepler* as an example, the reader realizes that you were very concerned with shape and how it works aesthetically.

JB: That's a big question. I suppose I should say once more, and this is a heresy, but I don't actually like the novel form very much. I'd rather have been a composer. But it always strikes me as remarkable that the novel form, the youngest form, is the one that seems to have been used up very, very quickly, indeed. After Henry James, after Flaubert, after *Ulysses*, is there very much left to do in the novel? What I thought I would do is take a form of the popular novel, and try something new on a thesis, something new in Ireland as well, that I would use this mode of thinking. I've always been infected with the virus of new ideas, probably the worst possible thing for a novelist. T. S. Eliot was right when he said it is no business of the artist to think but to feel and express, and I think that's true. I've always had big difficulty fitting ideas into fictional form. I suppose it's what keeps me going, writing too many books. When I see them on the shelves now, I have a pink wash of shame. So many mistakes, so many sins. But I keep doing it.

I find more and more that writing fiction is very, very like breathing. My brain doesn't wake up until about two o'clock in the afternoon. I can't tie my shoelaces before noon. I can't make a cup of coffee in the morning, but I can write. It's the kind of thing that carries over from the dream world into the world of fiction. The best analogy for writing a novel is one of those life-changing dreams you have four or five times during your entire lifetime, those dreams that seem to contain everything you mean and everything you are—even though you can't understand them. You get up the next morning and tell the person across the breakfast table, and, of course, after two sentences this person begins to yawn because there's nothing more boring than other people's dreams. But if you tell the person, "All right, I'm going to spend three to five years writing this dream in such a way that when you will not be reading about the dream, you will actually *have* the dream. That is my way of doing fiction. And I think anything less than that is really not worth doing.

LI: The intangible world . . . the world of perception . . . the world of dreams . . . coincidences. How do you deal with this in your everyday life and in your fiction?

JB: When I was younger, when I thought I knew everything, I thought everything moved rationally. The older I get, the more confused I get, and I find this confusion quite creative and stimulating. I like the confusion I am in, that gradual sleepiness that comes over you as one gets into what Gore Vidal calls the "springtime of senescence." I'm approaching midsummer now. My brother who is eight years older has nothing but beautiful dreams now, soft, caressing dreams. And he feels it's gentle death's way of saying, "Let's start preparing for the end, for the brilliant light, by taking little sips of the brilliance in the night." And I like that state, find it very creative.

LI: What fascinates me as a reader is the opening of your novels.

JB: I believe that a work of art has its own language and every novel has to teach the reader how to read in a new way. I spend a great deal of time with the opening pages; the first paragraph of *Mefisto* took me about six months. I was looking for a tone, for a launching pad. Once you've got the tone, once it clicks, you can hear it here in your head. I spend a lot of time getting the rhythm right, to get the reader used to the rhythm. Auden said, "The poem is the only work of art that you either have to take or leave." You can't read a poem and do your knitting, as you can do when you are listening to a piece of music or looking at a painting or reading a novel. What I've tried to do is make novels that have that same denseness and make the same demands on the reader as a poem so that the novel says to the reader, "You really must not skip any of this, and you must read this in a particular way." There is one form of a novel that continues to be written, and so it should, in which you can pour everything: questions of society, politics, morals, the way we live now, anything. There is another kind of fiction, which is my own, closer to poetry than to prose. "There is prose, there is verse, and there is poetry, and poetry can happen in either form," John McGahern says. "But mostly in fictional form."

LI: Could you tell us about the source of your themes, and is there a relationship between theme and the construction of the characters?

JB: There is in each book I write a progression from one to another; before I finish a book, the next book is started in my head. I have a terror of not having a book going, of having it on a low boil.

LI: Could you talk about your beliefs in the effects of humor? How does it work?

JB: I think the books are funny, and nobody else does. I do funny books that are grotesque, but life is grotesque. Three or four years ago, I was driving through Dublin the day after Christmas day. The city was entirely empty; everyone was home sleeping off their meals. I was driving on Pearse Street, a long straight avenue, entirely empty, not another soul, just me driving the car, and three albino men standing on the street corner having a conversation. And I thought, if I wrote that in a book, they would all say, "Oh, there's Banville." I thought, Where did they come from? Is there some sort of a convention?

My mother's death was tragic, the first close relative I had lost, probably the most important person in my life as I was growing up. But the day of her death was an absolute farce. She died of a heart attack while strolling out in the garden. I was the first who was taken to the hospital. They showed me the wrong body, which looked very like my mother. The doctor said, because it was a formal identification, "Is this your mother?" And I spoke, "Not unless death can leave you looking strange," and I could see him looking down the corridor, saying, "Oh Jesus!" looking for the porter, who came around the corner with another trolley, like a salesman, saying, "Try that one," and *that* was my mother. And it got more and more grotesque because we decided that we would not have an open coffin. The next day, when the people came for what's called "the removal of the remains"—an absolutely wonderful phrase. I love that, I think I'm going to call a book *The Removal of the Remains*—in a little chapel attached to the hospital, I was the first to walk in. And there, in an open coffin, was the woman they had shown me first the day before. I was in horror, and I felt I should stand in front of the coffin and go [gestures with his hands waving others away]. Perhaps I was saving myself from grief by recognizing the grotesque humor. My mother would be highly amused by the whole damned thing. She would have loved to hear that story, and she did hear it somewhere. But that seems to be life. When people say, "Your books are grotesque," I say, "Have you looked around you lately?"

And just to finish this answer, yesterday I was saying to a TV interviewer that the only direct statement I've ever made in any of my books is in *The Book of Evidence*, when the character says, "I've never gotten used to being on this earth. I think that our presence here is a cosmic blunder. I think that we weren't meant for this gentle world. It is too nice for us. We must have been put here by mistake." And then he [the character Freddie Montgomery] wonders about the people who were meant to be here. Are they homesick and lost like us? And he says, "No, of course, they'd be extinct by now because how could they survive in a world meant for us?" That's true, I have never got used to the extraordinary beauty of this world; we are richly undeserving. God knows we are the most dangerous species in the universe.

Questioner: You've talked about the beauty of this world. Am I right in thinking that somehow in the midst of your desire to construct order or have your characters construct order—though they are never able to—if you believe there is a great beauty in the chaos and that the chaos is necessary to the order and that we can't be whole unless we embrace the darkness. That seems to be in your books.

JB: Imagine how dull life would be if we did things completely rationally. Asymmetry is even in science. Physicists are coming to realize that asymmetry is an absolute necessity in the universe. It is the creative impulse. It may have been the impulse that started the whole bloody business in the first place, some imbalance in empty space, some tension. The rage for order, the divine creator, all of that is constantly undermined by the glorious incoherence of reality. The carnivalesque keeps breaking in. And I wouldn't have it any other way. We think we would love to have an ordered life—we say, "next year." Teleology is the way we live. We keep thinking there will be an end, a point at which to come to a complete rest. Everything will be perfect, the sun will shine, my family will love me, they won't require me to do things that I'm incapable of doing, and everything will be nice. The end comes, as we know, but that's not what we are seeking. And, when people say, as they frequently do, that my books are cold, passionless, and so on, I think, What books have they been reading? [laughs] Because, to me, the books are awash with shameful emotion; they embarrass me they are so raw, with all the things that keep battling upon me and keep me alive. I don't think there's any point in making art unless it's an effort. You say let the darkness in, but for artists, letting in the light is probably more problematic. Felix is a character perhaps of darkness, but he's quite funny, not all evil, wickedness.

Q: Most of your protagonists are either professional actors, or they are clearly histrionic and acting for themselves. Question one: Is this acting integral to your idea or belief? And question two: Does this have anything to do with your fascination with *commedia dell'arte*?

JB: I think it's in every book, in one form or another: characters stop and say that everyone else knows the secret, a huge secret but so simple that nobody can tell me; it can't be put into words. They just stand back and look at me and say, "Isn't it a pity that he doesn't know?" I suspect we all feel that; I know I certainly do. And, of course, they *act*. Look at this gathering. Have you smiled so many times in the past year as you have in the last three days? Everybody is nice; everybody smiles at everybody else. It's a wonderful thing to do, of course. But people put their face on when they are smiling. And that awful moment when you arrive home late at night, after another reception, another dinner, and you are slightly drunk, but you are still smiling. Your face is fixed. [crowd laughs] And you open your door and go in and fall face forward across the bed. You feel your face cracking like a glass mask. Then you say, "Never, fecking Jesus, never again." Because of the strain of pretending, as the English poet Philip Larkin said he would never be this perfect, and he wouldn't do poetry readings because he refused to go about the country pretending to be himself. And this is what I do: I sit here impersonating. As I sit here, I feel that I'm actually sitting somewhere beside myself, looking on in amazement and some embarrassment, and a certain contempt as well for the person sitting here, giving these glib answers to questions really looking for something more than just a performance. But I think that I have never learned how to step down off the stage. I suspect none of us do.

The Book of Evidence is immensely popular, especially in Ireland, not only for what it seems to be about. It's a book everybody can understand, easy to read, funny, and so on. This time people said, "Freddie's angst is exactly how I feel, and he recognized it too." Essentially, the inauthenticity of the self, the so-called "self," because there is no self. I don't believe there is a private self that we call the soul. The psychologists and psychiatrists have a name for it, but I don't believe there is any single coherence. Nietzsche has pointed out "there is no being; there is only becoming." There is no point at which we can stop ourselves or take a cross-section of ourselves and say, "That's me." There is no point. Even as I'm giving you this answer, I'm changing because I'm making tiny, tiny adjustments all the time. There's never a point of rest until the last moment arrives. I often look at the books and think, God Almighty, I keep hammering away at this bloody cliché: everybody knows we're all actors. Why do we keep on with the masks? I'm going to stop that and write a simple book about my childhood. I'm going to start again. Now that I have been practicing for about forty-five years, I think

I'm just beginning to learn how to write. So, I can now move on and start writing what I should have tried to write when I was seventeen or eighteen and see if I can apply the knowledge that I've gained, the knowledge that I have made words work; apply it. There will be no masks, no actors, no business of the theater, and I realize that's absolute nonsense. Of course, they'll be masks; of course, they'll be actors; it will be the same bloody book again in a different form.

But what was the second question? Oh yeah, have I a fascination with *commedia dell'arte*. You know, I do. I was talking to Fintan [O'Toole] yesterday about the theater, and I was saying, theater, to me, has to be carnivalesque. It has to have a great carnivalesque sense of excess; life is too much; the world is too much. It can't be contained in this form. And to some extent, I try to do that in fiction as well. I love the notion of *commedia dell'arte*. I love the notion of mask. I don't take it terribly seriously. A friend of mine who is a photographer was doing a series of photographs about the Carnival in Venice. We were going to do a book together, but the plans fell through. I would love to have written something about all those people she knew who came down and spent a fortune on their costumes and their masks for the few days every spring in Venice. And I love that notion, and I also love shallowness. That's where the real depth is, in the surface. Wasn't it Nietzsche again who said, "Give a man a mask and he will believe in the truth"? And Yeats, of course, recognized that it's only when you get the mask that you become real; you become authentic. I love the irony of that.

LI: This morning you mentioned that your favorite book is *The Newton Letter*. What is it that gives you so much pleasure in that book?

JB: It's not that I think it's particularly good, but it's the book that ended up being as close to the initial conception as I ever got. Technically, it is quite well done. It's a misconception that I love every sentence in the book. The narrator is wrong about everything, just continuously wrong, exuberantly wrong, and, of course, the narrator has absolutely nothing to do with all his mistakes. That's why I selected it as my "favorite." It's probably no coincidence that it is short rather than long because I probably succeed at distances as a sprinter rather than a long-distance runner. But I like the way it moves; it's rather cold, but I liked it for technical advances.

LI: Could you tell us something about your new projects and your new book that is coming out?

JB: The new book is called *Shroud* because it's largely based in Turin. It is not a sequel to *Eclipse* but a kind of parallel because it's in part the story of Cass Cleave's last months. She is a character in *Eclipse* who dies in the end of *Shroud*. It's a lot of other things as well. I don't want to think on it. I hate it, of course, especially in the period between having finished it and its being published. You think, "If only I could haul it back and do it right." But then I've said that many times before. I have this fantasy that I'm passing by a bookshop and I wave a wand and click my fingers and all my books go *clickety-clack* so that I can start it again and do it right the next time.

Shroud will be coming out in October, and then I'll have to start again very quickly. When I send a book to the publisher, I have a week of absolute panic, when I think I'd like to say to them, "Ignore that one. I'll write another one very quickly. I'll work for the next four months, and I'll give you a better one." Radical. Very insecure. Later, I'm doing some possible film projects. I'm writing a book about Prague, which is an interesting thing because I've never done that kind of writing before. But it's almost a relaxation to work that way. I've probably taken on much too many things, and I'll probably be a raving lunatic by Christmas trying to keep up with these projects. I must be going through a phase; it must be the change of life. Maybe I'm finding some new direction; I really don't know, but I find it interesting to watch my progress over the next few years. If I don't fall on my face in the meantime. Writing is like anything else in life. We think we are making decisions, making plans, but we really just drift into doing things. I'm also the kind of person who can't say, "no." If somebody asks me to do a project and will give me money to do it, then I just can't say, "no." I have to keep working. If I stop, something dreadful will happen. My heart will simply stop beating.

John Banville, the Art of Fiction: No 200

Belinda McKeon / 2009

Originally printed in the Spring 2009 issue of the *Paris Review* and used by permission of The Wylie Agency LLC.

When I first arrived at his Dublin city-center apartment, John Banville was working at his writing desk. The apartment, with its neatly aligned furniture and its orderly piles of books, is not Banville's home but his office, in which he works every day. Banville rarely gives interviews in his office, and after our first session he decided that meeting in local bars and cafés might be less "intense." During the next three interview sessions he was more relaxed and more forthcoming. As he surveyed the surroundings, he gave vent to the dry wit that at all times underlies his dour bearing. This black humor threatened to overtake the conversation completely during a meeting held just before Christmas. Amid the bustle of shoppers, Banville's brow stood acutely arched. He is a merciless observer, and his narrators are the same way: cold-eyed, callous, caustic.

Banville is sixty-three. He was born in Wexford, in southeast Ireland, to a father who worked as a garage clerk and a mother who worked in the home. He published his first book, the short-story collection *Long Lankin*, at the age of twenty-five and has since published a novel every three years or so: thirteen under his own name and, more recently, three under the pen name Benjamin Black. Following the early novels, he wrote two acclaimed trilogies: the first, consisting of *Doctor Copernicus* (1976), *Kepler* (1981), and *The Newton Letter* (1982), focused on men of science; the second, with *The Book of Evidence* (1989), *Ghosts* (1993), and *Athena* (1995), took the world of art as its touchstone. *Doctor Copernicus* won the James Tait Black Memorial Prize, *Kepler* the Guardian Fiction Prize, and *The Book of Evidence*, the

Guinness Peat Aviation Award. *The Book of Evidence* was also short-listed for the Booker Prize, an award that Banville won in 2005 for his novel of childhood and memory, *The Sea*. Banville has worked as a journalist since the late 1960s, when he became a subeditor at the *Irish Press*. He later worked as a subeditor and then as literary editor at the *Irish Times*. He remains a prolific book reviewer for publications including the *Guardian* and the *New York Review of Books*.

As a novelist, he is famous for his difficulty. In their architecture and in their style, his books are like baroque cathedrals, filled with elaborate passages and sometimes overwhelming to the casual tourist. For this, Banville makes no apologies—he says he is committed to language and to rhythm above plot, characterization, or pacing. Being Benjamin Black, however, allows him to play more loosely with character and storytelling; in interviews and in correspondence, he refers to Black ("the rogue") fondly and mischievously, delightedly playing this identity against his own. As Black he has written three novels in as many years: *Christine Falls* (2006), *The Silver Swan* (2007), and *The Lemur* (2008). Although the company of Black diverted him awhile from the agony of producing what he calls "a Banville book," a new novel under his own name, *The Infinities*, is forthcoming.

Interviewer: When did you first know that you wanted to write?
Banville: It must have been in my early teens. My brother was living in Africa at the time, and although he has no memory of this, he would occasionally send me books, one of which was James Joyce's *Dubliners*. The book was a revelation to me—the idea that literature could be very elevated but still be about life as I knew it, about the rather grim, gray, mundane life I was living as a boy in Wexford in the fifties. When I finished *Dubliners*, I started writing terrible pastiches of Joyce on an enormous black Remington typewriter borrowed from my aunt Sadie. I threw them all away many years later, of course, but I remember the opening of one of them: "The white May blossom swooned slowly into the open mouth of the grave."

A boy in his teens! What did I know about death? This is a problem for Irish writers—our literary forebears are enormous. They stand behind us like Easter Island statues, and we keep trying to measure up to them, leaping towards heights we can't possibly reach. I suppose that's a good thing, but it makes for a painful early life for the writer. Anyway, hunched there over my aunt Sadie's Remington, I was starting to learn how to write. Now, fifty years later, I'm still learning.

Interviewer: Was Wexford a good place for a writer to grow up?

Banville: Auden said that children should be loaded with as much trauma as they can bear, because it's good for them. I think that's certainly true of children who are going to turn out to be artists. My traumas were Wexford, Ireland, the fifties, and especially the Catholic Church. The first thing the Catholic Church does to a child is instill guilt in his little soul, and guilt is a good thing for an artist. As for Wexford, I never even bothered to learn the street names, because I knew I was going to be out of there as soon as I possibly could. I hated it because it was boring and provincial. Of course, now I feed on it—*The Sea* is a direct return to my childhood, to when I was ten or so. The book is set in a fictionalized Rosslare, the seaside village where we went every summer as children. Looking back now it seems idyllic, though I'm sure 95 percent of the experience was absolute, grinding boredom. I feel a kind of intellectual regret, not an emotional regret, at having left my parents and that world behind. But it's not a great weight on my soul. In a way I wish it were. To leave one's background without guilt is an indication of shallowness of character, I suspect.

Interviewer: Did your parents read books?

Banville: My parents were good, decent people, intelligent but not well educated. My father read cowboy books. My mother was afraid of the books I wrote, afraid of what she would discover if she read them. My father didn't care what I wrote about. He read some of my early work and quite liked it, I think.

Interviewer: You painted in your teens. What did you paint?

Banville: Oh, hideous pictures, hideous pictures. I was in my mid-teens and I was really into Dylan Thomas, and therefore I painted scenes from Dylan Thomas. It makes the hair stand up on the back of my neck in embarrassment as I think about them. Dreadful pictures. But trying to be a painter did teach me to look at the world in a very particular way—looking very closely at things, at colors, at how things form themselves in space— and I've always been grateful for that. You have all this space, and you have a figure: what do you do with it? And in a way that's what all art is. How do we find a place for our creatures, or inventions, in this incoherent space into which we're thrown?

Interviewer: What attracted you to novel writing?

Banville: Language. Words. The world is not real for me until it has been pushed through the mesh of language, and this was as true then as it is now.

I also had that wonderful conviction that writers have at the beginning that the possibilities are infinite. I didn't realize just how difficult it was going to be. I thought that within five or six years I would be a fully-fledged writer. Here I am now, at the age of sixty-two, still diligently practicing. But I loved, and still love, the craft. I am a graphomaniac. I cannot not write. If I find myself with a spare forty-five minutes at the end of my working day, I will turn to adding a few sentences to something. One of the reasons I love doing journalism—that is, reviews and literary articles—is that I can do it quickly. It gives me a craftsman's pleasure. Fiction doesn't do that. Fiction is just a constant torment and an embarrassment. I loathe my fiction. I have a fantasy when I'm passing a bookstore that I could click my fingers and all my books would go blank so that I could start again and get them right.

Interviewer: Do you really hate your own novels?

Banville: Yes! I hate them. I mean that. Nobody believes me, but it's true. They're an embarrassment and a deep source of shame. They're better than everybody else's, of course, but not good enough for me. There is a great deal more pain than pleasure in writing fiction. It's only now and then, maybe once every three or four days, that I manage to write a sentence in which I hear that wonderful harmonic chime that you get when, say, you flick the edge of a wine glass with a fingernail. That's what keeps me going. When I read the proofs of a new novel—which is the last time I will read or even glance at it—I approach it with one eye closed, so to speak, thinking, God, what am I going to find here? And I find horrors, horrors that can't be fixed. Everything in the text now seems hopelessly flat and deadened. Where I imagined a dancing rhythm, I find clumping and stumbling.

Interviewer: Your first book, *Long Lankin*, was a collection of stories and a novella. Why haven't you returned to the short-story form?

Banville: Nowadays everybody wants to have a rock band or write a film script, but back then our sole desire was to have a short story published in a little magazine. A beautifully produced journal, the *Kilkenny Magazine*, published my first short story. Following Joyce's example with *Dubliners*—of course, I was and still am fascinated by *Dubliners*—I put together a collection of connected short stories. Not that they had the same characters, but they were connected by theme and by chronology— one set was about childhood, another about adolescence, another about maturity. The novella was mortifyingly bad, and I've since suppressed it. I knew nothing about life, but I was writing it as if I were fifty years old—world-weary and cosmopolitan. But you know, I was learning to write. I was learning my capabilities and my limitations.

Interviewer: Were you in school when you were writing these early stories?
Banville: Yes, in school—you can image what a pain I was to my English teachers—then later I moved to Dublin. I never went to university. I'm self-educated. I didn't go because I was too impatient, too arrogant. I managed to fail my matriculation exam because I didn't want to go to college and be an architect, which was my mother's ambition for me. I thought I could do it all for myself. If I could have gone to Oxford or Cambridge I would have gone in a shot. In those days in Catholic Ireland, you had to get permission from your archbishop even to go to Trinity College, Dublin's "Protestant" university.

Looking back, I don't think I would have learned much more, and I don't think I would have had the nerve to tackle some of the things I tackled as a young writer if I had been to university—I would have been beaten into submission by my lecturers. But I think I would have been a little more relaxed. After high school, instead of attending university I took a job as a clerk at Aer Lingus, the Irish airline. I wanted to be free, and working for an airline allowed me to travel. I didn't socialize with literary people. Instead I would work every day, and I would write every night. I've been doing that ever since. I've only very recently become what's known as a full-time writer. I was a working journalist for thirty-five years, as a copy editor on the newspapers and then as books editor at the *Irish Times.* I can't complain about that because a day job gives you freedom.

Interviewer: Where do you think your discipline came from?
Banville: I am essentially a religious type. In my teens I gave up Catholicism, and at the same time I started writing. Writing keeps me at my desk, constantly trying to write a perfect sentence. It is a great privilege to make one's living from writing sentences. The sentence is the greatest invention of civilization. To sit all day long assembling these extraordinary strings of words is a marvelous thing. I couldn't ask for anything better. It's as near to godliness as I can get.

Interviewer: Do you revise?
Banville: When I finish a sentence, after much labor, it's finished. A certain point comes at which you can't do any more work on it because you know it will kill the sentence. The rhythm is set. The meaning is set.

Occasionally I will leave behind a sentence that I know is missing a word, and I'll go back to it later. I wrote a sentence like that yesterday. A man is talking about his wife who's a singer. She has just woken up in the morning, and he says, "Even half asleep like this, she sounded a true, dark note, a thrilling . . ." I put in "cadence," but I know it's not the right word—so the sentence is just sitting there, waiting for me to find the right, the exact, the only word.

Interviewer: Is rhythm as important as word choice to you?

Banville: It all starts with rhythm for me. I love Nabokov's work, and I love his style. But I always thought there was something odd about it that I couldn't quite put my finger on. Then I read an interview in which he admitted he was tone deaf. And I thought, that's it—there's no music in Nabokov; it's all pictorial; it's all image-based. It's not any worse for that, but the prose doesn't sing. For me, a line has to sing before it does anything else. The great thrill is when a sentence that starts out being completely plain suddenly begins to sing, rising far above itself and above any expectation I might have had for it. That's what keeps me going on those dark December days when I think about how I could be living instead of writing.

Interviewer: How tied are your books to the time in which you wrote them?

Banville: *Long Lankin* came from the early sixties. But Ireland in the sixties wasn't the sixties as Americans think of it. When I look back now to the sixties here, it's like looking back to the Middle Ages. It was a primitive world. But it's good for a novelist to cross periods in history in one lifetime. When I was writing *Kepler* and *Doctor Copernicus*, looking back to Europe in the Renaissance, I only had to think back to Wexford when I was growing up there to get a feel for what a primitive world was like.

Interviewer: What drew you to Renaissance Europe?

Banville: Oh, I wanted to get away, to do something different. When I did *Birchwood*, which I regard as my "Irish" novel, I couldn't think where to go afterwards because I didn't want to be labeled as an Irish novelist. I thought that I might give up fiction and do something else altogether. Then I started to write a book about the Norman invasion of Ireland in the twelfth century, and that somehow turned into a novel about Copernicus. Don't ask me how—I don't know. Fiction is a strange business.

Interviewer: What was your idea of an Irish novel?

Banville: One written with a brogue. One of which reviewers could comfortably say, "Well, here's the latest novel from Ireland." The usual charm of the Irish. And the charm of the Irish is, as we know, entirely fake.

Interviewer: Who are the chief offenders?
Banville: Good writers, but they were and are nothing more than good writers, and anybody can be that. It's not enough—you have to be more than that. Doing what you do well is death. Your duty is to keep trying to do things that you don't do well, in the hope of learning. So, I decided, with no cosmopolitan experience, to turn myself into a European novelist of ideas: Banville, the modern European master. I was young. I was reckless. There are people who tell me they think *Doctor Copernicus* and *Kepler* were my best books, but I feel now that in those novels I took a wrong direction, that I should have done something else.

Interviewer: What made you change tack?
Banville: *Mefisto.* That novel was originally intended to be the fourth book in the series that included *Copernicus*, *Kepler*, and *The Newton Letter.* My wife says I had a nervous breakdown during the writing of *Mefisto.* Maybe I did, but what's a nervous breakdown for a writer? For a writer every day is a nervous breakdown. Still, *Mefisto* was a big shift for me. I began to write in a different way. I began to trust my instincts, to lose control, deliberately. It was exciting, and it was frightening. The writer who wrote *Mefisto* was a writer in deep trouble. He didn't know what he was doing. He was striking out into new territory—for him, at least. It was painful at the time, and it was hideous in many ways. When the book was finally published, it was completely ignored. In those days they used to review four or five novels in one go and in one or two of those my book was dismissed in a half inch at the end of the column—this was the only review attention it got. Commercially it failed miserably. That was a traumatic time for me. The book came out in the spring, and I remember I spent that following summer digging my garden—Voltaire would have been proud. I made a wonderful garden. Grew beans, lettuces. I was healing myself from some kind of traumatic process that I don't pretend to understand. All right, let's agree with my wife and call it a nervous breakdown.

Interviewer: Where does the comedy in your work come from?
Banville: The world is a dark place, and I find it endlessly funny.

Interviewer: This seems the right time to turn to Beckett. When did Beckett become important to you and why?

Banville: Very early on I read *Molloy*. Like *Dubliners*, it was a great revelation to me—the idea that a writer could speak in such a completely self-absorbed way, not dealing with characters or human interests—the usual stock-in-trade of the novelist. It was great to discover that linguistic beauty could be pursued as an end in itself. *Beauty* is a word that we haven't mentioned yet, but it's crucial to me. It's what I'm after constantly. Beauty is an almost nonhuman pursuit. Readers ask me, "Why are you always telling us about the weather and how things look?" I say, "Because how things look and the beauty of how they look is just as important to me as the people who are in the foreground." I don't see human beings as essential to the universe. Human beings in my work are figures in a landscape, and the landscape is just as important as the figures.

Interviewer: But human beings—characters—are still the business of fiction, aren't they?

Banville: When I was young, art for me was a new religion. Now I see the aims and ends of art as less grand. If I can catch the play of light on a wall, and catch it just so, that is enough for me. I don't want to write about human behavior. Art now seems to me in many ways the absolute opposite of psychology. It's simply saying, "This is how it is. This is how it looks, how it feels." To describe things well is far more worthwhile than the kind of cheap psychologizing, or even expensive psychologizing, that the novel so often indulges in. One of my favorite entries from Kafka's diaries: "Never again psychology!" Of course, my books are about life—what other subject is there?—but life is so much more than psychologizing. Even so, my books seem to me to heave with the most embarrassing emotionalism and sentimentality, yet many readers consider them cold and distanced from human beings. I often wonder what world people live in if they think that my writing is not about life. To me, my books are completely realistic. They're the world as I see it.

Interviewer: The science trilogy, did you feel that you might have been weighed down by all your research?

Banville: *Copernicus* stuck very closely to the facts but in *Kepler* I invented freely, and it's a much better book because of that. I doubt that I will ever do another book based on a real person. I think that I've moved into another area—pure invention. I now think that research deadens fiction. Flaubert is a case in point. Flaubert read too many books, and in consequence some of his own books stagger under the weight of his erudition. He said he'd read some preposterous number of books to prepare for the writing of *Salammbô*, and you can feel them dragging the novel down. It would have been much better if he'd made it all up.

After all, who knows what the distant past was like? About *Kepler* and *Copernicus*, people often say, "You captured the period so well!" I always want to ask, "How do you know? You weren't there either."

Interviewer: Who are the philosophers that matter to you? In many of your reviews you mention Nietzsche.

Banville: As a young man I considered myself a Wittgensteinian, but for the little that I read of Wittgenstein, I understood even less. I read Nietzsche when I was a teenager and then I went back to reading him when I was in my thirties, and his voice spoke directly to me. Nietzsche is such a superb literary artist. One of my favorite Nietzsche aphorisms is—and I always trot this out when people ask me about some other writer who's having a huge success for some cheap thing—"You will never get the crowd to cry hosanna until you ride into town on an ass." Even in English that's wonderful.

In the last four or five years, I've begun to read the indigenous American philosophers—Emerson, Thoreau, William James, John Dewey—and I have found in them a very congenial view of the world, skeptical but not despairing. I especially love Emerson. Each of his essays is a collection of impassioned sentences. It seems as if there's a sense of order in the usual sense, but in fact there are just wonderfully rich congeries of sentences. I am inclined to think that the value of a philosopher's thought is always reflected in his style—mind you, where does that leave Kant and Hegel?

Interviewer: You said earlier that you hate your novels. Is that true of your book criticism—which you insist on calling "book reviews"?

Banville: It's not criticism. Critics do a different thing. The job of the critic is to place a work within the tradition; the job of the book reviewer is to introduce new work to the reading public. It's a much lowlier occupation, but it's a decent one. It's an honorable craft, if it's done honorably, and it's probably the form of writing that I get the most satisfaction from. I love rounding off a review and being able to say, "Yes, I've written a good, solid, carpentered piece of work." At least it's finished, as a piece of fiction never is, and I've done the best that I could. But even in this kind of work I lack confidence, and when I send in a review I wait on tenterhooks until the editor writes to say he will accept it.

Interviewer: How do you make the decision to accept or reject a book for review?

Banville: I will only turn down a book if I know I won't be able to muster enough interest to read the bloody thing. Or if I realize that I despise the author and that I'm just going to become hysterical in my dispraise. A couple of times in my life I've disobeyed my own rule, and later regretted it.

Interviewer: Are you referring to Ian McEwan's novel, *Saturday*, which you called "a dismayingly bad book"?

Banville: Let's just say that a couple of times in my life I've taken a flying kick at a book, and I shouldn't have done it. It's a delicate business. All too often, if one writes a favorable notice, it's seen as a product of the old-boy network, and if one dispraises a book, it's seen as envy. Nobody seems able to accept that I review books as a book reviewer, not as a competing novelist. When I review, I'm being as honest as I can. And I'm saying to the reading public—the minuscule segment of the reading public that reads reviews—that this is my judgment. You must understand, and I always assume that readers of book reviews do understand, that a review is an early, provisional reaction to a book. I've reviewed books favorably that a year later I've said to myself, My God, how could I ever have thought that rubbish was any good? And I've given bad reviews to books that later I've regretted. That's why book reviewing is so different from criticism, which provides, or seeks to provide, the long view. That's the reason I refuse to bring out a collection of my book reviews.

Interviewer: If you don't want your book reviews to be remembered, is there a single novel that you would like to be remembered for, more than the others?

Banville: Perhaps *Shroud*. It's a dark, hard, cruel book. It's the novel in which I got closest to doing what I aimed to do at the start of writing it. That had only happened once before, with *The Newton Letter*. Everybody hated *Shroud*—even, I think, the people who admired it. It was favorably reviewed, but it was not and is not a book a reader could readily love. *Shroud* is my monstrous child whom I cherish but who horrifies others. The odd thing is that, for all its harshness, it's a love story of sorts. I never thought I'd write a love story—what an idea! In my romance an old man and a young woman, both damaged, meet and develop a strange, violent, destructive rapport. And what is love if not strange, violent, and destructive? In love the loved one is the gilded mirror in which the lover admires himself. In the early stages there is tenderness and gaiety and fun, but these rapidly fade, and we go into possession mode, trying to grasp the mirror and frequently smashing it.

Interviewer: In your next novel, *The Sea*, you returned to your childhood. Did you decide to do this beforehand?

Banville: Yes. *Shroud* was the latest in a series of novels of mine in the first-person, all of them about men in trouble. I knew I had to find a new direction. So, I started to write *The Sea* in the third-person. It was going to be very short, seventy pages or so, and solely about childhood holidays at the seaside—very bare. I worked on it for about eighteen months, but I couldn't get it to work. And then, out of nowhere, the first-person narrative voice made itself heard again. I suspect that the reason I don't really believe in the third-person mode is that I'm such an egomaniac. Unless it's me speaking, it's not convincing—to me, that is.

Interviewer: Many of your readers found Max, the narrator of *The Sea*, much more sympathetic than your previous narrators. Did that surprise you?

Banville: I didn't think that Max was more warmhearted or approachable than any of my other narrators. He is weaker, and in a more devastated position in his life. Very many readers of *The Sea* cite to me the line, "The past beats inside me like a second heart." I wonder why it has such appeal. I've written better sentences, but this one seems emblematic of whatever it is in the book that caught people's imaginations and—dare I say it?—needs. I think what affects readers most immediately in the book is the theme of childhood. Most of the people who talk to me about the book dwell on the childhood sequences—I suspect they race through the grown-up sections in order to get to the next bit about the seaside. It's understandable. Those childhood loves that we experienced when we were ten or eleven were entirely pure, in every sense of the word. When we were at that age, the emotions we felt were pure because we were experiencing them for the first time. We didn't know how to do sex, we didn't know what to do with our bodies, but we thought there was some great secret that we might crack in about five years' time. As we find out, of course, the secret never gets cracked. But that's another story—another novel.

Interviewer: After you won the Booker Prize for *The Sea*, you said it was nice to see a work of art win the Booker Prize. It was a controversial statement.

Banville: Let's give it its full title, the Man Booker Prize—after all, the Man people are the ones who put up the cash. The first thought that occurred to me, that night when I heard the chairman of the jury announce my name, was, Just think how many people hate me at this moment. Naturally, I wanted to annoy those people even further by being arrogant. But I did also mean what I said. Whether *The Sea* is a successful work of art is not for me to say, but a work of art is what I set out to make. The kind of novels that I write very rarely win the Man Booker Prize, which in general promotes good, middlebrow fiction. The prize sells more books than the Nobel does, and these huge sales benefit not only the winner, but all of us in the trade. I understand why some people were upset when *The Sea* got the prize. I won in a year rich in strong, attractive, middlebrow novels, all of which had their advocates. I don't think a book like mine should win every time, God forbid. The prize would die, and it's a very important prize—to publishers, to authors, to editors. But every now and then, it's also important that a book like mine should win because, for instance, my editor can go to the money people at his publishing house and say, "Nobody thought Banville was going to sell, or win the prize, but look, he's won, and now I happen to have a book by a twenty-four-year-old kid, kind of like Banville." A good editor needs all the help he can get, in the current publishing climate.

Interviewer: When did you begin to write your Benjamin Black books?
Banville: I finished *The Sea* in September 2004, and it was published in April 2005. I started writing *Christine Falls* in March 2005, and it went very quickly. I was staying at the house of a friend in Italy. I sat down at nine o'clock on a Monday morning, and by lunchtime I had written more than fifteen hundred words. It was a scandal! I thought, John Banville, you slut. But then I remembered it was Black, not Banville, who was writing. I had fun doing it and I thought, If this has to be my day job, if Benjamin Black is going to earn some money so that John Banville can have freedom, then this is no more difficult than working in the newspapers.

On the day *The Sea* was short-listed for the Man Booker, my agent handed my publisher the manuscript of *Christine Falls.* No one knew it was coming—I hadn't announced my new project to anybody. My publisher was just beside himself with glee. Of course, everyone tried to persuade me not to use the pseudonym, but I wanted people to realize that this wasn't an elaborate postmodernist literary joke, but the genuine article, a noir novel from Banville's dark brother Benjamin Black. It was pure play when I invented Benjamin Black. It was a frolic of my own.

Interviewer: Do you read thrillers?

Banville: The impetus for Black came from my having begun to read Georges Simenon for the first time—not the Maigret books, which I think are slapdash, but what he called his *romans durs*, his hard novels: *Dirty Snow, Monsieur Monde Vanishes, Tropic Moon, The Man Who Watched Trains Go By*. I think they are extraordinary, masterpieces of twentieth-century—I hesitate to use the word, but I will—existentialist literature. Better than Sartre, even better than Camus. I thought, My God, look what you can do with a small vocabulary and a lean, straightforward style. I wanted to try it and try it I did. Of course, I would never be able to achieve the kind of economy that Simenon does.

I had been reading other thrillers all my life. When I was a boy, I read Agatha Christie, Josephine Tey, Dorothy Sayers, Margery Allingham—all of those polite British ladies with murder in their hearts. I moved on from them to Raymond Chandler, Richard Stark, and James M. Cain. High art can happen in any medium. I think that Simenon's *Dirty Snow*, for instance, is high art.

Interviewer: Where did Quirke, your amateur sleuth hero, come from?

Banville: First of all, I wanted somebody who would be my physical opposite. Quirke is a huge fellow, blond, broad-shouldered, irresistible to women. He's like me only in that he doesn't have much of a personality. He's mainly interesting as the center of something.

Interviewer: I find him a complex character.

Banville: Really? But don't you think the complexities of Quirke's character are rather clichéd?

Interviewer: They have to be for the book to work.

Banville: Yes, that's one of the many things I hate about life, that it's a hideously clichéd business. And Benjamin Black is bent on being as true to life as possible. Quirke—he has no first name, by the way, which is to say his first name is not known to us—is consciously crafted, whereas John Banville's characters sort of drift out of me, as if out of my dreams. It was interesting for me to discover the possibilities, and the limits, of this kind of fiction. For Black, character matters, plot matters, dialogue matters to a much greater degree than they do in my Banville books. One can, with skill and perseverance, give a sense of life's richness and complexity in noir fiction.

As to the limits, it troubles me that humor is so hard to do in a crime book. I don't know why this is so, but it is. And Benjamin Black can't do the kind of subtle, skewed humor that John Banville does. If you try humor in crime fiction, it comes out as smart-alecky. Most of the thrillers that I pick up, after three pages I throw them at the wall because the wise-guy tone grates on my nerves. Every hero in crime fiction knows everything about everything. Nothing surprises or baffles him. What I like about Quirke is that he's rather stupid, like the rest of us. He misses the point of things; he stumbles over clues, misreads people. He's far too dim to be a Philip Marlowe. But this is what I treasure in him—his human frailty and the curious kind of dogged honor he can sometimes display.

Interviewer: Were you surprised by how much you enjoyed being Benjamin Black?
Banville: I really didn't think it would be so easy to write mainstream fiction. I thought that when other writers talked about the difficulties of their lives, that they were telling the truth. Obviously, they were all lying. It's so bloody easy.

I'm being slightly facetious. If it's easy it's easy because I've been practicing my craft for forty or fifty years, and I'm now using that craft to make different kinds of books—books I am much more proud of than I am of my hated Banville books. Isn't that odd?

Interviewer: Is Benjamin Black's process really so different from John Banville's?
Banville: If I'm Benjamin Black, I can write up to two-and-a-half thousand words a day. As John Banville, if I write two hundred words a day I am very, very happy. A Banville novel will take me up to five years to write. When I'd finished *The Lemur*, the third Benjamin Black book, and sat down to become John Banville again, I worked one Friday for six hours straight, and I ended up with one sentence. Not a particularly good sentence, either. But I was thrilled to be back, working in that strange, deep level of concentration. That's the distinction—what you get in Banville is concentration, what you get from Black is spontaneity. I know there are readers who consider Black a better writer, certainly a better novelist, than Banville, and perhaps they're right.

Interviewer: Do you worry you might never be able to get back?
Banville: I've spent my life being a journalist, a copy editor—in other words, a technician. I have always been two people, professionally. Going back and forth between John Banville and Benjamin Black is just an extension of that.

Interviewer: Do you have sympathy for the characters you create?

Banville: I suppose it's possible that a writer would have feeling for his characters, but I can't see how, because writing is such a meticulous, intricate, technical business. I wish I could say that I love my characters and that frequently they take over the book and run away with the plot and so on. But they don't exist. They're manikins made of words, and they carry my rhythms. They have no autonomous life—surely that's obvious? I distrust those writers who claim to have feeling for their characters. They're liars or fools.

Interviewer: It makes you sound arrogant to call novelists liars and fools.

Banville: I am arrogant, and I'm also intemperate. I'm trying to be honest here. I'm not going to pose as a caring novelist. Art is a hard business. It's a matter of sentiment, but not sentimentality. I do it for myself. The coincidence is that what I do for myself chimes sometimes with the experiences and emotions and desires of other people. This is a kind of miracle, but I don't intend for it to happen—it just does. Art is like sex: when you're doing it, nothing else matters. Away from his desk the novelist can care deeply about the social, political, moral aspects of what he is writing but when he sits down to write, all those concerns fall away and nothing matters except the putting down of one carefully chosen word after another carefully chosen word, until a sentence is finished, then a paragraph, then a page, then a chapter, then a book. When I'm working I don't care about anything, not even myself. All my concentration is directed towards the making of the thing on the page. The rest is just stuff—even though it is the stuff of life.

Katherine Wootton Interviews John Banville

Katherine Wootton / 2009

From *The Literateur* (www.literateur.com) 8 October 2009. Reprinted with permission from Kit Toda, Dan Eltringham, and Katherine Wootton. Katherine Wootton interviewed John Banville 9 September 2009 in London.

Katherine Wootton: You write reviews, and you were a literary editor and section editor for a while. How do you feel about things moving online and the newspaper books sections slowly diminishing or being put online?

John Banville: Well, I think it's a pity, but then I grew up in the era of hot metal. I was talking to a young woman the other day, I mentioned carbon paper, and she said, "What?"

Things have changed so much in my lifetime. The thought that I would finish a book and press a button, and it's in my agent's office, my publisher's office. I used to laboriously type those things up, with carbon paper. I don't really think about online things; I'm sorry to say it doesn't occur to me. It's the access that's extraordinary.

I had a funny experience a little while ago. I went to Theakston's Old Peculiar Crime Writing Festival in Harrowgate in Yorkshire. I went because the name was so wonderful. And I like Yorkshire. I went to the festival as Benjamin Black, obviously, and there was a question-and-answer session. I said that I wrote very slowly as John Banville and write quickly as Benjamin Black, and this seemed to annoy people. Bloggers wrote about how incensed people were, and they weren't, in fact. I mean, this is all patent nonsense, nobody said anything to me, I didn't hear anybody in the audience being annoyed by this, but it caused a great kerfuffle. I was in much odium with crime writers and readers and so on.

I'm quite proud of my Benjamin Black books, as a craftsman. My John Banville novels I loathe and despise. I think they're better than everybody else's, but they're not good enough for me. They're a standing affront to me—because I couldn't get it right.

The problem is there's very little chance of checking the accuracy of these blogs. In the Harrowgate question-and-answer thing, I made a rather dim joke and said I fully expected Benjamin Black to win the Nobel Prize, while I would be forgotten. This is reported by a blogger as me saying I have much more serious things to do than crime writing; I'm going to win the Nobel Prize as John Banville. Which bore no relation to the truth. But what am I supposed to do about that? I can see interviewers coming to me and saying, "I believe you think you're about to win the Nobel Prize."

Also, of course, there's the question of access, everybody's opinion now can be heard, and most people haven't got opinions; they just have received ideas, but they seem to have received most of them from taxi drivers.

Apparently, in a Sunday newspaper in Ireland, I was quoted by the interviewer as saying I thought budget airlines were a bad idea because they brought people to places they shouldn't be in.

What I meant was I didn't think they were made happy by foreign travel. Did you ever see happy tourists? They'd be much better off staying home.

In fact, I have a plan, when I finally can't write anymore. When I have to do a real job to make money, I'm going to start a travel agency, the stipulation being that you may not travel beyond twenty miles of your home so you discover your own place. So, this is my plan.

But this was reported in the paper as me saying that the poor shouldn't be allowed to travel.

There's a hugely popular phone-in program in Ireland, late in the afternoon, and I'm told that this is what got on: the guy running the show said, "Banville says you people shouldn't be allowed to travel. Aren't you aware of that?" So, here I'm now pilloried for this as well. When I was growing up, if you phoned up a radio station, you were regarded as a crank, and they would hang up on you. Now, you can speak on the radio for minutes on end.

On the other hand, I have to say, the internet and word processing and all that is incredible. It's incredible that people can be in instant communication with each other, that people can check facts, even if the facts are slightly woozy.

You can check almost anything on Google and Wikipedia and so on. That can't be bad. If I lived in a totalitarian country—Thailand or China—I would be very glad of the internet.

With instant access to information, it'll be harder for tyrants to keep the truth from them, from the people.

KW: You talked a bit about the Booker yesterday (at a reading at the London Review Bookshop on September 8), because people were upset that you weren't nominated for it. How did the Booker help you as a writer, or did it make a difference in what you were able to write?

JB: My bank manager wasn't waking in the night when he thought about my overdraft.

It's a wonderful prize to win. In the English-speaking world, it's still the most important one there is; it probably sells more books than the Nobel Prize does. It's that big red fire engine that you want for Christmas. You know, I'm a little boy; I want that fire engine. We all do because it makes a fantastic difference—certainly for the particular book, but also one's reputation goes up a couple notches afterwards.

So, it's a wonderful thing to have, but as far as the writing is concerned, the writing is no different. It's always work, makes no difference whatsoever to it. I've never been pressured by publishers; nobody's ever tried to tell me what I should write or what I shouldn't write or that I should write by a specific time. Maybe I've been very lucky in my publishers, but I've always found them wonderful to work with—with one or two exceptions, obviously, but I suspect I've been very lucky.

The Booker prize is very good for publishing. Publishers need to sell books, because nobody's going to be able to afford to do that slim volume of poems, if at the other end they haven't got big blockbusters, selling lots and lots of books. So, it's very important.

It's also important for editors. Because my editor believed in my book *The Sea*, and against all expectations, it won the Booker prize, my editor then could say to the money people, to the accountants, when he gets some twenty-four-year-old with a book that's difficult and awkward and not an obvious bestseller, he can say to them, "Well, you know, this book is a little like Banville's book and Banville's book won the Booker Prize"—it strengthens their hand as well, so all down the line it does an awful lot of good.

Now, the downside of it is, if you're not on the list, you can forget about it, so it's reduced the number of books in a year to six. It makes it very difficult to sell *The Infinities*, because it wasn't on the longlist.

But, as far as the writing is concerned, it makes no difference whatsoever. Well, everything in life makes a slight difference. We're constantly being shifted and changed and carried away, so of course, it has some, but not a notable difference.

KW: Have you read any of this year's nominees?

JB: No, I haven't read any. I read very little fiction. I don't like novels; I read poetry, philosophy, and history. I should read more fiction, but when I do, I'm usually disappointed.

And you know, I'm getting to an age where I'm starting to reread novels. It's a phenomenon: everybody over sixty starts to reread, turns into an old codger who doesn't want to read new stuff. I'm sure there's a whole world of wonderful new writers out there; I don't read them.

KW: Are there any writers that you particularly enjoyed that you thought were unsung or underappreciated or underpublicized?

JB: Well, I've been championing [Georges] Simenon's *romans durs*, his "hard novels," and I've been championing Richard Stark's Parker novels, far superior to crime novels. These are wonderful.

The University of Chicago Press has just brought out six of them, reissued, and they're masterpieces. There are at least a half-dozen I've read that are as good as anything being done in so-called "literary fiction"; he's a wonderful writer. Richard Stark—powerful books. Start with *The Outfit*, which I think is the first one.

KW: After writing the Benjamin Black books and coming back to your John Banville fiction, was there anything that you were really keen to do, now that you weren't writing within the trope of the genre? As you were saying, you don't particularly like the idea of genre . . .

JB: Well, most of my books have plots, despite the fact that people say that they haven't.

The Sea is full of plot, there are twists at the end. *The Infinities* has a twist at the end. It's more common than we think—Beckett, for instance, does that all the time. Beckett was a great fan of *series noir* French crime fiction. And all his books have plots, even the most abstruse and the most apparently arid, and they all have twists at the end.

In *Company*, there's talk about all this stuff and at the end he says, "alone"—it turns out that all this is invention. It's a wonderful thing, [and] falls apart at the end.

In *Molloy*, he has the character Moran who is on a long, long quest. He starts out by saying, "It is midnight, rain is beating on the window." After this immense quest, he comes back and says, "I sat down, I wrote 'it is midnight, rain is beating on the window.' It was not midnight, it was not raining," and again the book collapses like a house of cards.

So, I see my books as quite straightforward, within the tradition. I'm certainly not an avant-gardist, you know: these are quite traditional books, but they have a particular inflection to them that strikes some people as strange because the prose is very demanding.

I try to make the prose as dense and as demanding as poetry, and I quote Auden as saying that the poem is the one thing that you either take or leave; if you listen to music you might drift away to think about your dinner or sex or something. The same is true of painting. The poem, you read or you don't read it, and I want my books to have that quality: you either read them or you don't. The mind can't drift.

I'm trying to re-create reality. I'm trying to get the reader to see, to hear, to smell, to taste, the world as it is—not as other novelists and poets tend to think reality is. I want to get at the real thing itself, which is behind our everyday concerns. I'm trying to get at the essence of the thing itself—it's not easy.

KW: What people find difficult about it [Banville's writing] is that it is written in a very poetic language, and people aren't used to reading poetry; they're used to reading workmanlike prose.

JB: People have said to me, "Why are you always talking about the weather? Why, why don't you just tell us the bloody story?" and I said, "Because the weather is part of the story."

I am, if I'm anything—people say I'm postmodernist, which I'm not—if I'm anything I'm posthumanist, because I do not see humans as the center of the universe. I don't think we own the place.

This is a hangover from the inculcation of religion into us when we were children. When I was six, seven years old, the most influential book in my life, I suppose, was the Catechism of the Catholic Church: Who made the world? God made the world. Why did God make the world? God made the world for man's use. All lies, all nonsense, but extraordinarily influential. Catechism was an amazing book. It has the answer to everything. Also, when you get to the end, it tells you all about concupiscence and lust and things like that, which you're never going to find out about elsewhere.

But I don't believe any of this. I don't believe that man is the center of the universe. We're highly evolved animals; we keep forgetting that. We think that at some point the connection between us and the animals broke and we floated away and became gods, and we're not.

We are immensely, immensely clever creatures. And we are the most successful virus in the world, but we're still animals.

It's a great tragedy that we've lost our connection with the animal world. I think that's a real disaster for us—this extraordinary arrogance that we have about ourselves and what we are and what we're capable of. We're capable of magnificence; we're capable of producing Johann Sebastian Bach and Einstein, Rembrandt, Samuel Beckett. We're also capable of many lesser things, but this arrogant attitude we have—we're destroying ourselves; we're destroying the world. This is my green speech. I do think it's a disaster that we've lost our connection with the larger world.

KW: In *The Infinities* your sometime narrator is a god, one of the Greek pantheon, who says, "I'm only omniscient sometimes." Is that a way of poking fun at the idea of the whole "the gods created the world"?
JB: Oh, no. I suspect the whole thing is taking place in Adam Godley's head; it's all made up. I wrote the gods in because I was originally going to base the book quite closely on Kleist's play *Amphitryon*. The skeleton of it is still inside the book. But no, I wasn't commenting on religion.

Of course, as a citizen, rather than a writer, I would say that monotheism has been a total disaster for us. All the war, mayhem, and power in the world—return to paganism would be a wonderful idea.

To call them Zeus and Hermes and Athena and so on is to give names to things that we don't understand—and the Greeks were very clever in that—because we live within a very, very narrow band of reality.

We don't even see things that cats and dogs can. They can see in the dark; they can smell things. We don't have any of that; we just exist in this tiny, tiny band. We don't see infrared rays, we don't see the neutrinos that are streaming through you and me, and through the entire world, even as we speak—we have no sense of any of this. So, there's a whole enormous version of reality out there that we know nothing about, that we don't see.

Einstein was always very interested in this. He was always very suspicious of the fact that mathematics—which is manmade, and we forget that. We think mathematics is this natural entity, but we invented it, that all these new discoveries about reality, they all fit in with mathematics. Einstein was always suspicious of that, which makes me think he might have been thinking in the same way as Wittgenstein. We only say those things that we have the words to express. Einstein was suspicious that we see only what we are capable of seeing and we take this to be the totality of the world and reality, but it's not. So, there are all kinds of things we know nothing about. To give them names is a wonderfully poetic way of dealing with reality.

My friend John Gray, the English philosopher, always insists that religion is a kind of poetry, and it is. It is a poetic version of the world. The trouble is, as we know to our cost, when people believe it absolutely—*they* have the right one, *their* god is the only one—things get very sticky, indeed. So, return to paganism.

KW: It'd be much more fun, anyway. Your character Adam the elder says that he hates his work. It's better than anyone else's, but it isn't good enough for him—
JB: Did I say that; did I put that in the book?

KW: You did, I can even tell you the page number—
JB: Oh, I believe you, I believe you.

KW: But then he goes on to say, "All my peers are dead"—how do you feel about that? Is that a continuation on a theme, or is that just Adam?
JB: I suppose I feel, to some extent, like Keats who wrote, "I'm living a posthumous existence."

The people whom I would have seen as my heroes, my exemplars, are all gone. I don't see a Joyce or a Kleist or a Beckett or a Henry James in the present world. We seem to be in a cultural trough.

But then, everybody over sixty says that—oh, in my time, there were giants striding the earth—but we seem to be in a period of rapid changes.

When I was growing up, life was very slow, indeed, and even in the fifties and into the sixties, artists were still regarded as figures of significance.

The artists are probably still there, but the significance has moved over into the *pop* word, pop music and all the popular culture. They are now the upcoming figures, and that is a world that I don't really understand. I never said that before; I'm not sure it's true. It sounds true when I say it.

People say to me, "How can you start a book talking about Zeus, Hermes, all this that people will have to look it up?" and I say, "Well, so what? Why shouldn't they look it up? Why shouldn't I demand that they do a little bit of work? It'll be good for them. They'll enjoy it." *The Dictionary* and the *Dictionary of Mythology* are wonderful books, full of adventure and play, sexy as anything.

KW: You're also assuming your readers aren't stupid or uninformed.

JB: Of course, I think that this is something that has happened in my lifetime. The audience has become completely despised, and I don't despise the audience.

The two best reviews that I've ever had: in 1989 when *The Book of Evidence* was shortlisted for the Booker, I had a period of notoriety—three minutes out of my fifteen minutes of fame. I was running for the train one morning going to the newspaper office, and there was a man on a bicycle, riding by, saw me, recognized me from television or newspapers, came towards me riding very fast.

I thought, Oh Christ, I'm going to be attacked, and just before he got to me, he said, "Great fucking book." And I thought, I'll never ever have a review as good as that.

The second one: my wife was in Marks and Spencer's in Dublin, and when she gave her credit card, the woman said, "Are you related to John Banville? Tell him *The Sea* is the most beautiful thing I ever read." And she said, "Tell him that came from a checkout woman at Marks and Spencer's." Isn't that wonderful? These are the people I write for.

I don't write for reviewers, critics, fellow writers. I write for the man on the bicycle and the woman at the checkout counter. There are more of them, and they are more receptive than people imagine. And they shouldn't be talked down to, and they shouldn't be written down to.

KW: You started to base your book on *Amphitryon*, and it went somewhere else. Hermes, again, is like that; he is portrayed in the story as sometimes interfering and making people . . .

JB: He says, "I'm only omniscient sometimes," yes . . .

KW: Do the characters get away from you? Do they start doing things on their own when you're not paying attention?

JB: Oh no, writers *say* that, but I always think they're either fools or liars.

Your characters are all me; they have to be. I'm the only person I know from the inside. *Know* is an ambiguous word there, too. But I'm my own material.

In this book I found myself curiously drawn to these little marionettes of mine. I liked Helen, who is sexy as anything; I liked Petra, poor Petra. And I almost missed them when the book was finished. This is very strange. It's probably to do with getting old. I miss my little people.

I think this book is something of a break with the books that I've been writing since the early 1980s. A lot of it's in third person. There are different perspectives. It's not just one maddened eye, as in *Eclipse* and *Shroud* and all those books, so I suppose it's probably closer to a traditional novel than many of the books so far.

So maybe I'm becoming traditional and soft—the new soft, caring Banville. But I did, I quite liked some of the characters and miss them.

KW: Did you not feel that way about your earlier characters. Do you loathe and despise them or hold them in contempt?
JB: Oh, no, I just regard them as my invention, the puppets at the end of my string. Of course, I tried to give them as much life and as much bone and blood as I possibly could. There's no point in writing fiction, if not.

I love Borges, I love Italo Calvino and so on, but I don't love their books very much because of the people in them. There's no blood there; they're just mind.

My project is an examination of reality. I came across a wonderful formulation in the Goncourt journals the other day. Jules de Goncourt wrote, "Flaubert and my brother and I have ushered in a new kind of writing," which he said is a scrupulous investigation of reality, in a prose that speaks the language of poetry. That absolutely sums up my project, but there's as much evidence put on this meticulous examination of reality as there is on the poetic quality of the style.

I'm trying to re-create reality; I'm trying to get the reader to see, to hear, to smell, to taste, the world as it is. Not as other novelists and poets tend to think reality is. I want to get at the real thing itself, which is behind our everyday concerns. I'm trying to get at the essence of the thing itself—it's not easy.

One way that I do it is by a highly developed prose style that wants to mesmerize the reader.

I imagine that my books are either you love them or you hate them. I imagine a couple of the Booker judges just absolutely hated that book—all that god stuff, what is he doing? I can understand that. I don't approve of it, but I can understand it.

But that's the risk that I take. Four years ago, the Booker panel saw what I was doing, or enough of them did for me to win the prize. And I like to think that readers see it as well, and they do, they come up and tell me that they do.

KW: A lot of your characters—certainly the primary male characters, somewhat less with the women—are somehow bifurcated. They've got their outside face, the person that interacts with the world, and then this sort of ogre within who's trying to get out and do something—

JB: Isn't this true of human beings?

The example I always use is the man who gets out of his lover's bed, walks into the street, and meets his worst enemy—they are two different people.

The person that you talk to now is not the person who will go and have lunch with my wife.

As Eliot says, we present a face to meet the faces that we meet. This is not a new discovery of mine, and, of course, we all need secret in our lives.

Our sexual lives are veiled, have to be; otherwise, there'd be no civilized society. And that is not just our sexual lives. I do have a strong sense that the inner life is another person.

Of course, Stevenson got it perfectly in *Dr. Jekyll and Mr. Hyde*. There is somebody else inside that has to be kept in; otherwise, there would be anarchy.

The only thing that I ever wrote in one of the books that was me speaking directly is a paragraph in *The Book of Evidence* where he says, "I never got used to being on this earth. I think our presence here is a cosmic blunder," and that we got the wrong planet. And he says, "But what about the people who were meant to be here? Are they off on the other side of the universe feeling unhoused and lost like us?" And he says, "No, they would have become extinct long ago, for how would they survive, these gentle earthlings, in a world made to contain us?" And that's how I think about it. I think that we got this extraordinarily beautiful place to live in by accident. We don't deserve it, we're doing our best to destroy it, but it keeps forgiving us.

I've been watching those trees across there. The gods have been playing in those trees since we've been talking here. Absolutely beautiful place. Astonishing and tender and cruel and so on as well, doesn't mean us any harm. The world will swipe us down. It doesn't mean us any harm. It just happens to be indifferent to us, which, of course, causes our fury. But I think that's what the books are trying to do; they're trying to be a celebration of this extraordinary place we live in, and of us as well. That's all any artist ever tries to do—to say, "Look, isn't it wonderful, isn't it terrible, but isn't it wonderful as well?

All the talk about the intellectual approach, all of that is incidental to that project: trying to, I suppose, celebrate . . . Isn't that what art tries to do, to celebrate? Anyway, that's my little testament for you.

KW: Thank you so much.
JB: You're very welcome.

The Millions Interview: John Banville

Anne K. Yoder / 2010

Reprinted by permission of Anne K. Yoder, staff writer for *The Millions*. Her fiction, essays, and criticism have appeared in *Fence*, *BOMB*, and *Tin House*, among other publications.

I had the pleasure of speaking with Banville over the phone last week about *The Infinities*, ambitious characters and their potentialities, the characteristics of great art, and the beauty of the sky.

Anne Yoder: *The Infinities* opens with Zeus's son Hermes narrating the goings-on of the Godley family, who have gathered under the same roof while the family's patriarch, Adam Godley, lies on his deathbed. The novel's title alludes to the immortality of the gods as well as Godley's Brahma theory of infinite infinities and interpenetrating universes that debunked the then-prevailing theories of relativity and quantum mechanics. For a book that addresses mortality, much of the focus is on the finite, particularly human mortality and the imminent death of Adam Godley. Why is there such a focus on death in a novel concerned with the infinite?

John Banville: First, all the science is just what we call "cod science" here. It's fake. And the book is not really concerned with quantum physics and those things, which is very frightening for all of us. It's a human comedy. We may be amused and fascinated and enthralled by scientific theories, but we have to live through our days in the world. And we have to face death, and death is what gives life its flavor. I'm absolutely convinced of this. Most of the philosophers have recognized that. Spinoza says the wise man thinks only of death, but all his meditations are a meditation upon life. Which is true. Death is not the point. Life is the point. But death is the beginning of what gives life its point.

Yoder: The elder Adam Godley nears godlike immortality as much as any human can, both through his Brahma theory and because he pursued a life committed to knowledge and thought. But on his death bed it seems like he begins to regret the life of action that he forsook. He thinks, "Doing, doing, is living, as my mother, my poor failed unhappy mother, among others, tried her best to din into me. I see it now, while all along I thought thinking was the only thing." Was his pursuit of ideas a waste of life? Or is his regret inevitable because man's life is finite, and his choices are limited?

Banville: Oh, it's not a wasted life. He has done marvelous things. He has had the most extraordinary intellectual adventures and some not-so-intellectual adventures as well. He's had a good life. But, of course, like everybody, he feels sorry for himself, especially at the end of it. I think that he would exchange all his worldly success and all his scientific and mathematical success to be young again and sleep with his daughter-in-law, Helen. In one of Yeats's last poems he's sitting and watching this girl and saying, what are Russian or Spanish politics to me, "O that I were young again and held her in my arms." It's very simple.

Life at its simplest is very simple. We spin the most extraordinary intellectual conceits and emotional conceits, but in the end, it's quite simple. We want to be happy. We want to be delighted. And, you know, a beautiful woman, as Helen is in the book—in many ways she's the center of the book. She's this wonderfully erotic, sensual creature. She's like those women by a great master like Tiepolo, one of those big, blonde women flying in the sky. And young Adam, for all his ineptness and all his silliness and all his sense of inadequacy, is going to keep her. To my great surprise, it's a happy ending.

Yoder: To my surprise as well. Picking up on Helen, and Roddy as well, I wanted to ask about their ambition. They share a common ambition in their potentialities—in their desire to make themselves something greater. Both are described as hard-hearted and relentless and share a common desire to alter their identities. They resemble other brooding characters from your previous novels, such as Victor Maskell, the spy and art historian in *The Untouchable*, at least in this way of altering identity. The younger Adam, in contrast, is simpler and less ambitious. Although he's plagued by more insecurities, he seems more content with his humanity. I was wondering what the link is between potentialities and ambition, artistic greatness and the human desire to be godlike.

Banville: Yes, these are good questions. Constantly in my work is the tension between the life of the mind and life in the world—the physical life, the life that we want to lead, the Helen side of things, that wonderful, erotic (and I mean *erotic* in the whitest sense of the word), that sensual sense of being in the world, as against the desire to speculate and to think and to make theories. Old Adam professes to have this dismissive attitude toward his son, but he's sort of puzzled because his son is the one who is living in the world. And the son, of course, is the one who believes in the possibility of good, the simplistic, that the simple life might be even more valuable than the life of the mind. It is a comedy.

Heinrich von Kleist, whose play *Amphitryon* is the skeleton of the book, had the ambition to blend Greek drama with Shakespearean burlesque. And that's what I'm trying to do as well. The great thinking, the great speculation, and the great notion of being alive only when one is thinking is constantly undercut by the simplicity of living in the world, the simplicity of desire, even of hunger, of being Rex the dog, who is pure animal. So, it is a comedy.

Yoder: I think you pull that off very well—the contrast of the Greek drama and the Shakespearean burlesque.
Banville: Why, thank you.

Yoder: I was going to ask about Kleist's influence because this seems like a departure from your previous novels, in its narration, in that it's a comedy, a story told in the classical mode with the presence of gods and an adherence to Aristotle's three unities. There's also an inherent playfulness and relative lightness in comparison to your previous work. I wanted to ask about your desire to base the story on *Amphitryon* by Kleist because you already adapted his play once for the stage in *God's Gift*. What is it about his play and this myth that has inspired you to rewrite it again as a novel?
Banville: On a very simple level, I think that Kleist's *Amphitryon* is one of the great works of European literature. Kleist is hardly known at all in the English-speaking world, with great sadness. Goethe is the one that everybody knows, but nobody knows Kleist. He lived but a quarter of the lifetime of Goethe, but he did astonishing things in that short lifetime. *Amphitryon* is his superb, dark masterpiece. It's comic and tragic, continually heartbreaking because Amphitryon loses everything. He loses his wife, his identity, even his name. This is a beautiful—it's an awful cliché to say it—*bittersweet* drama that one never knows quite whether it's tragic or comic, dark or light. And that's what I wanted to catch because that's how life is. Life at one moment is tragic, at another it's comic, at another moment it's extraordinarily erotic and sensual, at another it's gray and dull. And that's what fiction, what all art tries to catch—what life actually feels like.

There's no message. I constantly say one of my absolute mottos is from Kafka, where he says the artist is the man who has nothing to say. I have nothing to say. I have no opinions about anything. I don't care about physical, moral, social issues of the day. I just want to re-create the sense of what life feels like, what it tastes like, what it smells like. That's what art should do. I feel it should be absolutely, gloriously useless.

Yoder: I noticed you pay great attention to physical details in this book, and in other books like *The Sea*, where the sense of smell is very prominent. And I found this interesting in the sense of juxtaposing the lives of the gods and humans. Love and death are the two human characteristics that the gods envy. And man, likewise, envies the immortality of the gods. In *The Infinities*, there's also a heightening of the corporeal, especially the human body in its many beautiful and grotesque forms—from the elder Adam's defecation that caused his stroke, to his hands which are like "a package of scrap meat from the butcher's, chill and sinewy," and the younger Adam's "prizefighter's rolling shoulders" and "weightlifter's legs." Is man's life sweeter in its sensuality?

Banville: Yes, of course. One of the saddest things that's happened in Western civilization is that in order to pretend we're something we're not, we've had to banish the body from philosophy. Our philosophy is all to do with the head, with thought, how we think, how we perceive the world. Very few philosophers, with the remarkable exception of Nietzsche, give due recognition to the fact that we are not pure spirit trapped in a mere body, but that body and spirit have an equal weight. This is one of the great things that art does. One of its duties is to remind people about our physicality, that we're not just brains trapped in this grotesque thing. The "grotesque thing," so-called, that this body is as much a part of us as our minds and is as much a part of our personality as our minds are. I love that scene where Helen is going to the lavatory in the morning. I really enjoyed writing that. I wasn't making a point of any kind. I just wanted to show that this is what people do every morning. I'm not saying we should dwell on this, since it's not a particularly pleasant aspect of our lives. But it *is* an aspect of our lives that we should not try to ignore and push aside

Yoder: And the gods always seem to envy this.

Banville: Well, of course, the gods envy this. The gods, of course, are Adam Godley's mind. They don't have any physical reality; they don't have any reality at all outside Adam Godley. The whole thing is got up by him. It's all happening in his head. It's the old argument which I've been writing about all my life: which is more important, the life of the mind or life in the world, or are they equally important?

Yoder: That's interesting. I noticed how Godley and Hermes seem to merge at a certain point in the narration. In the novel, Hermes is the narrator, and his role as the narrator allows for a greater breadth of perspective than the first-person narrators of many of your previous novels, which are limited to one, sometimes unreliable, point of view. Hermes's omniscience lets the reader penetrate the minds of many characters, even the family dog, Rex, and the comatose Adam. The result is a kaleidoscopic perspective that undermines man's tendency to place himself at the center of the universe. I was wondering how this decentering fits into your greater plan for the novel.
Banville: People used to say I'm a postmodernist in days when postmodernism was still fashionable. It no longer is. If I'm anything, I'm a posthumanist. I don't see human beings as the absolute center of the universe. One of our tragedies, and maybe our central tragedy, is that we imagined that at some point in evolution we reached a plateau where we were no longer animal—that we had left the animal world and become pure spirit, unfortunately tied to this physical body we have to carry around.

This seems a very bad mistake. We should admit our physicality. We have lost contact with the animals, which I think is a disaster. We should realize we are immensely intricate animals, but we are animals still. And we should not lose sight of that. This sounds like my social plan for the world, you know—let's go back to the animals and everything will be fine. We're talking about a novel which is meant to delight and stimulate. As I say, I have no philosophy other than the philosophy of trying to live as well as we can. This is what my characters are doing. Even in my darkest books, my characters are trying to live as well as they can, and to live as rich a life as is possible. That's what art is for—it's to say to people, "Look, the world is an extraordinarily rich place. Look at this extraordinary place we've been put into, this world."

Somebody phoned me the other day, a charity for the blind, and said they're running some series where they're getting people to say in a sentence what is the thing they would miss most. And I said, apart from the faces of my loved ones and the paintings that I love, what I would miss most is the sky. This extraordinary thing we have above us all day long, all night long, is the most amazing thing. It keeps changing. With the seasons it changes; it is constantly beautiful; it is constantly mysterious. And to think we live our lives under this absolute miracle, day after day, is an astonishing thing. And all I try to do in my books is to celebrate this world and our place in it, our predicament in it, for good or ill.

Yoder: The sky is something I take for granted, and that's something that comes up in the book.
Banville: Where do you live?

Yoder: I live in New York, in Brooklyn.
Banville: Oh, you see, there's not much sky in New York.

Yoder: No, the skyline is more prominent than the sky.
Banville: One of the great advantages of living in Ireland is that we have these enormous skies because the buildings are tiny. Don't get me wrong. I'm going to Manhattan on Monday, and I can't wait. Wonderful, wonderful, wonderful city. But I do find myself walking along Fifth Avenue looking at the sky, which is like looking at the bed of a luminous river.

Yoder: Man's incapacity to grasp the world aligns us with the animals. Adam Godley's Brahma theory provides almost too much knowledge for mankind. As Adam remarks, " . . . we had enough, more than enough already, in the bewildering diversities of our old and overabundant world." Hermes comments, too, that man's inability to grasp the immensity of existence comes from a "defective imagination" that makes living possible. As a result, many of the characters hold opinions that are often based on false notions of the world (such as the younger Adam's espousal of the Christian conceit of good battling evil). Much of the time humans are deluded by their own conjectures, so what are humans to make of life? And can science only take us so far?
Banville: My goodness, these are very deep questions you're asking me. Why don't you ask me what my favorite color is or my favorite pop group?

Yoder: Well, the final question is a fairly easy one.
Banville: Again, the essence of art is that it's always light, in all senses of the word. What kills art is solemnity. Art is always serious but never, never solemn. Good art recognizes our peculiar predicament in the world, that

we're suspended in this extraordinary place. We don't know what it's for or why we're here. We know vaguely, but there is no answer to it. It's simply that by just some chance of evolution, we evolved beyond the other animals. We got consciousness of death, which gives all life its flavor. This is peculiar to us, so far as we know. Who knows, the animals may know that they're dying, but it doesn't shape their lives in the way that consciousness of death shapes ours. But art, as I say, has to be light, it has to be frivolous, and it has to be superficial in the best sense of these words. Nietzsche says about the surface that it's where the real depth is, and I think that's true. I never speculate; I never psychologize; I just present, so far as I can, the evidence—this is what one sees; this is how the world looks; this is how it tastes and smells. In other words, I don't know how to answer your question.

Yoder: In this book, in particular, names seem significant. There's Adam and his son Adam, the "clay men," named after the first biblical Adam. There's Dr. Fortune, Petra, who is a stone in her mother's breast. The act of naming is mentioned multiple times, including the older Adam's disinclination to call people by their names. So, what is in a name here?

Banville: For a novelist, it's important to get the names right, simply on a technical level. Once you have the names and all the characters right, then you've got the book. And in my other life, as a book reviewer, I always know a book is flawed when the names don't suit the characters. There's no science to this, there's no way of saying why a character is suited to a certain name, or vice versa, but it's simply true. John Le Carré, for instance, not a great novelist, but he has a genius when it comes to names. All the names in his cast are absolutely perfect. Henry James is similar. You can tell when a novelist is not comfortable with the material if he gets the names wrong. But that's the mystical thing, because I don't know how it works.

I was calling Helen something else for a long time—I can't remember what it was. But then I thought, of course, she has to be Helen. It's a very simple name, it's straightforward, it's all those silly references back to the Greek, and so on. But it was the right name for her. She only came alive for me when I found her name. It's no great science; it's a quite simple thing.

The naming of names, of course, is what literature does. It names things, and it examines a name. It brings back to attention the question of what it is to be called something. We all have that curious sensation of when a word slips away from its context, when it becomes a grunt. That's a very scary phenomenon. This is one of the things art does, literary art does, is to name things well.

Yoder: And, therefore, the writers are the "relentless taxonomists," as Hermes calls man in the novel.

Banville: Oh, yeah. And by the way, my favorite color is blue.

Yoder: Which explains why blue is prominent in the novel. Here's the easy question: *The Infinities* is the first novel published under your name, John Banville, since *The Sea* which won the Booker Prize in 2005. In the meantime, you published three literary crime novels under the name Benjamin Black.

Banville: Don't say they're "literary." Just call them crime novels.

Yoder: Well, they have been called "literary." How did writing those novels inform this one, if they did at all? And do you plan to continue publishing novels under both names?

Banville: Oh, yes, I have a new novel coming out shortly under Benjamin Black's name. It's a completely different discipline. I like doing it, it's an inglorious craftwork that I enjoy immensely. And, yes, I'll keep doing it. It's an adventure I've embarked on, and whether I'm making a mistake or otherwise, I don't know. But we stumble along in darkness. We think that we're deciding to do things, we think that we're directing our lives, but we're not. We're just being blown hither and thither by the wind.

John Banville with
Paula Marantz Cohen

Paula Marantz Cohen / 2010

Content from the Drexel InterView provided courtesy of the Pennoni Honors College, Drexel University, recorded 26 February 2010, in the A. J. Drexel Picture Gallery, Drexel University, Philadelphia, PA, USA. Permission to print transcription granted by Paula Marantz Cohen.

Paula Marantz Cohen: Hello and welcome to the Drexel InterView. I'm your host, Paula Marantz Cohen, speaking to you from the Drexel University Picture Gallery. Today our guest is the prolific and much-acclaimed author John Banville. John Banville has written seventeen novels under his own name and several more under his penname, Benjamin Black. He is also a playwright and a critic. His 2005 novel, *The Sea*, won the Man Booker Prize, the highest literary award in Britain. His latest novel, *The Infinities*, was recently published by Knopf. John Banville, welcome to the Drexel InterView.
John Banville: Nice to be here.

Cohen: You are a very *prolific* writer. You've written seventeen novels, as I said, and you've also written plays, short stories, and reviews. It seems to me that you must be writing all the time, and I wonder if it is a compulsion.
Banville: Maybe I'm not so much prolific as just old, and I've been around for a long time.

Cohen: But you don't seem that old. [laughs] Seventeen is a lot.
Banville: It *is* a compulsion, of course. I can't stop doing it. If I did, I'd fall off the edge of the world. It's a way of life now. People ask me sometimes, "Why do I write?" And I say, "You may as well ask me, 'Why do I read?'" I can't *not* do it. There's a sort of pathos in it, really. I think that, for me, the world is

not real until it's been pushed through the mesh of language. It's a way of validating reality for myself.

Cohen: So, do you think about experience all the time as grist for your writing?
Banville: The English playwright Alan Bennett said once that the bad things that have happened are not quite as bad for the writer as they are for other people because, for the writer, no matter how bad the event is, it can always be used as material. And, yes, everything is grist to the writing mill. I remember, years ago, when my wife and I were together first, we were driving somewhere. And we were having one of those arguments that you have when you're together first, when both people are trying to sort the other one out. She was in magnificent rhetorical flight and absolute fury, and I said to her, "That was wonderful. Can I use that?" [laughter] She said, "You monster. You're an absolute monster." And I said, "I know I'm a monster, but can I use it?"

Cohen: Your writing is really quite extraordinary. You have been called "a writer's writer," very much a craftsman.
Banville: Oh, God.

Cohen: I know you must be tired of that. But, to me, as a reader of your work, you're also very much involved with moving plot forward. You balance style—word choice, and so forth—with plot. You often have, not just in your thrillers but in your literary books, a mystery, a surprise that the reader is led to. How do you balance that, and do you think about those two facets of writing consciously as you write?
Banville: I'm glad to hear you say that you see the plots in my novels. Lots of people complain that there's no plot. I can never understand this. They seem to be embarrassingly forward plots. [laughter] The novel form requires a plot. Ian Forrester said, "There must be a story." All novelists would rather write about nothing. But, in the best sense of the word, the novel is a vulgar form and requires story. It appeals to that aspect of ourselves which needs story. We all need bedtime stories, even if they're told to us at midday. We never quite grow up in that aspect, and some of us need to *tell* stories. So, yes, it has to be. There is no point in having a novel which is all style. Flaubert tried to do that. Joyce tried to do it. But they couldn't succeed. Even *Finnegans Wake* has a plot of sorts. So, a plot is absolutely necessary.

Cohen: You said that many novelists do not want to have plot. Yet I think that there is this undertow: you are a novelist because you want plot. Otherwise, you'd be a poet. Wouldn't you?

Banville: Yes. In a peculiar way I don't find the novel form very interesting from an artistic point of view. It's rather clumsy. It is at a certain level, as Henry James said about *Middlemarch*, "a loose, baggy monster." But loose, baggy monsters have their attractions. Elephants are amazing creatures, and the novel is a kind of elephant. But I like being able to make that elephant dance on a quarter.

Cohen: You've written short stories, but not many. I wonder why not because that would seem to be a more congenial form for you.

Banville: Well, you see, when I was starting to write seriously in the late fifties and sixties, all our ambitions were to have a short story published in a little magazine. Now, as far as I can see, everybody wants to be a pop star or make a movie, earn vast amounts of money from things. We were very modest in those days. Everybody started out by assembling a book of short stories. You would get that published, and the publisher would accept your book of short stories *on* condition that you would give him your first novel because, of course, short stories didn't sell. I now don't know how to write short stories. I've lost the knack. I can't think in that compressed way that you need to for the short story.

Cohen: I understand that. Quite a number of your novels have a historical element; they involve research. I'm thinking particularly of your trilogy: *Doctor Copernicus*, *Kepler*, and *The Newton Letter*. I wonder about the balance, again, of historical fact. If you have too much of it, you sound like a pedant. If you have not enough of it, of course, your reader doesn't know where you are. How do you handle *that*? Is that something that you've struggled with?

Banville: Yes, that's a good point. I remember when I was writing *Doctor Copernicus*, the first novel that I did that could be called "historical," I didn't realize it was historical until I was halfway through the damn thing. I realized I would have to start doing some "research," quote- unquote. But I remember my wife saying to me, "Look, don't be frightened by the facts. A fact is just a fact. It's not necessarily the truth." [laughter] And she's absolutely right. Frequently the truth lies somewhere outside or behind the facts. So, yes, one has to be very careful not to load the book with all the research you've done. Flaubert boasted that for his book about Carthage, *Salammbô*, that he had read ten thousand books, exaggerating as usual. It's a great novel, but you can feel the weight of those ten thousand books he read *weighing* the thing down. It's really much better to imagine. You know, Henry James said a wonderful thing. He said that a young lady of polite upbringing walks past a soldiers' barracks. She glances in one window and then another window. She can then go home and write a three-volume novel on the military life. And it's true. The imagination is what counts, not the facts.

Cohen: Well, Henry James did talk about the germ and the importance of removing it from reality quickly enough so that it wouldn't be contaminated by too much reality. I think that is so true, as a novelist myself, that too much can really deaden the imagination.

Banville: Oh, yes, there is nothing more deadening than that, as you said, too much reality. There's another nice story of W. H. Auden, the great English poet, in a train with friends going through the Alps. He's reading something, as usual, and the friends are saying to him, "Look at the view. Look at the view." And Auden says, "Yes, one look is enough," and goes back to his book. Which is *true*. The world is made in the mind.

Cohen: I want to talk a little bit about your 1997 novel, *The Untouchable*, which is based on the great British spy scandal, the story of "the Cambridge Five." Your book uses that scandal as a codebook. You use that and then you embroider it imaginatively. The main character, Victor Maskell, is based on Anthony Blunt, who was uncovered lastly as a spy in 1979, and he was the curator for the Queen's paintings. Fascinating character as you create him. I wonder about your use of this. What drew you to this? It's certainly a very provocative and interesting story, but what drew you to write a novel and imagine these people the way you did?

Banville: Well, I was sitting watching a documentary about the great painter Poussin. Anthony Blunt was a great expert on Poussin. The program started with some footage of Blunt on the day that he'd been named as a spy by Mrs. Thatcher, and he was doing a press conference. He was sitting in a long, narrow room, just sitting alone on a chair. At the other end of the room, all the journalists were getting their notebooks ready and their cameras ready, preparing for this "press conference," so-called. Blunt didn't realize that there was a camera off to the side that was running. And Blunt, who was completely impassive, was just watching the journalists. Then this tiny smile crossed his face as he watched them. You could see him saying to himself, "These people think they're going to get things out of me that some of the best interrogators in MI5 spent years trying to get. What fools they are." And I thought, I have to write about this person. It was just that little smile. *That* was the germ in that book.

Cohen: That was the germ. Well, you make Blunt into an Irishman, even though he wasn't, and you, of course, are. That's one of the few *clear* deviations from the record. Tell us about your choice to make him Irish.
Banville: First of all, I realized that I was going to have to write about an *almost* contemporary Englishman, and I just didn't feel safe enough to do that. I knew that all the reviewers would catch me out on tiny details, so I decided to make him into an Irishman. But his great friend was the Irish poet Louis MacNeice, and I had just read a biography of Louis MacNeice. So, I took MacNeice's childhood and gave it to my character Maskell. And I worried a bit about this, but, as I said, Blunt was a great expert on the painter Poussin. When I was thinking about using MacNeice as the Irish side of my character, I took down a volume of MacNeice's poetry. The first poem was called "Poussin." I thought, That's a message from Louis MacNeice. He's saying, "All right, go ahead and use my life." But *you* know yourself this is how fiction is made. It's made out of bits and scraps.

Cohen: Yes. I think you did a wonderful job with that character. I want to talk about *The Sea*, which, I have to say, of the books I've read of yours, is my favorite. I think it's a fabulous book, and it did win the Man Booker Prize. I wonder if *you* feel that it's your best book.
Banville: Oh, I don't *know*. I hate them *all*.

Cohen: I know you hate them all. I've read that you loathe them all, and you don't reread.
Banville: They're standing affronts to me.

Cohen: But you must have had a feeling. I know, as a writer, that when you're writing, you have some sense, even if you don't fully acknowledge it, of how good you think the book is.
Banville: Well, I'll tell you, when I finished the book and sent it off to the publishers, I waited in great trepidation because I thought they wouldn't publish it. I thought they would say, "John, we don't really like this. Put it away in a drawer, and we'll wait for the next one."

Cohen: But when you're writing, there is that sense, isn't there—I don't know what point it is—where you feel that you are doing something very sig-nificant? It may dissipate by the time you're done, and it may not be there at the very beginning, but isn't there a point in the writing when you feel that?

Banville: Oh, yes, it's always there for me at the beginning. At the beginning, I could do anything. I've just started a novel, and it's going to be the greatest novel of the twenty-first century. It's going to amaze everybody. I'll be given two Nobel Prizes. [laughter] It will make pots of money. I know, rationally, that when I come to the end of it in three or four years' time, I'll regard it as just another botched job. But, for now, I'm full of optimism, fizzing with optimism. Otherwise, we wouldn't start.

Cohen: I also wanted to ask you about your portrayal of women in your novels. It seems to me they divide into two sorts. They're either intensely attractive and desirable or extremely not.

Banville: Well, I'm really not evading your question when I say that I don't see very much difference between men and women. My women characters are not, to me, women characters. They're just characters. When women ask me about my treatment of women in my books, I say to them, "Look at my treatment of *men* in my books; it's far darker, far worse."

Cohen: Well, that's true. They're both darkly represented. You're abso-lutely right.

Banville: But I've never felt a great distinction between men and women, apart from the obvious distinctions.

Cohen: It's hard to believe you did not attend university, yet you are one of the most extensively read novelists alive today. There are echoes of Proust, Joyce, Beckett, Kleist, Nabokov in your work, as well as scientific informa-tion. I wonder, then, if you would recommend that writers not go to the uni-versity and simply read, as you seem to have done, voraciously and widely.

Banville: No, no, no. I deeply regret now that I didn't go to university. I wanted to get away from my family. I wanted to be free. I wanted to leave all that behind me. So, I went to work for the airline [Aer Lingus], which would give me cheap travel, and I would be independent. But *now* I realize, and I realized when I was in my thirties, that that was a mistake. I should have had that three or four years of being a student.

Cohen: What do you think it would've given you?

Banville: I think it would've given me more of a sense of ease in the world.

I think that's what university does. That's what an education does. It's not for training you to be a doctor or a scientist or a novelist. It's for putting you at ease with the world and with yourself, and I missed that. I miss it now. So, I would not recommend that. I'm pushing my own children to go to university and have that three or four years. Even if it's just fun, do it.

Cohen: I'll have to think about that. I want to talk about the sense of mystery in your books, and the fact that you write mystery novels under a penname, Benjamin Black. Why this distinction between your so-called "literary novels" and your genre fiction. Why *do* you have a penname?

Banville: Well, just when I had finished *The Sea* in 2004, I began to read Georges Simenon, whom I had not read before. Not the Maigret books, which I have never succeeded in finishing one of them, but what he called his *romans durs*, his hard novels. The publishing wing of the *New York Review of Books* had begun to reissue some of these, so I read them for the first time. I was completely bowled over by these *extraordinary* works. Very limited vocabulary, very straightforward narrative style, but the effects that he achieves are just astonishing. I think at least half a dozen of those *romans durs*, those hard novels, can stand with any twentieth-century literature, not as pulp or detective, but up there with Camus and Sartre and the rest of them. I thought, if this can be done in this simple, straightforward, narrative style, I would try something myself. I had a television script that wasn't going to be made, so I thought, I'll turn it into a novel. I didn't know if I could do it. I sat down one Monday morning in the house of a friend of mine in Italy, and by lunch time I had become Benjamin Black. I found that I could do it.

Cohen: So, the more minimalist style is part of the identity of Benjamin Black, as opposed to the more poetical and literary style of your other novels.

Banville: Oh yes, and I write in a completely different way. Banville writes very slowly, very slowly indeed, scratches out maybe a couple of hundred words a day. Whereas old Black sits down, knocks off two thousand. But Black is a craftsman, and I admire him for that. I quite admire his work. I like Black's work. I don't like Banville's. [laughs] Don't let me make a mistake. I regard Banville's books as better than everyone else's, just not good enough for me. Okay?

Cohen: I see; I get a sense of that, yes. I think there is an ego there lurking somewhere.

Banville: Do you? Did you suspect that? Yes? [laughing]

Cohen: I suspect it. I don't know you that well. Will you reread Black? You won't even look at Banville.
Banville: No. Why would I reread Black?

Cohen: Right, you can write another novel. Why bother rereading? Finally, I want to ask you about the comic aspect of your writing. There is comedy there, very dark, for the most part, but there are these wry and comic asides. I wonder if you've ever thought of writing a novel that was purely comic.
Banville: Oh, I don't think I'd know how to write a comic novel. I'd make terrible jokes. [laughter] They'd all be lumbering and unfunny. Comedy arises from narrative; it arises from the language. You spot an opportunity, and you seize on it. Especially for an Irish writer, it's usually to do with wordplay and using enormous and, in many ways, ridiculous vocabulary. People constantly criticize me for using big words. I always say, "Do you mean big words like *screwdriver* and *marmalade*?" But I say, "Look, you have to realize that Irish writers are almost always ironic, and that their most grandiose poses are frequently completely undercut by irony." The comedy, as I say, arises from the irony, from the narrative, from the language. It's not imposed. I wouldn't know how to do it.

Cohen: Yes. Are you an Irish novelist, in quotation marks? I know you now live in Dublin. You have, I guess, for most of your life.
Banville: Yes, I was born in Ireland; I live in Ireland, and I write in what we call Hiberno-English, our version of English, which is very different from *English* English. It's as different as American English is different from *English* English. It's a wonderfully supple and rich literary mode to work in. Irish writers love the ambiguity of language. We love the imprecision of language. We love, especially, the richness of the English language, which is one of the greatest languages in the world. Of course, we are deeply scarred by the fact of having lost our own language, having lost the Irish language in the middle of the nineteenth century. But we made the best of it. We have changed the basic English that we were given, which is rather like the Latin of the Roman Empire. It's a language of command, of narrative, of straightforward statement, and we changed that into something rich and strange.

Cohen: That's very eloquently put. Now, your latest novel, *The Infinities*, is a very interesting novel, the story of an Irish family. It is narrated by the Greek god Hermes, whose father was Zeus. Zeus makes an appearance, as well, at various occasions in the novel. It borrows from von Kleist's play

Amphitryon, where mortals and gods interact. It's a very tricky conceit, it seems to me, and you carry it off. Tell me about your decision to write about this. Did you feel that it was difficult to do?

Banville: Well, all novels are difficult, as you know, but not particularly. I had always admired Heinrich von Kleist's play *Amphitryon*. He's a very great dramatist, almost unknown in the English-speaking world. I would put him up there with Goethe. In fact, I think *Amphitryon* is better than anything Goethe could have written. And I was going to base the novel quite closely on *Amphitryon*. Kleist's ambition was to blend Greek drama with Shakespearean burlesque, and in *Amphitryon* he succeeds in this. It's a wonderful play of wonderful comedy and manners. Very light, very playful, but very dark and dangerous, as well. In *Amphitryon* the central character loses everything. He loses, even, his identity. So, it is quite dark. That was, if you like, the inspiration for it. It certainly gave me the structure for the book. But I also wanted to look at human life from a different perspective. And the Greek gods have always appealed to me immensely. The great genius of the ancient Greeks was to find a mode by which to account for everything in human life. There's a god for everything, much more sane and much more workable than monotheism, which has caused so much damage to our world, as we know. So, I loved the idea of the Greek gods, and I loved the idea of Hermes as a narrator because, of course, all us novelists think of ourselves as gods, at least demigods. [laughter] And it was fun to do that, yes.

Cohen: It seemed like it was fun. I read somewhere that you've said that you are not a psychological novelist. I would say that's true. You say that Henry James, too, is not a psychological novelist, and I agree with you there, as well. But here, it seems to me, you're pushing "nonpsychological" to the furthest point, in some ways. On the other hand, my question to you here would be, we tend to think of the psychological as a synonym for the complex. Without that, what makes complexity? I'm not quite sure how to frame this question.

Banville: Oh, I know what you're saying, yes. But look at the world. Look how complex the surface of the world is, without pretending that we can go beyond that. I'm an antipsychologist because we cannot *know*. All we can know is something about the insides of our own minds. We can know nothing about the insides of other people's minds. We can conjecture. And we can guess, but we can't *know*. But what we *can* know is what we see. I think that art is, in the old Christian sense, a matter of witness. You bear witness to what you've seen. My books are the record of what one man saw in his little moment on earth and gave his witness of it.

Cohen: I want to thank you very much, John Banville, for talking to us today, and giving us your sense of witness.
Banville: Thank you. I enjoyed it.

The Greatest Invention of Humankind: The Sentence

Jill Owens / 2010

First published on Powells.com on 5 April 2010, following the publication of *The Infinities*. http://www.powells.com/post/interviews/john-banville-the-powells-interview. Reprinted by permission.

Jill Owens: *The Infinities* is based in part on *Amphitryon*, the play by Heinrich von Kleist, which you had already adapted. What made you decide to go back and adapt it into the form of a novel?

John Banville: Kleist's play is one of the great dramas of Western literature. It's hardly known at all in the English-speaking world. In fact, Kleist is hardly known in the English-speaking world. Kleist died at the age of thirty-two in the early 1800s. His ambition was to blend Greek drama with Shakespearean burlesque, which was quite a task, but he succeeded, I think, in *Amphitryon*. Zeus comes to Earth because he has fallen in love with the wife of Amphitryon and spends the night with her in the form of Amphitryon, so she thinks it's her husband. The next day, Amphitryon himself comes back unexpectedly, and there follows a wonderful comedy of errors. It's very dark, but a great piece of literature.

So, I thought of modeling a novel on it. I was going to stick fairly closely to the drama, but, of course, fiction has its own rules and requires different methods. But *Amphitryon* is still there, clandestine, within the book.

Owens: I would say that *The Infinities* is a kind of comedy as well, even though it's pretty dark; it's about death and mortality.

Banville: Well, it's about life.

Owens: True. [laughter] The tone is lighter than in some of your previous works. At one point, Hermes describes the gods as being playful, but not benign, which I thought actually described the tone of this book fairly well. How did you think about tone and voice in this book?

Banville: Yes, it is playful. I have always tried to avoid solemnity. I like to think I am serious, but never solemn. I think solemnity is the death of art. But yes, it is playful and lighter. I didn't really see that until I'd finished the book and some people said, "This is quite funny and quite comic." I looked back over it and thought back over it, and I realized that yes, it was. Frequently, an artist doesn't really know what he's doing. We stumble along in the darkness. There's a wonderful quote of Kafka's, I wish I could remember it. It's something like, "I don't think as I speak; I don't speak as I write. I don't write as I should, and it all goes on in deepest darkness."

I wasn't intending to make a comedy or a tragedy. I preferred to make a book and that's what I did. It did, for some reason, come out more playful and, I like to think, funny. That's what I would like to give people. If people don't laugh, hopefully they smile very hard.

Owens: The point of view is interesting as well, and this may go to what you just said about not thinking too hard about it as you were writing it. It's in third-person through several different characters, and then between first-person with Hermes and then first-person with Adam . . . and then it gets very blurry. I was wondering how you decided to structure the point of view in that way?

Banville: Again, I didn't decide. I'd like to claim that I did. It's like life itself; we're so adrift. We think we're in control, and we're doing this and doing that, making this decision or taking that direction—but in fact, we're just drifting along. The older I get, the more I like to let books find their own direction. I feel that my instinct now is such that I can work along and trust it.

I sometimes think that the entire farrago is taking place in Adam Godley's mind as he is lying there preparing to die—the invention of his very active mind. But as well as referencing Kleist, of course, it's intended to be Shakespearean. The names are just ridiculous—Adam Godley and Benny Grace and so on. There is a very high level of irony in it. I think that anyone looking for a straightforward novel is not going to find it. I hope they find this more interesting and somewhat delightful.

It is not a straightforward work and it is, as you said, very playful. It's full of tricks and little reversals, odd terms. That's the way I try to write fiction; it's always playful. If you look at even what's in the darkest works of Beckett, for instance, they're very playfully structured. Beckett was a great fan of French crime fiction. He used to devour those books. All his books have a peculiar kind of detective story plot, and they all have a twist in the end. For instance, in *Molloy*, Malone's action starts at midnight, when he is peeking in the window. After a long and devastating journey, he comes back to find his world in ruins. He says, "I went in, I sat down and wrote, 'It was midnight when he was peeking in the window.'" It was not midnight, it was not raining, and the whole book collapses like a house of cards, with this wonderful trick, this twist in the end. So, even in the darkest work, it is always playful.

Owens: One of main themes in this book is that the gods are jealous of our humanity because of our life force and temporality, which gets back to mortality. And I love the description of the humans from the dog Rex's point of view.
Banville: Everybody likes that. [laughter]

Owens: I was trying to figure out an excerpt from it because the whole paragraph worked so well together. A few lines that might sum it up: "They are afraid of something. Something that is always there though they pretend it was not . . . Their laughter has a shrill note, so they seem to be not only laughing, but crying out. When they weep, their sobs and lamentations are disproportionate. So, what is supposed to have upset them is just a pretext, and their anguish springs really from this other frightful thing that they know and are trying to ignore." Was Rex meant to be kind of a counterpoint to the gods' perspective?
Banville: Yes, he's a kind of god himself. But whereas the gods can't understand love and can't experience mortality, Rex doesn't hold that mortality, and he misses the dark secret that torments the humans around him, one that he can't quite figure out. He feels sorry for them, and he doesn't understand why they're so overwrought all the time. I suppose that is one of the deeper themes in the book, the price that we pay for our self-consciousness is that we get the consciousness of death, which sweetens every single act in our lives. It's just momentous. The fact that all this will end.

So yes, that would be a theme, but again I try to treat it lightly. Rex is a comic character, and I like to see him as a very Shakespearean dog. He's also very kindly. He knows his people, his human beings. He takes them for walks; he eats the awful, unpalatable food they give him. He wants to treat them well.

There are a lot of benign feelings in this book. As human beings, they're trying to think of each other and tolerate each other. In a way, if you look at the book closely, the human beings are the gods and the gods are something else. They're kind of frozen in immortality, unloved and incapable of loving, driven by lust, by anger, by jealousy, by all the things that we're driven by, but without the compensating delights of ordinary love and mortal life. In a sad way, the book is trying to celebrate the beauty of this world and the extraordinary miracle it is to be alive. [laughter] I don't want to get carried away here, but that is what I am trying to do. That's what all art does, even the darkest of it. It celebrates what it is to be alive.

Owens: I think the book does that wonderfully. It's interesting because the title itself is referring to infinities both in space, time, and potential. The idea of other selves on other worlds and the image of the boy on the train, which seems to refer to old Adam in his youth, is an enormous subject to try to write about fairly concretely, which I think you do here.

Banville: Yes. The science is all completely fake and ridiculous. [laughter] Of course, who knows? The most ridiculous thing that you can think of tomorrow turns out to be true. Physics is a very strange world, with very strange discoveries. It might well be that somebody will start manipulating the infinities in equations tomorrow, or the next day, and come up with an extraordinary discovery. That, again, is one of the great joys of being alive. There is always something new. There are infinities of new things, always. I am interested in physics. Twentieth-century physics is often full of beautiful ideas and notions and images that are more interesting in many ways than the ideas in twentieth-century philosophy.

The beauty that drives physicists and the beauty that drives the novelist is absolutely fascinating. I realized when I was very young that science and art come from the same source. Once they react to that source in the human intellect, they change. There are advantages and disadvantages on both sides, art and science. But they do spring from the same source. So, though I can barely add two and two, I know how a mathematician's mind works, because I do the same kind of thing in my much humbler way. I don't speak the language of the gods, which is mathematics, but I aspire to the condition of mathematics.

Owens: The world of *The Infinities* is slightly different, or possibly later than our own. I read the book twice, and the first time I read it, I thought that it was a slightly overlapping parallel world—which includes a bellicose Sweden, the prominence of von Kleist as an artist, and then, of course, the physics. When I reread it yesterday, I thought maybe it was a little bit in the future, but I wasn't sure which interpretation was correct.

Banville: Any interpretation that you want to put on it is correct. There are as many versions of *The Infinities* as there are readers to read it. Every reader remakes the book; every viewer remakes the painting; every listener remakes the music. The thing stays itself, at some level, but our interpretations make new things of it. As far as I can see, *The Infinities* takes place under no time. There are telephones, but the postal system is still run on the Thurn and Taxis. I had a lot of fun doing that, knocking Goethe off his pedestal. I had fun, as I say, inventing these silly names of people. I would hope that the book would be read in that spirit, to go back to the word we've been using, in that *playfulness*.

Owens: Yes, I think it absolutely is. I was wondering if you chose that setting, which is both familiar and alien, to introduce or reinforce the theme of the uncanny.

Banville: Yes, I think so. I do think art is a process of making the familiar unfamiliar, showing us how the ordinary is, in turn, extraordinary. If you read Freud's little essay on the uncanny, that's essentially what it is, bringing back familiar things in unfamiliar shapes, showing them to us, in Freud's view, in a terrifying way. But also, from the point of view of the artist, showing it to us in a delightful way. We certainly discover the things we thought were ordinary are not ordinary at all. This is what good art does. It takes a pebble in the road or a human being, and it concentrates on them until they begin to glow. I think the concept and the notion of blushing is very important in art, and in my kind of art. You know, the artist concentrates on the detail of the object until it blushes in the way the love object blushes when a lover gazes at it with that particularly intense gaze. That is what art should do. It should make the world blush and give up its secrets.

Owens: That's a wonderful way of putting that. I love that metaphor. There is a sentence in the book: "How to conceive of a reality sufficiently detailed, sufficiently incoherent, to accommodate all the things that are in the world?" This seems to get to the heart of writing to me, of creating an entirely new and entirely familiar world, all at once.

Banville: Yes, that is the difficulty of writing. When we're very young and start writing our first short stories, or whatever, we're shamed by the difficulty of it, by that awful realization that all the things in your head cannot be put down on the page. It has to be done word by word, line by line, paragraph by paragraph. One has to find some way of encompassing this. I always think that reality is square, but art is round. Trying to encompass that square reality with a round method is terribly, terribly difficult. It always involves sleight of hand, a marvelous trick.

You can be sitting in a room reading about Leopold Bloom, for example, and the person you're reading about, the thing made of words, will seem to you more real than the person sitting across the fireplace from you. Art can summon up an extraordinarily vivid and intense sense of reality. How is that done? It's impossible to say. This is just a string of black marks on a white page and yet what it does to our imagination is much more miraculous than the miracle of the loaves and fishes.

Owens: You were quoted as saying that you would like to give your prose "the kind of denseness and thickness that poetry has." How do you think about your prose, while you're writing, paragraph by paragraph and line by line?
Banville: I work by the sentence. That's the unit for me, not the word or the paragraph. Joyce, for instance, was a master of the paragraph. *Ulysses* is a masterpiece of paragraph-making. But for me, it's the sentence. I have to have the rhythm of the sentence before I can feel the true meaning of the sentence. Do you know what I mean? It's not that the rhythm is supreme, and I give up sense in order to have rhythm. That's allowed to the poet, but prose has to make sense. But there has to be a rhythm there. The meaning both shapes the sentence, but also to some extent is shaped by the sentence. This is a strange process that I don't understand.

It's very difficult when you start thinking about the sentence or trying to talk about the sentence. It is an extraordinary thing. I have said before that if I were asked to name the greatest invention of humankind, I would say it's the sentence. You can do without the wheel. There have been civilizations, like the Incas or the Aztecs, that had no wheel, but they had the sentence. That's where everything comes from—our thinking, our communication, our adoration of the gods, and our abjuration of the devil. It's all done through the sentence. So, I feel extraordinarily privileged to be making some sort of living and making my life vocation through making sentences. It's an extraordinary thing. I'm a very, very lucky person.

Owens: The sentence is sort of the atom of humanity, then.
Banville: That's it. [laughter]

Owens: I was curious who you considered influential writers. You've named Beckett and Joyce already. D. H. Lawrence came to mind while I was reading this book, in places.

Banville: I greatly admire Lawrence as a poet, more than as a novelist. He is a marvelous, marvelous poet. His poems are not terribly shapely, but my goodness, they're intense and they do conjure up the world. His poems about animals are absolutely superb. People always talk about me being influenced by Nabokov and Joyce. But who I'm most influenced by, if I'm influenced by anybody, is Henry James.

Henry James is the supreme stylist. He may not be the greatest artist as a writer, but he is certainly the greatest novelist. If you look at the body of work that he left behind, and those last three novels, where his style becomes so opaque and so cloudy, I think he may have found more interesting modernistic ground even than *Ulysses*. *Ulysses* is a kind of throwback to a medieval world. But Henry James, in those late novels, really catches something of what it is to be conscious. That strange fuzzy sensation that we have, where we're not thinking words, we're not thinking in images, we're not thinking in feelings, but we're thinking a strange whipped-up egg white of all these things. We seem to claw our way through this strange cloud of knowing, of barely knowing. Henry James came as close as anybody has come to what it is to be conscious, an incoherent state. So, if I were to admit to any influence, it would be to Henry James.

Owens: I happened to be in Mexico this past week with some friends, and we were talking about dead writers that we would bring along to a desert island with us.
Banville: Oh, I wouldn't bring Henry James! [laughter]

Owens: One of my friends did pick him.
Banville: Well, he would be a marvelous conversationalist, but you might have to wait forever for him to get to the end of his sentences. He always reminds me of that wonderful cartoon about the German language where there are two men, one of whom is in an absolute rage, and he's strangling the other. The man who is being strangled is perfectly calm and the caption is, "He's waiting for the verb." I think with Henry James, you'd have to wait for a long time for him to get to the end of the sentence.

Who did you pick? Writers are not very good company. [laughter]

Owens: I picked Keats.
Banville: Oh yes, Keats would be wonderful, wouldn't he? Did you see that movie [*Bright Star*], Jane Campion's movie . . . ?

Owens: No, not yet.

Banville: It's quite good. It is worth seeing, but it doesn't catch anything of Keats, because Keats was such a feisty little guy. He was tiny, but he was always picking fights with people over matters of honor and principle. He was an absolutely wonderful creature. I would love to have known Keats.

There's another influence. I'm certainly influenced by Keats. Of course, one has to be very careful being influenced by somebody with such a rich imagination and such rich language. Christopher Ricks has a great book, the title of which is wonderful: *Keats and Embarrassment.* And you know, Keats's poetry is sort of embarrassing. You read it as a teenager and you feel you should be in a locked room reading it, it's so voluptuous. [laughter] But he was an influence. He was one of the earliest people I started to read.

Owens: Switching gears, I had never read much mystery or crime fiction, but I picked up *Christine Falls* a few years ago and I was utterly drawn in by the language. How did you start writing those mysteries and why under a pseudonym?

Banville: The pseudonym, first of all, was so that people wouldn't think that I was pulling a postmodernist literary hoax. I wanted people to realize that what you see is what you get. These are straightforward books. They are not meant to be literary endeavors in the way that Borges would sometimes write detective stories and so on. These are straightforward mystery novels. So, I took the pseudonym but never intended to hide behind it. I simply wanted people to realize that this was just an entirely different direction that I was taking.

I had finished *The Sea* in 2004, and I began to read some Simenon, which I hadn't read before. Not the Maigret book—which I've never actually managed to finish—but what he called his *romans durs*, his hard novels, such as *Tropic Moon, Dirty Snow,* and *Monsieur Monde Vanishes. The New York Review of Books,* the publishing wing, has reissued about a dozen of them. I was bowled over when I started to read them, to see what could be achieved with such very spare vocabulary and a very direct style. No psychologizing, no speculations, just straightforward narrative. I thought I would try to do something similar. I would not have Simenon's extraordinary spareness and his capacity to summon up a scene in half a sentence. It's an extraordinary gift. I don't know how he manages it. But I was greatly taken.

And I'd read other people, like Richard Stark and his series of Parker novels, most of which were written in the early sixties. Again, I think they're masterly works, not of crime fiction, but of literature of any sort. I'm very glad to see that, partly with my encouragement, the University of Chicago Press is reissuing Richard Stark's books.

Owens: I've seen them; they're very well done.
Banville: Aren't they wonderful? And then there's James Cain. *The Postman Always Rings Twice* is an extraordinary book. I think he dashed it off in a weekend. It's a frightening, dark, and absolutely true book.

I don't like the notion of genre. For me there's just good writing, and then there's writing that isn't good. A lot of very good writing, indeed, happens in the so-called "genre of crime fiction." So, I wanted to join the ranks and try my hand at it, and I found that I could do it. I could do it with extraordinary fluency. I would write a Benjamin Black book extremely quickly, whereas a John Banville book takes years to scratch out. It's an entirely different way of working.

Owens: I guess my last question would be, what are you reading lately that you are enjoying?
Banville: Certainly the American books that I have read very recently that have impressed me most are Robert Richardson's three biographies of Thoreau, Emerson, and William James. I think those three books together, which I suppose could be called a trilogy, are an amazing work of contemporary American literature. People make this whole separation between creative and noncreative writing, which I never understand. These are as creative as any fiction. They're beautifully done, and they're exciting.

I just finished reading Roberto Calasso's book *Tiepolo Pink*, which was reviewed in the *New Republic*. It's a marvelous book about a marvelous painter. That's the marvelous thing about books. There's always something else that you haven't read! I have nothing but sympathy and compassion for people who don't read, because it is such a wonderfully rich world. There is always some new, exciting thing to be discovered.

An Interview with John Banville

Hugh Haughton and Bryan Radley / 2011

Modernism/modernity 18:4 (2011), 855–69. Johns Hopkins University Press. Reprinted by permission of Johns Hopkins University Press.

The following interview with John Banville took place on 23 June 2011, as part of the *Samuel Beckett: Out of the Archive* conference and festival at the University of York. Before the interview, Banville read an extended extract from *Ancient Light*, to be published in 2012.

John Banville: Two inquisitors! This is more like Kafka than Beckett . . .

Hugh Haughton: Thank you for that tantalizing prelude to the new Banville novel. Like so many new Banville novels, it appears to be, in a sense, a postlude, or part of the afterlife of earlier Banville novels, in this case *Eclipse* and *Shroud*.

JB: We're back with the Cleaves again, Alex and Lydia. Yes, for those of you who haven't read these books—and these guys read everything—the book revisits Alex Cleave, an actor, who first appeared in *Eclipse*, and his daughter Cass, who had committed suicide in *Shroud*, in which my great monster Axel Vander is, to some extent, implicated in her death. But I should, I suppose, say that . . . I'm playing a lot of games in this book because Alex Cleave, having retired as a theater actor, has been asked to star in a movie based on the life of Axel Vander . . . but, of course, he doesn't *know* this. He gets a suspicion of it but then realizes that this couldn't possibly be the case that Axel Vander had known his daughter. So, it's very complicated, and the reviewers will be absolutely *furious* that I require them to go back and read earlier books. But it's always good to annoy the reviewers.

HH: You are a reviewer yourself, of course . . .

JB: Yes.

HH: Are you so easily annoyed?

JB: Annoyed? No, not at all. Not at all. I'm the most gentle of reviewers, as you know.

HH: You once began an essay by claiming that you didn't think you were a novelist; can you explain what you meant by this?

JB: Well, I wonder if any novelists think of themselves as novelists; you know, we all want to be someone else. I, of course, have that wonderful, vulgar desire to tell stories, as we all have, to tell stories and to be told stories. And Beckett, you know, famously, when somebody asked him why did he call *Company* "Company," said, "The book is company." And it is. When you wake at four in the morning, you don't have to think about your bank balance or death or sex. You can think about the book. So, it keeps one company. But, you know, I like to think that I do something else. I make sentences, this is what I do. I don't work by plot or dialogue or character. I work by sentence, and each sentence generates the next one. That seems to me analogous to the way—I would *think*, because I don't know how it's done—in which a poet works from line to line.

Bryan Radley: Why are you so haunted by Cass?

JB: Ah! The other one . . .

BR: Yes, I know, over here . . . Actually, we *could* talk about double acts in your work, because it strikes me that in the new Benjamin Black novel there are a pair of cosh-wielding guys, people who waylay other people in streets, who are very reminiscent of the people who waylay Axel Vander.

JB: Yeah, I wonder whether this is something built in, because again I notice in Kafka, and as I say here we are, with my two cosh-wielding interlocutors . . . I don't know actually why that should be. I wanted to go back to Cass because I felt she's unfinished business. A Spanish friend of mine—actually, an Argentinian who lives in Spain, a novelist—always said to me that he assumed when he saw the name of *The Sea*, that this was going to be Cass's book, because he says, "This is the book that you haven't written." This is not it either, I'm afraid, but I've made it up to him by putting him into the book under an anagram of his name. I have quite a few anagrams in this book; I had a lot of fun doing this book. When you get to my age, you can have fun. You say to yourself, "It's not going to *sell*, they're all going to hate it anyway, so just have fun."

But Cass, I suppose, is unfinished business; Cass is very like Phoebe in the Benjamin Black books. My agent says that I'm in love with Phoebe, but, in fact, I think Phoebe is *me*, and I think to some extent Cass is me as well. I always feel—well, I'm of an age now where I can admit such a thing—but I always feel that I'm more female than male. I certainly have more affinity with women. Their minds seem to work in the way that mine works. As I say, if I were twenty years younger I would never admit this because, well . . . the night is young, but . . . [laughter]

But now, it doesn't matter. So, I feel a deep affinity with Cass. Of course, she's dead, but in *Eclipse*, which I thought was quite a nice fancy that I had, that in *Eclipse* she's haunting—the father doesn't know that she's dead or shortly to be dead—she's haunting him from the future, and he's seeing ghosts that he doesn't realize are his daughter . . . Why do I write such complicated books? Why can't I write simple books that people would like, you know, and *buy*? [laughter]

Well, Black tries to do that, and he doesn't seem to be doing too well either . . .

HH: You talk about your sympathy with women, and female characters, and Cass—and she is a very powerfully present figure in *Eclipse* and in *Shroud*—it's extraordinary to have her resurrected in this form. But, when writing in your first-person, you have always written in the first-person of a garrulous, intellectual, ambitious, and rather monstrous *male*—well, pretty well always, though not *always*; can you explain that?

JB: Well, I am an ambitious, garrulous, and monstrous male, of course—as well as being a woman. You know, Dame Edna—here I am with the gladioli.[2] Look, I mean, books—even the Benjamin Black books, which I try not to brood on too much—they all come from somewhere very deep inside oneself. No book is made from the surface of the mind or from the surface of the self or the surface of the sensibility; they all come from very deep, indeed. So, in a way, I'm the last person to explicate them. I don't know what's going on in them. And increasingly, the older I get, the more I allow things to happen that I wouldn't have in the old days, when I thought I was in control of everything. Now I'm hopeless. I almost remind myself of one of those galleons that's lost all its sails and I'm a floating hulk. But I imagine that the life of the vermin on a floating hulk would have been marvelous, and I'd like to think that these are verminous books, that they are doing all this stuff while the hulk floats on. That's a nice image, isn't it? I must remember that; do you mind if I make a note? [laughter]

BR: If the books are becoming more dreamlike, and you've been talking increasingly about the sense of this nocturnal world permeating, more and more, your working day, and in a sense of you losing control, the one area where you do retain an extraordinary level of control—you hinted at it in terms of your use of anagrams—is *naming*. And naming seems to be particularly important to you.

JB: Oh, I think every novelist knows this, that once you've got the names, you've got the thing beaten; you've wrestled it to the ground. And when I used to review fiction, which I don't really do anymore, I could get a novel in the first ten pages. If the names were wrong, I'd know that the rest of the book was going to be wrong as well, because somehow the novelist hadn't blended with his material. Now, I don't know; this is completely inexplicable. There's no way I'm saying why a name is right and why a name is wrong. If you look through Henry James's notebooks, he goes through lists of names after names until he hits the right one. And, you know, he did find some wonderful names.

HH: Hyacinth Robinson, for example, as a revolutionary in *The Princess Casamassima.*

JB: Yeah, or Mrs. Condrip.

HH: Thank you for that.

JB: Henry James did it! I didn't imagine it . . .

HH: I know, I know! One of the things that is mysterious and appealing to both Bryan and myself about your work is its comedy, and it seems to be raising its lovely head in your conversation, too. I wonder how much you think comedy is of the essence of what you're doing. Because, on the one hand, you seem to be doing very dreamlike excavations of unknown, hallucinatory stuff, and in what you've just been reading you talked about a "luminous mirage," and "half-frantic consciousness" and hallucinations. That seems to be the world you operate in. But, on the other, there is often a very strong sense of the ridiculous, the oneiric, and the ridiculous together. And I wonder how they relate.

JB: Well, you know, in our dreams most men haven't got their trousers on. And we're flying, as well. It's a horrible thought, really. [laughter]

But yes, I do think that in a way—I'm not sure about this—but I think that the novel essentially is a comic form. Even at its most tragic, it's still in some way comedic. Again, I can't explain this, but I feel this more and more. That doesn't necessarily mean that it's laugh-out-loud funny. But I suppose that as I get older, the comic side of life comes to take over more and more from the tragic. Well, I still feel that . . . I'm trying to figure out what I think about this. I feel viscerally that the novel is a comic form, that it's essentially a burlesque form.

Let's go back to the very beginning, where you were talking about me and my pretentions to be a poet. You can be as poetic as you like, or tragic, but the form itself will drag you back into the world, will make comic moments, absurd moments, ridiculous moments. Look at the man we're all here for. Beckett is absolutely wonderful. I always remember the first time I read in *Molloy* this extraordinary paragraph—I suspect he must have written in a kind of rhapsodic trance—about making a little creature, and then I'll eat it—and then he says, "Well, I'll be buggered, I wasn't expecting that." And it's wonderfully comic; I laughed out loud. And it's a superb paragraph, but that wonderful little moment of comedy in the middle of it gives it a kind of human element that would have been missing otherwise. I think that's what comedy is for, to constantly drag us back to how funny we are, how funny in our awful, tragic sense.

I have a line in this [*Ancient Light*] where the boy in it, the narrator, is remembering when he was fifteen and having an affair with the thirty-five-year-old mother of his best friend at school . . . This is a complicated book. The place where they meet, he and the woman, is an old house in the woods, and there's this broken-down lavatory outside. And he says, in an aside, "We need not go to the Greeks; our tragic predicament is written down on a lavatory roll." And I think that's the truth. You were supposed to laugh at that. [laughter]

Ah good, yes, yes!

BR: Actually, that leads on quite nicely to when you did a recent review of DeLillo, I think it was of *Point Omega*, maybe, for the *New York Review of Books*. You talked about the fact that there were two DeLillos, and the one you seemed to prefer was based on a sense of humor, shot through with ambiguity. And you talked about diffidence being important, where one could confuse something which could have been especially tragic, and that in actual fact it might turn out to be the punch line. And, considering we've got many Beckett scholars here today, I think particularly of that sense of painful comedy, which you described when you wrote on Beckett for the *New York Review of Books*, but also that sense of comedy that you might not be getting the joke, or that the point might be not to get the joke.

I think this has to do with a sense in which so many of the possible jokes in your work, the moments that I think are particularly funny, occur when you're not sure that you're supposed to be laughing, and you're not even sure that there's a joke there in the first place. I know that you've complained over the years that people haven't grasped that sense of humor and that for a long time you were considered quite difficult, etcetera, and that people seemed to have a tin ear for the humor. Do you think that's changing now? Especially after, for instance, *The Infinities*, which seems to me to be a romp.

JB: Well, it is, I mean, it's a very complicated and deep romp . . . [laughter]

BR: . . . but a romp, nonetheless . . .

JB: . . . but a romp, nonetheless. I don't know if you noticed, but that book sank like a *stone*. My best friend, I was having lunch with him one day, and he said that to me. He said, "Loved that book, you know. Sank like a stone, though, didn't it?" Your best friend always tells you things like that. No, people didn't get that joke at all. I mean, it got good reviews, they tell me, but it didn't go anywhere because the point of it was missed, that it was an elaborate, I hope, delicate, *and* tragic comedy, but if you foist something like that on the public nowadays when they want something . . . Anyway, let's not go down that road . . . Sorry, sorry. Why did you mention that book?

Yes, it's funny that you should say that . . . Comedy is always tentative; there's nothing less funny than the broad joke, but the tentative joke is always . . . I used to love Tommy Cooper, who would stare at the audience in like a trance of terror, with his tarboosh on his head, making these awful jokes that were not funny . . . and that was what was funny about him. I'd like to be that kind of comedian. Broad jokes are not for me. I wouldn't know how to do them. If I set out to write something funny . . . [laughs] I can imagine how it would sound. It would be completely leaden. Comedy is always, humor is always of the moment. You know, "Well, I'll be buggered; I wasn't expecting that."

BR: Pursuing your mention of *Molloy*'s comic double-take, how has your sense of Beckett—and his influence—changed over the years?

JB: Yes, of course—everything changes over the years. I once revered Beckett as a superhuman artist, but, of course, there are no superhumans, or not visible ones, anyway. I still consider him one of the greats, but I recognize now that his venture was an entirely human one, for all his genius, his erudition, his scholarship.

HH: There is a vein of theatricality in all your work, and you have adapted Kleist for the stage as well as scripted a screen adaptation of a novel by Elizabeth Bowen. How does the theatrical Beckett figure in your own work?

JB: I do not rate B.'s theater work as highly as I do the fiction. I'm inclined to agree with B. himself, who said that the plays were little more than footnotes to the novels. This notion shocks lovers of his theater, but I hold to it. Yet there are passages in the plays that, as I go about my days, I chant to myself to savor their tragic beauty—Didi's "astride of the grave" speech, Clov's "They said to me . . ." etcetera. Oddly, perhaps, I find the novels almost more "theatrical" than the plays—or perhaps I simply mean more rhetorical? And I suppose if I am anything, I am in the rhetorical, which would include Wilde, Yeats, Beckett.

BR: You have spoken of the novel as an essentially comic form and have acknowledged the influence on your work of English comic writers such as P. G. Wodehouse and Evelyn Waugh. Critics also often note strains of Beckettian and Nabokovian humor in your work. How are such fundamentally different forms of comedy related, if at all?

JB: Comedy and the comic in fiction—in art—are to me highly mysterious. In fiction or the theater, it is impossible to be comic, I think; the comic just happens, as a part of the flow of invention and of language. Although I have reservations about Wilde, I do think he is the key here—Beckett owes vastly more to Wilde than he does to, say, Synge. That style of high rhetoric and high irony is an essentially comic style in Beckett and, if I may dare to put myself into the same sentence, in my work, also. (Picture puny novelist with jacket pulled over his head, tiptoeing shamefacedly off.)

HH: You talk about the novel as an inherently comic form, going back to Cervantes, in the beginning the poetic and the comic might well be in alliance. But the novel has also been a very material form . . . responding to a world of things and commodities, and related to the bourgeois, the history of the bourgeoisie, and so on. And I think your fiction *is* orientated and anchored in a world of things, but you seem to have been, from very early on, also quite keen to *dematerialize* the novel, or move it towards an ontological or epistemological space . . . It's a place of undoing and, really, *de*materializing. I'm always conscious of both the outer weather and the inner turbulence of your characters. But it seems to depend upon a kind of dematerialization. Does that make any sense?

JB: Yeah, I like that. I'll steal that. I've been stealing various things from Hugh all afternoon. Yes, the outer weather and the inner turbulence, that's nice, I like that . . . You mention Cervantes. I'm inclined to agree with Nabokov, who said that Cervantes is only funny if you think that people puking in each other's faces is funny, or if making fun of a sad old man . . . To some extent I agree with that. I'm not a great fan of that great novel; it *is* a great novel, but I'm not a great admirer of it. It's a tricky business that I'm involved in . . . should one try to dematerialize the novel? Isn't the very essence of the novel that it is a loose, baggy, monstrous form, that it can accommodate . . . anything you want to throw at it? . . . Anything that you want to throw into that great bag, it will accommodate it; it'll bulge, but it will still hold it. I always remember Nathalie Sarraute saying that there are all kinds of novels: you can have the *nouveau roman*, but you can also have big, loose, baggy monsters . . . that's the wonderful thing about the novel: it's a house with many mansions in it. And I'm working in a very small cubbyhole up in the attic. [laughs] But I'm doing my little bit, yes, to give the novel the force and—I've said this many times before—the force and the denseness of poetry. Auden said that with all the other art forms you can take them or leave them. You can look at a picture and think about your dinner, you can listen to music and think about that beautiful woman walking past, but the poem, you either read it or you don't; you take it or you leave it. And I would like to think the same is true of my books: you take them or you leave them; you read them or you don't. Your attention can't slip when you're reading my books. That's why I work for so long on the first paragraph, because the first paragraph is saying to the reader, "This is how this must be read, and if you don't read it this way, go and do something else." And most people, amazingly, go and do something else. [laughter]

HH: One of the things you have done recently is do something else. And I wonder, in the light of this, can you say a bit more about the birth and astonishing vitality of Benjamin Black, who seems to be operating in the areas, or kind of the genres that, in a sense, what you are talking about disowns. But you have, through this, owned it; I think these are deeply Banvillean novels . . .

JB: I know, and that's what's really troubling me . . .

HH: . . . but by a side-route.

JB: . . . and they're doomed, forever . . . as that. Well, a friend of mine, a sympathetic friend in Dublin, says, "You're doing what Beckett did when he moved to French," you know, "Pour écrire sans style." "To write without style." I think that's very fanciful. I didn't do that. I did it essentially to have a day job; I invented somebody to do my day job for me. But as I said at the start, *no* book comes from the surface; every book, even a bad book, comes from the very depths of the novelist. If the novelist is shallow, then the deep's not very deep; but still, they come from the deepest deeps that novelist has, and Black may not be . . . very deep . . . I hope he's not. But I had read Simenon, and I loved the books. I wanted to do something like that, and I set out to see if I could make that kind of book. Now I'm becoming interested in it. I had a fascinating experience recently. I was doing a Q&A like this at a thing in Dublin a couple of months ago, and a young woman stood up in the audience and said, "I'm an epileptic; I have seizures." Then she said, "Before I have a seizure, I have this very strong sense of smell. I don't know what it is, but it's a very strong sense of smell," and she also said, "I also feel that I've discovered the secret of the universe . . . unfortunately when I come 'round from the seizure, I can't remember what the secret was." But she said this, "I don't get any smell from Quirke, your character Quirke." And I said immediately, "That's because he's one of the dead." Then afterwards, I thought, No, that's not it; it's because . . . my character Quirke has been among the dead; he's lived among the dead all his life. And maybe it's my project in this series of books to bring him back from the underworld, to bring him back to be among the living. Now, if that's the case, Banville will have to be called in. If I'm going to get interested in Quirke's existential predicament, Banville will have to do it, and Black will stand back gnawing his knuckles. [laughs] So, I hope I won't. I hope I can find a way of doing it. But that makes him interesting to me, in a way that . . . This was a kind of *jeu d'esprit* when I started. I didn't know what I was doing. But then, one never knows what one is doing. One stumbles along as Kafka says, "in deepest darkness." I wish I could remember that wonderful quote, "I don't write as I think, I don't think as I should think," and so on, so everything goes on in deepest darkness. That's how art is made. Thank goodness. Because if we knew what we were doing, it would be flat and dull. It's the sudden eruptions of the darkness and the ignorance into one's process of making art that makes art . . .

BR: Are you worried at all . . .

JB: . . . Was that a good enough evasion of the question? I think I did pretty well there.

BR: Are you worried at all that there might be more permeability between the worlds of Banville and Black . . .

JB: Oh yeah.

BR: . . . than your performance of the two might suggest? Hackett coming from *The Book of Evidence*, for example.

JB: Well, you see, I didn't remember that; I'm now of an age where I don't remember anything. Yes, as Gore Vidal wonderfully said about Ronald Reagan, he was "in the springtime of his senescence." Now that I'm in the springtime of my senescence, I find that at about three, three thirty, in the afternoon my eyelids get heavy, and if I'm being Black, Banville will lean over and say, "That's a very interesting sentence." Or the other way about, Black will lean over and say, "Just get it written; stop fiddling around with it." And that has to be stopped because the two are completely different. If Banville were to write a sentence in a Black book, or if Black were to write a sentence in a Banville book, it would not work. I'm not saying that one is lesser than the other. I love that there's a note in one of Darwin's notebooks, a little margin note that just says, "Never say higher or lower."

And I'd like to think that . . . it's one of the things that makes me love Darwin . . . "Never say higher or lower," isn't that wonderful? "Never say higher or lower." And here was the man who had written *The Origin of Species*, but things are as they are. So, I don't say that Black is higher or lower than Banville. They're two separate ways of working, and I would like to keep them separate.

BR: What is it that draws you repeatedly, I think in both guises, towards questions about secrecy and the illicit, and that sense of ferreting out, of detecting? Quirke always seems to have an itch to scratch. And there's a sense in which people like Axel Vander seem equally driven.

JB: Well, I can't imagine! I mean, I'm a novelist. I can't imagine why I would be driven by the itch to know other people's secrets! I was sitting in a little restaurant today at lunchtime, and I was watching everybody. And, of course, I wasn't watching them to *use* them; I'm simply watching them with this strange hunger. I'm sure we all do this—but I was watching them with this strange desire to know. Because other people seem to me absolute mysteries. There's me in the world, and then there are all these other people. It's very, very strange. And, of course, we all feel that. But I remember when I was a child, traveling on the train—I used to come to see my aunt in Dublin, and we would go back in December on the trains through the darkness. The wonderful thing about trains is they go through the backs of places, the backs of houses, and you look in, and you see people who don't realize they're being seen—not doing anything in particular, just leading their ordinary grubby little lives—but their grubby little lives are transformed and transfigured by the fact that one's looking at them. That, it seems to me, is what a novelist does. A novelist is always saying, "Look, this is a completely ordinary life, but if I look at it long enough, and if I train the glare of my spotlight on it for long enough, it will begin to glow; it will give up its secrets." Because, of course, there's no such thing as an ordinary life, an ordinary person. One of the reasons that I love Joyce is that he said, "I've never met a person who was a bore." I think Joyce is exaggerating a bit, but one took his point. One took his point because nobody is a bore if you can get beyond the surface that we all erect—that I'm erecting here, that you're erecting here. We're all acting. Behind that, there is a shimmering creature biting its nails saying, "Oh my god, I'm going to be found out." *That's* what novelists do. So, why wouldn't I be fascinated by secrets?

BR: I like that sense of the back end of things, because it reminds me of the beginning and the end of *The Newton Letter*, for instance, the train going down and coming back . . .

JB: Jesus, you remember everything. This is really eerie. [laughter]

BR: . . . but that sense of . . . particularly with the increasing fascination, maybe, with the 1950s, and unearthing a particular . . .

JB: But before you go on, let me say something to do with *The Newton Letter*. The point about *The Newton Letter* was that—at the start of it he says about trains, you see the back end of things, but the point of that book is that the narrator sees none of the back end of things. He only sees the surface, and he's completely wrong about everything. And I have a friend in Dublin whose emotional life is absolute chaos, and she phones me up, or she used to, and she says, "John, tell me what to do, my life is . . ." And I say to her, "You're asking the wrong person." I may be able to write about it, but I know nothing about life. I don't know how it works. I can write it, but I don't know how it works. And that's where again it's analogous to dreams. We can dream the most extraordinary things that in our waking lives we know nothing about. Sorry, I interrupted you. Can you remember the question?

BR: No, no, not at all. Is that why you're interested in intellectuals then, because you like to write about people who might know very little about life? [laughter]

JB: Well, I can only write about myself. I have very little interest in people per se . . .

I need to explain this. I have an interest in how people work and how they function. But—you know how doctors talk about diseases presenting themselves, patients presenting themselves? I have no interest in how people present themselves to me. That's just the stuff that we have to have in order to live, in order not to kill each other, to have a civilized society. But behind that, there's all this . . . as I say, we're all crouched behind it, biting our nails, worrying that we'll be found out—that's what interests me. That's what interests any novelist. But I can only write about it, and I know the question you're asking. I do like to write about people who have some sense of themselves and how they think. I do like fiction that thinks. And this is a great failing. It really is. To be infected by the bacillus of philosophizing, of thinking, is a bad thing for a novelist. Eliot says it is no business of the poet to think and to a certain extent I think he's right. Of course, being Eliot, he didn't say what it *was* the business of the poet to do, but I presume he meant to feel. And, you know, if you look at Eliot, supposedly one of the twentieth century's greatest intellectuals, you read lines like "Garlic and sapphires in the mud / Clot the bedded axle-tree"—wonderful to say, especially for an Anglo-Saxon (I can imagine Seamus Heaney reading that line, "Clot the bedded axle-tree.")—it doesn't mean a damn thing, but it sounds wonderful. I feel that this is the thing about being a novelist. It *has* to make sense. Otherwise, there's nothing there. Otherwise, it's just windbag stuff, going on. Words, words, spilling out.

HH: But there is a vein in your work, and it's there from as early as *Copernicus* and *Kepler,* and it's there in *The Newton Letter* in the crisis of the poor, hapless would-be biographer not able to write because of his own eternal disarray, and it's there also in *The Untouchable* with the Blunt figure and in *Shroud* with the versions of Paul de Man and Althusser . . . there is a side of your work that is interested in major, shaping intellectual figures, and inhabiting them, reimagining them. So, in some sense, in a less—well, more *and* less skeptical way—you are continually investing in the role of the intellectual and exploring that, or exploring whatever's behind it. And that's an unusual feature of your work. Someone like Thomas Mann will do it, or Thomas Bernhard, but it is unusual. And it is a real strong dimension of your work. And that doesn't quite fit with what you've been saying.

JB: Me and the two Tommys, yes . . . I don't see why it should be strange. After the great efflorescence of the nineteenth century, after that huge burgeoning of storytelling, of middlebrow fiction, it couldn't be sustained. It was too weighty; it had to collapse under its own weight. And the pivotal figure that I see is Henry James. James is the one who got us out of the nineteenth century, and out of the Victorian novel, into the twentieth century. I see him as the first real modernist. And I think we talked about this before: in a way he was a strain of modernism I wish we had followed. I think we're scrambling now to catch up with James's modernism, but we decided for whatever reason to follow Joyce and Beckett into experimentalism. And I have doubts about that. That piece [from *Ancient Light*] that I read today, Beckett would have loathed it. He would have said that was the worst kind of literary platitudinizing, and, in a way, he would be right. But the trouble about the avant-garde is that it walks very fast, but it only walks for a short time, and then it comes to a terrible stop. It seems to me now that it is the time for retrenchment. We have to go backwards. I would go back to Henry James, who caught—in a far more serious way than Joyce did, for instance— the sense of what it is actually to be conscious. Because when you read those late novels of Henry James, you're wading through this fog that is exactly like life, whereas in Joyce you know exactly what Bloom is thinking, you know exactly what all these people are doing . . . so, yes, why not be interested in intellectual things like that? We're losing that in the world. As Rilke said, the things we can live with are falling away. We should be interested in how the mind works. We let our minds go soft if we don't. The intellectual is still an extraordinary adventure. And how privileged we are; my god, how privileged we are to be able to think about who we are and what we are and how we are in the world and what it is to be in the world. And I'm not ashamed to say that all my books are aimed at going behind mere human *doing* to the question of what it is to *be*, the question of being in the world. And that's what all artists do, however they work. There's my creed, my God . . .

I hope this is not being recorded, is it? I could be blackmailed with it forever.

BR: Perhaps this would be a good moment to open the discussion up and take some questions from the floor.

JB: This is the existential moment I love. [laughs]

Q1: In your novel *Birchwood*, you make a character say what might be taken as an encrypted declaration of intentions. You have him say, "I will stay here, but I will be different from the rest." Is that still valid for you, that you feel different from the rest of Irish writers?

JB: I'm very touched that you should remember that. My God, *Birchwood* seems to me to have been written in, you know, 1740 or something. It's prehistoric to me. Yes, that was my little aesthetic declaration, and I suppose in a way a political declaration. I wrote that I would stay here, that I would live in this house, but live a life different from anyone who has lived in the house has ever done. I have tried to do that. It hasn't profited me very well. But I couldn't have left. The great ones left; they always went into exile. No Irish writer ever *emigrated;* they all went into exile, shaking their fists [*shakes fist*] at the back of the ferry as it headed towards Liverpool. I feel that the only exile for me is internal exile, to be in Ireland . . . On a very simple level, I can't do without Ireland because

I can't do without the climate, I can't do without the look of the place . . . the light . . . I know you frown, you must be from the South, are you? Who could love the Irish climate? But I love it . . . it's an absolutely perfect climate, it's absolutely beautiful, it's ravishingly beautiful to me. And that is important to me for some reason. I mean, when I was a teenager, I tried to be a painter, and failed miserably, but I learned to look at the world in a particular way. So, the look of things is very important to me. I can see people reading my books saying, "Why is he constantly talking about the bloody weather? Why doesn't he tell the story?" But the story to me is consequent upon the weather, part of the weather, the human figures are figures in a landscape, and the landscape is always important. I tried to live life differently, yes, and I tried to be an Irish writer without being an Irish writer. And I still loathe that playing of the Irish card. You know, "We're wonderful, we're Irish . . ." I loathe that. I think Irish writers should try to be international while remaining Irish. But, I didn't have to leave for that reason. I am glad you remember that, my little declaration. I was twenty-three or something, God! [laughs]

BR: At about the same time, you said that a lot of Irish writing was like a form of literary knitting?

JB: We say a lot of things when we are young. This is why my fellow writers love me in Ireland.

Q2: Can you write under both names at the same time, or do you have to finish what you are writing in one persona, and move on to the other?

JB: No, I tried to do that, but I couldn't. No, I could only be one or the other. I worked in journalism for thirty-five years. I was a subeditor; I would write at home in the morning. This is the wonderful thing about working for the newspapers . . . I never wrote for the newspapers; I was the guy who tinkered with them. An editor of mine in those days defined a subeditor as someone who changes other people's words and goes home in the dark. Which I thought was nice. I liked doing that, I like being a technician. But I would work from 5:30 or 8:30 in the evening, until the early hours. Then I would go home and struggle out of bed in mid-morning, and work until 5:30, or 8:30, and I would have to be two people— the guy who went into the office and the guy who wrote . . . and I'm still that way with Black and Banville.

Q3: Could you say a little more about exile, and your sense of the earlier great Irish writers' need to go into exile?

JB: It's always fascinating about Hemingway, for instance. We think of him as the quintessential American writer, but nearly all the major novels—only one of the major novels is set in America—are set in Europe, apart from *Across the River and into the Trees*, which is not exactly a masterpiece. That was necessary for him. I feel exiled in Ireland, but I think an artist is exiled everywhere. This is a grand nineteenth-century, unreconstructed Romantic notion, but I do feel that we are unhoused and I wouldn't want to feel in place. I wouldn't want to feel part of any country. I wouldn't want to feel part of any society, really. That seems to me essential. They were all weaker than I am, they all had to go away into exile. I can stay where I am. Maybe I was just cowardly; maybe I was afraid of the world . . . didn't want to take it on.

Q4: Were the predecessors you were referring to going into exile from a different Ireland than the Ireland you live in? Has Ireland changed to allow you to stay, or is it the same place that Joyce fled from, Beckett fled from? Is Ireland different?

JB: Yes, of course. But Joyce had to go because he had to preserve the Dublin in his head. If he were to come back to Dublin, the version of Dublin in his head would be tainted. Of Beckett, to some extent, the same thing is true. I mean, Beckett was much more badly treated by Ireland than Joyce was. Joyce was always whining and moaning about how badly Ireland was treating him—"the old sow who eats her farrow"—but nobody ever ate him. He went off because he wanted to go off and have a good life elsewhere. Beckett was badly treated when he came back to be a witness for his friend Sinclair against Gogarty. As we all know, he was very badly treated. So, I can imagine him going away and shaking his fist at Ireland. But then he went back to Paris and immediately he was stabbed in the street. So, nowhere welcomes the writer. [laughs] Yes, Ireland has changed, but again that is not of any real significance to me because I don't feel part of Ireland. And the Irish resent this very much, I think. I'm not regarded as an Irish writer, especially now that we're in such trouble, and we're all broke. I think it's not that writers should be writing about Ireland and our crisis and so on. That's not what artists do. I don't think it's even what novelists do. For instance, people say to me, "Why aren't you writing about the present day?" And I say almost all novels are historical novels. All the great Victorian novels are historical. They're not set in their own time; they're not commenting on their own time. Things have to settle down before the novelist can address them. So, I suppose I might leave Ireland now if I didn't have so many family commitments. But I wouldn't leave in any fist-shaking way, I'd simply slip away, and nobody would notice . . . Nobody would care either. I know that seems a frivolous answer to a serious question, but the fact is that the frivolous answer is the real answer, because I feel frivolous about Ireland.

HH: If I can come in here, I was just thinking that the Quirke Dublin novels curiously really do return to Ireland—in the past, it is true, as historical novels, but to some of the issues that now, from the present, look to have constituted a kind of disastrous internal climate for Ireland . . . like the child abuse that lurks in *Elegy for April* and the sense of the Dublin mafias where the heroes of 1916 might be involved in terrible political and other acts. It seems as if, under the name of Benjamin Black, there is a more politically conscious writer about the historical Ireland?

JB: I wish that I could agree with you, but I don't feel that. I really believe that any writer who imagines he has a social voice is in trouble. If you mix politics and art, you get bad politics and bad art. I can imagine, of course, if, for instance, it seemed to me tomorrow that the Civil War in the North would make a subject for a novel for me, that I could write it as a novel rather than a commentary on war, then I would do it, but that would be incidental. I think this is always true. For art, subject is always incidental, or at least secondary, to the work itself.

Q5: You used the phrase, "delighted us enough," which made me think of Austen. I wonder if you could say anything about the influence of women writers on your work.

JB: That's the high point of Austen for me. It goes downhill after that. I can't say, really. I don't think, for instance, that Virginia Woolf is . . . Oh God, I won't say anything about Virginia Woolf. I don't distinguish between women writers and men writers; I really don't. To me Elizabeth Bishop is a great poet of the twentieth century, so is Lowell. They're completely different poets, but I don't distinguish between them. I just don't think about this; it never enters my mind whether this is a woman writer or a male writer. This is probably the reason for my lack of success as a Casanova over the years. [laughs] They're all the same to me.

BR: There's just time for one more question.

Q5: Does hate motivate your writing at all?

JB: Hate? That's an interesting question. No . . . no particular emotion works in art. Art works on all the emotions. Of course, the things I hate in the world influence me and the things I love in the world influence me, but, you know, people say to me, what's your book about, and I say it's about everything. It's not about something, it's about everything. And that's the point of art. It's not one thing, it's everything. It tries to be everything. Not that it's compendious as *Ulysses* and *Finnegans Wake* try to be compendious. The tiniest aphorism by Kafka can be about everything. The artist is not there. [laughs] When I do readings, book-signings, I can see the disappointment in people's faces when they approach me. I'm older than they thought, I'm shorter than they thought, I'm not good-looking . . . and I want to say to them, the person who wrote the book that you love is not me. He ceased to exist when I stood up from my desk. And he has no affects at all. There's nobody there. This is a marionette you see before you, trying to represent . . . This is true, the person at the desk is as great a puzzle to me as he is to you. I don't understand what he does. Frequently, the next day I go back to read over what I wrote the day before; I don't recognize it. I can't remember writing it. Time is strange. I always tell this story: I was writing one day, and my wife put her head in the door of my study and said, "I'm going to the shops," and closed the door. She opened it again and said something else, I said, "I thought you were going to the shops," and she said, "I've been to the shops." There was no sense of a gap, you see, between. As I always say, it's closer and closer to being in a dream state. You know, you're awake until five to seven in the morning, and you fall asleep until ten past seven. And you have this extraordinary world of dreams that's huge, and it's happened in ten minutes. Fiction is like that. That's the way, for me, making art and making fiction is.

HH: I think that's a great note to end on. I'd like to thank John Banville for a wonderful account of the strange dream-work of the novelist.

Notes

1. "Oblique Dreamer," an interview with John Banville published in the "Observer Review" section of the *Observer* (Sunday 17 September 2000), 15.

2. In his introduction Haughton compared the double-act of John Banville and Benjamin Black to Dame Edna Everage and Sir Les Patterson.

Marvelous Masks

Kevin Breathnach / 2012

Kevin Breathnach's interview took place during a web call with John Banville in Dublin, Ireland, while Breathnach was in Gwangju, South Korea. The interview appeared in *Totally Dublin*, 28 June 2012. Reprinted with Kevin Breathnach's permission.

Breathnach: *Ancient Light* is the third book in a trilogy. Did you have to go back and read *Eclipse* and *Shroud* before you began writing?

Banville: It's not really a trilogy. It could be considered that way, but I didn't intend it. In fact, it's funny because now that you've said it, it's the first time I've thought of it as part of a trilogy. I've built in the references to previous books as a kind of game with myself. But it's certainly not necessary to have read the previous two books. Of course, it would be nice if people did go back and read them, but this is a stand-alone book. Myself, no—I couldn't read my past work anyway. That's why I keep making mistakes, forgetting things, and getting the colors of people's eyes wrong. No, I couldn't go back and reread. Fiction is fiction anyway—it's not like writing history. I'm not that interested in accuracy.

Breathnach: That's appropriate, given that the unreliability of memory is one of *Ancient Light*'s central themes.

Banville: Well, yes. I've become more and more convinced that we don't actually remember things as they actually happened. We make models of things which we carry into the future and which account for the fact that, when we return to a place or meet a person we once knew, the place or the person is different—not entirely different, of course, but in strange ways. Rooms have moved around; the color of their eyes has changed. It's because we don't actually remember these things. The brain is constantly modeling what it scans. That's what memory is—a series of models.

Breathnach: The ineluctable modality of the past?

Banville: Nicely put.

Breathnach: Is it the most Banvillian novel you've ever written?

Banville: Ha, ha. All my novels are Banvillian novels. They have to be. I can't write them in anybody else's voice. They all seem of a piece, part of one large volume somebody will perhaps bind into an enormous doorstopper after I've gone. There is continuity between them all, even though some of them are very different. That's inevitable, since when I finish one book I'm starting another. I couldn't have a gap.

Breathnach: There are so many figures in *Ancient Light*, and still more names than that. When it comes down to it, though, there seems to be no more than two or three essential identities at play. Do you have to map something like that out before you start writing?

Banville: No. I used to do a lot of planning when I was a young man. When I wrote the first line, I would know what my last line was going to be. But it's much looser now. I trust my instincts. I let the thing drift. In my early days, writing was a process of thinking; now it's a process of dreaming. And I think it's good to follow one's instincts, to let unexpected things happen. It gives spontaneity and lightness to the page.

Breathnach: Your characters spend a lot of time in the half-space of guesthouses. What role does the guesthouse play in your fiction?

Banville: I hadn't been conscious of that, to be honest. This is the great thing about doing interviews; you always learn something new. I was certainly conscious of the fact that all my novels seem to be set in particular houses. The house seems to be a very important symbol for me—I use the word *symbol* with caution. I don't pretend to understand it. This is another thing about getting old: one imagines that one would become wiser, but one actually becomes more confused. That's okay, though. Confusion is a good thing for a writer.

Breathnach: On the subject of the guesthouse—

Banville: You're not going to let this thing go, are you?

Breathnach: Not yet, no. Can I ask when you began writing *The Sea*?

Banville: I suppose it was around 2001.

Breathnach: It's just that *Vertigo* by W. G. Sebald, a novel about memory by a writer you admire, was translated in 2002. The protagonist of that book, clearly based on the author, stays in a guesthouse, which decades before had been his family home and where many of the significant events in his child-hood occurred. Meanwhile, *The Sea*'s protagonist stays in a guesthouse, which decades before had been the summer-home of childhood friends and where many of the significant events of the protagonist's childhood occurred. W. G. Sebald did not like his first name, Winfried. Instead, he asked that his friends call him Max. And, of course, the protagonist of *The Sea* is called Max. Is there any connection?

Banville: Ha. You should be a detective. I can't remember when I read *Vertigo*. It would have been after *The Sea*, I think. There's a very curious thing about one of Sebald's books. The narrator is in Ireland, where he stays in a guesthouse, a rather ghostly place run by an Anglo-Irish woman. There are a couple of lines in it that are quoted directly from *The Book of Evidence*. It's very odd. I had a very strange sensation when I came across that. But with writers, you know, there's stuff in the atmosphere that we don't know about. It drifts in and out of our minds. I certainly wasn't making any reference to *Vertigo*, but things imprint themselves in the mind. One keeps things that one doesn't realize one is remembering. I'm not even sure *remembering* is the right word for it. But if I had taken stuff from *Vertigo*, I would be perfectly willing to admit it.

Breathnach: "How fragile is this absurd trade," your narrator writes, "in which I have spent my life pretending to be other people, and above all pretending not to be myself." Have you considered doing any further not-pretending to be yourself, doing memoir or perhaps more travel writing?

Banville: In that sort of book, I think one is pretending even more than in fiction. In fiction one is presenting one's naked self. I remember meeting a friend of mine on the publication day of one of my previous novels. "You're looking a bit grey in the face," she said. "What's the matter?" "It's publication day," I said. "I feel as though I'm walking down the street naked." "Yes," she said, "and carrying your X-ray plates under your arm." Fiction is an X-ray of the self, whereas travel-writing and memoir are both marvelous masks. I do have a plan to write an autobiography—though, of course, I shouldn't be telling you this, because it's no good if it's known—but to write an autobiography in which everything would be slightly false. Instead of a brother and a sister, I would have two brothers. Instead of being born in Wexford, I'd be born in New Ross. Upon publication, I would insist that it was all true.

Breathnach: On the subject of nonfiction, is there any chance you could be persuaded to put out a selection of your essays?

Banville: No. Because I don't write essays; I write book reviews. If I were an essayist or a critic, then I would publish books of essays and criticism. But I'm a book reviewer, and book reviews are not meant to be preserved. They're meant for the day.

Breathnach: You've spoken of having changed your mind about books you've reviewed in the past.

Banville: Well, I don't often do it. But, yes—sometimes. The thing about reviewing is that you're reading a book that nobody else has read, so you can't talk about it to other people. It's a purely subjective, individual judgment you're making about a book. Afterwards, when you look back on it, when you talk to other people and read other reviews, you think, Oh God, I didn't see this, or I was wrong about that. I'm quite willing to admit I've made mistakes—in a positive way and in a negative way. I've written bad reviews of books, which I discovered later to have much more in them than I saw—and vice versa. One has to be open. It would be very foolish to be a book reviewer and have a closed mind.

Breathnach: Do any of these mistakes of yours appear now as blurbs for other people's books?

Banville: Probably. You have to keep in mind, though, that blurbs are favors one does for friends or praise for books one admires; they're a way of encouraging people to read, a way of bringing a book to the attention of people. They don't necessarily have to be an absolutely final decision on a book. I could give a blurb to a book and then think a year later that I shouldn't have. Or again, vice versa: I could end up thinking that I should have given a blurb when I was asked, but I refused. One changes as life goes on; one changes one's opinions. The worst thing to have would be a closed mind. There are no books that I've given blurbs to that I feel embarrassed about or ashamed about. And, of course, blurbs are always overstated. Wasn't it Dave Eggers who called one of his own books *A Heartbreaking Work of Staggering Genius* or something like that? I thought it was a very clever idea.

Breathnach: Do you still read newspaper reviews?

Banville: Not of my own work, but of other people's I do. I don't keep up as I used to, mind you. I worked as books editor in the *Irish Times* for ten or eleven years; you get a bit jaded after that. I suppose I don't take the newspapers as seriously as I used to either, which is sad. I don't have as much time. Time's winged chariot is behind me, flapping its wings faster and faster. But I do think reviews are important. I still do a lot of them myself and will continue to do so. Reviewing serves a public function. It brings good new work to the attention of people who might not have noticed it otherwise. It is a very worthwhile trade, and I take great satisfaction from my reviewing—far more than I do from writing my books.

Breathnach: Do you actually read fewer novels these days?

Banville: Again, that is the effect of age. As one ages, one reads fewer novels. It's a well-known phenomenon. I don't know why it is. Nobody quite understands it. But what fiction offers is something I don't seem to need as much as I used to. I'm fascinated to read history now. For instance, I've just discovered recently the essays of the great historian, Hugh Trevor-Roper. Those are beautifully written. I'd give three bad novels for one of his essays. There is a lot to be read besides fiction—psychology, poetry, philosophy, letters. On the other hand, I just finished reading Richard Ford's latest book *Canada*, which was absolutely masterly. I would be very sorry not to have read that.

Breathnach: You mention philosophy. Of course, Axel Vander is based on a number of theorists. Have you ever had much time for critical theory?

Banville: No. Of course, I was mesmerized when I was young—as we all were—by structuralism, by this-ism and that-ism. Now I'm not. I mean, I think literary theory is useful for literary critics. It's a useful tool for approaching imaginative work, but I think it's very dangerous for a writer to dabble too much in theory.

Breathnach: There's a note in the second volume of Susan Sontag's diaries in which she writes about having to reduce her reading to write more. Do you find it difficult to strike a balance between reading and writing?

Banville: Oh, yes. There were writers I couldn't read when I was writing. I couldn't read Henry James. I couldn't read Yeats. I couldn't read Nabokov. I couldn't read Beckett. I couldn't read them because their voices would have gotten into my head, slid down my arm, and come out the end of the pen. One has to beware very much of influences. One has to beware of the people one admires. I started rereading Nabokov recently. Of course, he's not as good as I thought he was (that always happens), but I can see how one could end up taking over that tone very easily. The greater the stylist, the easier it is to parrot his style.

Breathnach: But what about in terms of time?

Banville: No. Reading is always secondary to writing. I keep office hours; I work from nine to six. I take a very short break in the middle of the day. I do that five days a week. I read on trains. I read sitting on the lavatory. And I read at night after I've had two or three glasses of wine—one eye open, one eye shut. I read when I can. And it's amazing how much reading you can get done. John McGahern used to always say it's really not asking too much of oneself to read for three hours a day. I think that's true, but life has distractions—and more and more distractions accumulate. I still love reading, though. It's still one of the greatest pleasures in life.

"Two Hats": John Banville and James Gleick

James Gleick / 2014

John Banville's conversation with James Gleick was recorded live at the Key West Literary Seminar, January 2014. It appears with the permission of Arlo Haskell and James Gleick.

James Gleick: I've become aware that some of you, having carefully read the program, expected to see three chairs. So I'll explain. My name is James Gleick. I'm the moderator. On my left you see John Banville, who has been called "one of the most imaginative literary novelists writing in the English language today." He has won the Man Booker Prize, the Kafka Prize, and, this year, the Irish PEN Award, and he's regularly mentioned every autumn when the Nobel Prize season comes around. Also, on my left is Benjamin Black, who is never going to win any of those prizes. [laughter] He's the author of—well, I just learned today that his next book is going to be called *The Black-Eyed Blonde*. That is not, if I may judge, a John Banville title. Benjamin Black's books are a bestselling series of dark thrillers, featuring a Dublin pathologist named Quirke. And actually, as you've gathered, Mr. Black looks a lot like Mr. Banville. But in his author photos, he's wearing a rakish fedora pulled down low over his brow. So, I have some questions for both of them, and I'm going to try to give them equal time. I'd like to start with Mr. Black. I imagine that you have every bit as much native talent as John Banville, and he gets all the prizes. [laughter] We know that some genre writers feel that they aren't taken seriously enough by what is laughingly called "the mainstream literary establishment." I wonder if you ever feel that way yourself?

John Banville: Well, no, because when I did the first Benjamin Black book, the first Quirke book, I gave it to my publisher. I was having lunch with her, and she said, "This is a wonderful book." I said, "It's a crime book," and she said, "No, this is not a crime book. This is a literary book."

And I said, "Oh, God, don't say that. That's not what it's intended to be." I wanted to do something entirely different. I was on the cusp of turning sixty. To embark on a frolic of my own at that age seemed a wonderful thing to do. I intended to do one book, and I'm still doing them. I seem to be unstoppable. [laughter] This beast is free and ranging about the wild, causing mayhem.

Gleick: But you did mean for it *not* to be a literary book, whatever that meant.
Banville: Well, look. I really hate this notion of genre. When I started publishing in 1970, way back in the Stone Age, there was just *fiction*. Now there's a thing called *literary fiction*, which is separated off, and I *hate* that notion because it makes a ghetto, essentially, a place in bookshops for people to avoid. "Don't go there, that dark corner." There's just fiction; there's *good* fiction. When I was very young, my brother, who's older than I am, introduced me to the novels of Raymond Chandler. And here was a person writing crime fiction, supposedly, but it was wonderfully stylish, wonderfully funny. It had a flair to it that I loved. And that's the kind of thing that I try to do. And then in about 2004, a friend of mine, an English philosopher, put me onto Georges Simenon. I hadn't read Simenon before, and I just discovered a whole new world—that's too much of a cliché—I discovered a new way of writing. Simenon has a very, very small vocabulary. There's a nice story that when Simenon finished a book, he would come out, line his children up, and shake the typescript. They'd say, "What are you doing, Daddy?" "I'm getting rid of the adjectives." [laughter] It was a revelation to me. What could be done without adjectives? Banville likes the odd adjective.

Gleick: Yes, I've heard that. [laughter] Let me address a question then to Banville, actually. I just want to read the opening of the latest Benjamin Black novel, which is called *Holy Orders*: "At first they thought it was the body of a child. Later, when they got it out of the water and saw the pubic hair and the nicotine stains on the fingers, they realized their mistake. Male, late twenties or early thirties, naked but for one sock, the left one. There were livid bruises on the upper torso and the face was so badly disfigured his mother would have been hard put to recognize him." Now, Banville is not just a novelist, but a critic. You were literary editor of the *Irish Times*. You've reviewed books of all sorts, fiction and nonfiction. You've written many essays for the *New York Review of Books* on Rilke, Kafka, Beckett, Strindberg, and our own Robert Richardson. But I'm not aware of your ever having stooped to reviewing thrillers. What do you make of this kind of writing? Is it lowbrow? Is it unliterary?

Banville: Well, it's a different way of working. It's a different kind of book. I think it's his craft. In a way, the world could do with more craftpersons, as we must call them nowadays, than artists. [laughter] I have tried to make them as beautifully done as I can. Not in the same way as Banville thinks of beauty. I like to think of it as a beautifully polished table, a beautifully done chair, which you can use but also admire. It's a different way of working. And the ways of working are simply that Banville concentrates, and what you get from a Banville book is the result of deep, deep, deep concentration. What you get from a Black book is the result of spontaneity. That's the best way I can put it.

Gleick: Do you write more quickly as Black?

Banville: Oh, yes. Black can do a book in two or three months. Banville would take two, three, four, five years to write a book.

Gleick: Is that because there is somebody censorious looking over Banville's shoulder, who goes away for the sake of Black? An editor with high standards or certain tastes?

Banville: I can't answer that because, forgive me, it's the wrong question. [laughter] I don't mean that to be critical. I mean simply that these are two entirely different ways of working. For most of my life I worked in journalism. I worked as, what you would call, a copyeditor. We called them subeditors at the daily newspaper. I worked at night, from five o'clock in the evening to one o'clock in the morning, sometimes eight o'clock in the evening to four in the morning. That gave me the daylight hours to do my *own* work. I was two entirely different people. When I got up from my desk and went into the newspaper office, I was a different person. So, becoming Benjamin Black wasn't all that difficult. But then we have this illusion that we are unitary beings. We have the notion that there is a pilot light inside us that is oneself. I don't believe this is the case. We're a collection of poses, of attitudes, of versions of ourselves. And thank God for that because that's what makes life interesting. It'd be dreadful if we were a unitary creature. We make ourselves up as we go along. This is what makes life interesting. So being merely two people is very easy. Now that I've written a Philip Marlowe book, a friend of mine said to me, "Oh, yeah, you were Banville pretending to be Benjamin Black. Now you're Banville pretending to be Benjamin Black pretending to be Raymond Chandler. [laughter] I could go on forever. It's not difficult to separate oneself.

Gleick: Was there something about choosing the name that helped the process along?
Banville: The name Benjamin Black?

Gleick: Yes, by creating a separate name. In theory you could have just kept going and published these books as John Banville.
Banville: Well, no, I wanted people to realize that it was something new that I was doing. It was a new adventure I was embarking on. I didn't want people to think that it was an elaborate, postmodernist joke. The first name I chose was Benjamin White. It was the name of a character in my early books, which, thank God, nobody reads anymore. But my publishers and my agent said, "We think *Black* would be better. It sounds better. Also, you'll get much higher on the alphabetical list of librarians purchasing this." [laughter] Look, it was an adventure that I started on. It was a *jeu d'esprit*, and in a way it still is. I sit down every summer now and I write one of these books. When I'm starting it out, I think, I don't know if I can do this. But I do it, and by the end of the summer, it's done. I've committed another one of these . . . sins.

Gleick: I don't want to get too obsessive about trying to tease apart the differences between the two types of books. But let me ask you this. Benjamin Black has said that, for him, character matters and plot matters and dialogue matters to a much greater degree than in John Banville's books. If I were John Banville, I would think that might be sort of an insult.
Banville: Oh, no, no, not at all, not at all. I don't think Banville really is a novelist at all. [laughter] My good friend the late John McGahern, the Irish novelist, used to make a wonderful distinction. He said there is verse and there is prose, and then there is poetry. Since he was a novelist, he said it happens more often in prose than it does in verse. That's the road that I follow. Banville tries to make his books as dense and as demanding as poetry, as verse. W. H. Auden said that the poem is the only work of art that you either take or leave. You can listen to a symphony, and your mind can drift away for a while. You think about what you're having for dinner, and you can look at a picture and think about other things. With a poem, you either read it or you don't. I want to make my Banville books to have that kind of demand on the reader: you either read it or you don't. It's amazing how many people decide not to. When I write the Black books, as I said, I want to make a well-crafted piece of work. I discovered when I started doing it, that I had a talent for plot, character, and dialogue, which I didn't

know I had before because Banville was never interested in these things. [laughter] I suppose it's a kind of surplus that these books are made out of.

Gleick: I want to read another sentence. This is from John Banville's latest novel, *Ancient Light*, and it's one sentence. If you want to think of a ridiculous thing to do, imagine taking the entire collected work of John Banville and choosing one sentence to read for illustrative purposes. So, I guess I should say this is not meant to be typical in any way. I chose it at random, but I think it pertains to what you were just saying. And, by way of context, it is part of a description of a woman's arms. We're starting in the middle. The arms have already been described for quite some length of words. [laughter] And the woman is Mrs. Grey. She's aged thirty-five, and the point of view is that of her lover, a fifteen-year-old boy. The arms: "They were lightly freckled on the backs, and the undersides were fish-scale blue, and wonderfully cool and silky to the touch, with delicate striations of violet veins along which I liked to slide the tip of my tongue, following them all the way to where they abruptly sank from sight in the dampish hollow of her elbow, one of the numerous ways I had of making her shiver and twitch and moan for mercy, for she was delightfully ticklish." Now, I was an English major, so I think I know what we are talking about here. But this afternoon I heard you say that one thing that you believe it is impossible to write about is sex. Do you stand by that?
Banville: Well, the erotic is entirely different to sex. Sex is a mechanical function. Our greatest sexual experiences usually don't take place when we are in the missionary position. They usually take place elsewhere. You know, the droop of an eyelid, the crease of an elbow, the light on the back of the neck. This is, of course, speaking from the man's point of view. God knows what women find in men to like. [laughter] But the sentence that you read probably took me a morning to write, and I'm still not happy with it.

Gleick: What on earth is wrong with it?
Banville: A sentence can always be better. I met a young Irish writer recently who gave me a great compliment about *Ancient Light*. He said, "That's a perfect book." And I said to him, "Young man, there is no such thing as a perfect book. It can always be better." And that's the point of art: you keep striving to make it better. You keep striving to get the perfectly clear, ringing sentence. You hit your nail against the rim of a wine glass: *ping!* That's what I want to get into sentences. Every now and then, it seems to me that I do. Then someone reads it aloud, and you go, "Ah, Christ." [laughter]

Gleick: I'm sorry. I won't read any more.

Banville: No, no, no. That was quite a nice sentence.—

Gleick: Until I butchered it.

Banville: I don't remember writing it. [laughter] This is one of the nice things about getting old. I suppose I should stop saying *getting* old, about *being* old. A friend of mine visited Samuel Beckett in the old folks' home in Paris, a couple of years before he died. Beckett was saying how his memory was decaying, how he couldn't remember anything. My friend began to sympathize, and Beckett said, "No, no, it's wonderful; it's wonderful. It's *all* going; it's *all* going." And the problem is, of course, that one's memory goes, all the *good* things. But you vividly remember the bad things. I can still remember—and sweat about—gaffes that I made when I was fourteen. I can't remember the good things that I did then.

Gleick: Well, I did want to correct what I think might've been a misimpression that had been left this afternoon. I think you're saying that when you don't write about sex, you mean that you don't write about the plumbing.

Banville: Exactly. Well put, very well put.

Gleick: But there is, in my view, a great deal of eroticism in both of these books, actually. There's a kiss in this book that is—I'm not going to give much away about this book—that's one of the most erotic kisses I have read about recently. I hope I'm not cutting into your sales here. [laughter]

Banville: Language is such a passionate and sensual medium. It's extraordinary. We invented this thing to communicate. It started out with grunts. As Sanskrit scholars tell us, it started out with lists of amounts of corn, and so on. And look what we have done with it? Look what we've made of this extraordinary medium? I always say this in public, that the greatest invention of humankind is the sentence. There have been civilizations. I think the Aztecs or the Incas or somebody didn't have the wheel. But they had to have the sentence. This is what makes us human. It's what we think with. It's what we imagine with. It's what we communicate with. It's what we declare love with, declare war with. The sentence is the absolute, essential monad of being human. And here am I. I get to spend my days working with this extraordinary invention. I feel immensely privileged. Even though, as I say, I don't get them perfectly right every time. But the privilege of being able to get to work in that is a pure joy. And everybody does that. You sit down to write a letter to your bank manager or your lover. You're working in sentences, and you're trying to get it as right as you can. So, it's wonderful. Language is a wonderful thing.

Gleick: At the risk of returning us to earth, I want to ask a little bit about, well, the machinery. We're here this week talking about crime fiction, also known as mysteries, detective novels, thrillers. We've never really been able to settle on a name for the genre, I don't think. But one of the things they have in common is the detectives. You have a detective, even though he's not officially a detective, called Quirke, who is a really remarkable character. I want to ask you about him. Either one of you, Banville or Black, can talk about him. As you said this afternoon: He's tall. He's blond.
Banville: He was. He's getting shorter. He's shrinking steadily.

Gleick: He doesn't like the rain. He drinks more than he should. Women are constantly inviting him into their beds. He doesn't even seem to ask. I'm not asking you if he came from something in you. I want to know why he's the way he is. You set out to build a central figure who is the one who solves the mysteries. What should we know about him?
Banville: It's a good question, actually. I've never thought about it before. He has to come from me. As I've said many times, I'm the only material that I have. I'm the only person I know from the inside. When I was young, I spent a lot of time trying to know people from the inside without much success. That's another story. He must represent some aspect of myself. I don't recognize it.

Gleick: He's an orphan. He had a terrible childhood. He's damaged.
Banville: Yes. I *didn't*. I had a perfectly normal childhood. There's a lovely story that Seamus Heaney used to tell. Poor Seamus that we all miss. He said that he was talking to a Finnish poet once. Finnish poets tend to be somewhat gloomy. [laughter] The Finnish poet was saying that he was having a terrible problem in his life because his parents were still alive, and he hated them. And he wished they would die. This was the big problem of his life. And he said to Seamus, "What about you?" Seamus said, "I like my parents." And the Finnish poet said, "Oh, you *really* have a problem." [laughter] And I see what he meant. A relatively happy childhood is a distinct disadvantage. But then I was brought up as an Irish Catholic so that sort of negated all the happiness. Whenever I went near the priests or the nuns, they would tell me how dreadful and guilty I was. Poor old Quirke, I think, has had all my guilt poured into him. It's as if he were an ink bottle, and I

poured all the black stuff in there. That's what it is, but I don't know and I don't want to know. When I was young, I felt that I was entirely in control, that I knew exactly what I was doing. My books were meticulously planned. I would know what the last sentence was going to be before I wrote the first one. Now I don't work like that. I let instinct have its moment. I let instinct take over. I remember reading Henry James: "We work in the dark—we do what we can—we give what we have." And I think that's absolutely true. I now work absolutely in the dark. I do not know what I'm doing. But that is the right way to work, I think. That is, after all, the most lifelike way because we don't know what we're doing. We think we do. We think we're living. We think we're making decisions. Whereas, in fact, we are just drifting. We're being pushed this way and that. And again, thank goodness we are. Look at the last century, the great monsters who knew exactly what they were doing and decided that they would do it. We've had enough of that. Let's hope it doesn't come again in our time. Just to drift and to allow things to happen and allow imagination to play over the surface of this strange world that we live in because, again, I find being here *extremely* strange. I have never ever gotten used to it. I've never gotten used to this world. The only direct statement of myself that I've put into my books was in *The Book of Evidence* where the character says, "I've never gotten used to being on this earth. I always think that our presence here is a cosmic blunder, that we were meant for somewhere else." He says, "I wonder how they're faring, the people who were meant for here. How are they faring in the planet that was meant for us on the other side of the universe?" And he says, "No, no, they would have been extinct long ago. How would they have coped, these gentle earthlings, with a place that was meant for us?" I think that's true. We're certainly the most successful virus the world has ever known. And yet for all our awfulness and for all our wickedness and for all the damage that we do to the world and to ourselves, we still manage to make a certain music. For every Hitler there is a Beethoven. In fact, for every Hitler there are ten Beethovens. We've done better than we deserve to have done. We've done better than we seem to have been capable of doing. And maybe we'll keep doing it. This is what art is always trying to do, trying to concentrate on how extraordinary it is to be here and how extraordinary we are. In, as I said, all our awfulness and all our pettiness, we're still extraordinary creatures.

Gleick: There is an awful lot of awfulness and wickedness in the world of the Quirke books. It's a very specific world. It's very vivid, and it's a particular time and place. Of course, it's Ireland, mostly Dublin. It appears to be the

1950s, although I don't think a date is ever mentioned. Why did you choose to root the books in the past?

Banville: Well, partly from cowardice and laziness. If I were going to have a pathologist as a protagonist, he'd have to know all kinds of science. That would mean I would have to do an awful lot of work, which I was not prepared to do. In the 1950s pathologists sort of cut the person open and rooted around to see if they could find why they had died, and then shut them up and put them away. There was none of this stuff that goes on now. At least it seems there is a lot of stuff going on now. I suspect they still cut them up and root around, but then pretend. [laughter]. But also, the 1950s was a fascinating time in Ireland, a fascinating time in the world. That huge sigh of relief that the world heaved in 1945, 1946, when those terrible, terrible wars were over, and there was a brief period of bliss that we'd gotten over this. And then it all started up again. In the 1950s, a very dark time—especially in Ireland, extremely dark—we didn't realize how deprived we were. We didn't realize how oppressed we were. The Catholic Church would tell us that we were free, and Eastern Europe was under the heel of atheistic communism and so on. We didn't realize that we were just the other side of the coin of Eastern Europe. We had in place of the Communist Party, the Catholic Church, who ruled everything, ruled everything! Politicians were terrified of the Church. So, we lived in exactly the same way that the oppressed peoples of the East lived, but we didn't realize it. We thought we were free. And it was a wonderful, wonderful time to set noir fiction. All that fog, all that cigarette smoke, all those secrets, all that denied sexuality, all those crimes that were covered up, as we've discovered now in the past ten, fifteen years. We discovered just how *terrible* those times were. I started writing these books when these investigations were going on into sending children abroad, and the crimes we have been capable of. Did I say, "capable of"? The crimes we have *committed*. We're astonished by it. We're still sort of reeling in shock from what we'd discovered about the 1950s. So, you asked me why do I set crime fiction in the 1950s? [makes a clicking noise] A wonderful time! [laughter]

Gleick: It's true that anyone who has read the Quirke books knows that, apart from any of the obvious villains who pass through the pages, there's one great malefactor that looms and is never brought to justice, and that is the Church. You do seem to have feelings about the Church.

Banville: Well look, it is very, very complicated. Religion is a great comfort to a great many people. The majority of men lead lives of quiet desperation. A certain majority of women lead lives of quiet desperation, and they did in the 1950s. The church was a comfort to them. As my friend, the philosopher, who put me on to George Simenon, says, religion is a poetic version of life, which in its way is very beautiful. But the Church in Ireland was a male power structure. I read a book recently by a man about my age writing about the 1950s, a journalist. In his introduction, he gives an anecdote. When he was about twelve years old, way back in the '50s, he was standing in a bus stop. A motorcyclist was coming on the street when a motor car did a U-turn. The cyclist whacked into it, was thrown over the car, and splattered on the street. The car stopped, and a priest got out, looked at him. A crowd had gathered around the poor motorcyclist on the ground, who might have been dead, probably was dead. And the priest looked at his watch, said, "Is he all right?" Then he got in his car and drove away. The power of these ghastly little men. They had absolute power in those days. There is no point in my pretending that I'm not furious about those people and what they did to us. What they did specifically to women, to young women in Ireland, is an absolute disgrace, and it's a disgrace that I don't think we have yet admitted. We haven't fessed up to it yet. We're still pretending that in some way this was an aberration; this didn't happen. But it *did* happen. It was a terrible, terrible time. I don't want to turn into a social commentator, which I'm not, but you asked me about the 1950s. That was the 1950s.

It was also a time, for me, of extraordinary gaiety. I suppose these books are set in the mid-50s. I don't really date them myself. Apart from anything else, I lose track of what age people are supposed to be. The eighth of December, the Feast of the Immaculate Conception, happens to be my birthday. They got it almost right, you know. On that day, everybody from the country came to Dublin to do their Christmas shopping, so, as a child, I would be brought to Dublin from Wexford, the small town about eighteen miles south of Dublin, on the early train, before it was light. We would stop somewhere along the way, and I would see the sun coming up, shining, across these frosty fields. I would get to Dublin—even still the smell of diesel fuel from buses seems to me a wonderfully romantic smell—and it was wonderfully thrilling. I wanted to go to Moscow, and Dublin was my Chekhovian Moscow. I would go to my aunt's flat. She had this decrepit flat in a big Georgian house in one of the most beautiful parts of Dublin. She would have the cake and so on. So, for me it was a romantic place, and I tried to get something of that romance into these books, as well as the darkness and the awfulness of it. I suppose it was simply that it was home for me. I'm not that old, but when I look back, it seems to me that I'm looking back into the Middle Ages. It could be something from Brueghel.

Gleick: Several people have made the point this week that there's some-thing about mystery fiction or crime fiction that makes it seem natural to reveal something about a particular place. There are a lot of crime series that we associate with a very specific locale. It does feel as though you've had the opportunity in this series of books to explore a version of Dublin, a dank and, as you say, smoky and rainy version of Dublin that is more vivid than . . . that's not what I mean.

Banville: I think in a way it *is* a more vivid version. Certainly, if you go back to comparing Banville and Black. Banville's version of Ireland is a fantastical place. It's very unspecific.

Gleick: And it changes from book to book.

Banville: Yes, of course, it does. I'm not interested in writing about Ireland. I'm not interested in setting books in Ireland. They're set in my head. But the Black books are set very specifically in a specific Dublin, and I had great fun when I started doing this. I used to try to remember the details, and it's extraordinary how much you can dredge up from your memory of when you were ten years old. I was amazed how much I could bring back. But details would infuriate me. In those days motor cars didn't have indicator lights in the back. They had a little orange arm that would stick out from the side of the car. I spent weeks and weeks trying to figure what the hell was the name of this thing, and a friend of mine said, "They were trafficators!" I said, "Yes! Trafficators!" I was able to drop that in like dropping a piece into a jigsaw puzzle, and, *click*! There's a great pleasure in that.

Gleick: And you can't just Google "1950s Dublin" to find out . . .

Banville: No, that's true. Although it's amazing, there was some restaurant or something that I was trying to follow up on and, in desperation, I Googled it. I got somewhat close to it in, what do you call it? Wikipedia. It's amazing how much is in Wikipedia. And it's perfectly suited to writing fiction because most of it is fiction.

Gleick: All right, that was cold. So, we've been playing with this conceit, at least I have, that literary fiction is one thing, and detective stories are a whole different thing. Literary fiction cares about style and sentences, and detective stories care about plot. Literary fiction being high art and detective fiction being low craft. But I think we both feel that this is wrong. As you say, the bookstores, in a better world, would arrange authors by alphabetical order and not create cubby holes. I certainly feel that the Quirke novels have more in

common with the Banville novels than I've said. One thing that occurs to me is that Banville describes light and color and shade and clouds more lovingly than any other writer I can think of, with the possible exception of Black. At least Black, I think, is capable of it. At the risk of depressing you yet again, I'm going to read one more sentence in hopes of making this case. "The heavy evening rain had turned to mist, fine and light as cobweb, that did not so much fall as drift vaguely this way and that through the dense and glossy darkness. On Ailesbury Road each streetlight had its own penumbra, a large soft bright ball of filaments streaming outwards in all directions, and the lit windows of the houses were set in frames of the same muted yet luminous gray radiance."
Banville: Yes, I think Black was off making a cup of coffee. [laughter] Banville nipped in. It seems to me that in any kind of writing you have to give a sense of where it's happening. Some people say to me, "Look, why do you keep telling us about the bloody weather? Just tell us the story." And I'll say, "But the story *is* the weather. The story is where the character is." You can walk out in the morning and be in a perfectly good mood, and it'll rain. And you'll suddenly be in a bad mood. The world affects how we act. We imagine that we're these autonomous beings, moving through a neutral world. We're not. We are like the rain in that we're drifted this way and that. It seems to me absolutely vital, whether it's crime fiction or my other fiction, that we have to know where we are. We have to know how things are, how it feels, how it smells, what it tastes like. Otherwise, what's the point?

Gleick: Maybe the only difference is that in the Benjamin Black books, after passages like this, you remind us that Quirke has no interest in the scenery.
Banville: No, but he is influenced by it without knowing. What we are skirting around here is the difference between the two. Black has to stop at a certain point. Black will write a sentence. and it will have a trajectory. It will have a force that's moving it on to the next sentence. And each sentence carries its nugget of information. In Banville there's no limit. I will sink down and down and down and down and down into the skeleton of the thing, into the very bones, into the genes of words. If I'm writing and it's three o'clock in the afternoon, I am so deep in the work that I don't know who I am. I don't know where I am. I will use a word that I don't know the meaning of. When I've finished writing, I'll have to look it up, and I'll discover it was the right word. I don't want to be mystical, but there is something strange that happens when you get to that level of concentration. As Black, I can't allow that plumbing of those depths. I just can't allow it. If I'm going to write that kind of book, I have to stop at a certain point. Does that make sense?

Gleick: I think it does. Before we send this audience out into the cold and dark . . .

Banville: The cold and dark of Key West.

Gleick: The foggy, smoke-filled streets of Key West. Let me ask one more question. I'm speaking to both of you now, and I'm going to oversimplify. It seems to me that all your books have one great theme, one great subject at their core. Of course, you write about many things, but it's not an accident, I daresay, that Quirke is a pathologist who spends his day rooting around in corpses and Banville, too—I am thinking of *The Infinities* and other books— seems to think a lot about death. So that's what I want to ask you finally: Do you think a great deal about death, and is that part of the business?

Banville: How long have we got?

Gleick: We've got one more minute.

Banville: Well, I was reading Spinoza again the other day, and he says . . .

Gleick: As one does.

Banville: Sorry, *glancing* through. He says the free man thinks of little less than death, and all his meditation is not on death but on life. And I think that's true. We are the creatures who are constantly aware that we are mortal, that we will die. This colors everything we do in life. It adds the sweetness to life. It was this self-consciousness which brought the consciousness of death. That's what made us into the extraordinary creatures that we are. I wrote a little play [*Todtnauberg*] about a famous meeting between the philosopher Martin Heidegger and Paul Celan, the poet, in Heidegger's hut in the mountains. Nobody knows what they talked about. Celan was a Jew. Heidegger had been a Nazi, probably still was a Nazi. And I wrote a little radio play speculating what they talked about. Celan says to him, "Why did you throw your lot in with the Nazis." And he says, "Because they give due weight to death. They recognize death stands at the elbow of the midwife, and says, 'Give me the child because I am the one that will give life to this child.'" Death gives us life. The awareness of death, the awareness that it will end, sweetens everything. Every moment that we live is informed by the awareness of death, but it's also intensified by the awareness of death.

Gleick: Please join me in thanking John Banville and Benjamin Black.

Banville: On that cheery note.

"I Hate Genre": John Banville's Interview with Jon Wiener

Jon Wiener / 2014

Jon Wiener's conversation with John Banville appeared in the *Los Angeles Review of Books* on 15 March 2014. Reprinted with the permission of publisher Boris Dralyuk and Jon Wiener, professor of history, emeritus, University of California, Irvine.

Jon Wiener: There have been something like fourteen John Banville novels, books that go in the literary fiction section of the bookstore and that win the Man Booker Prize; and as Benjamin Black you have now written eight books, and they go into the mystery section. So, we have high and low, art and craft, poetry and plot; is that an okay way to talk about Banville and Benjamin Black? **John Banville:** No. I hate it. I wish they didn't do that. This genre of literary fiction is new since I started writing. It's usually in a corner of the bookstore, and it may as well have a neon sign saying: "Don't read this stuff." My ideal bookshop would have no sections, just alphabetical, and not just fiction, but all the books next to each other. You would discover things.

Wiener: You've said you started writing the Benjamin Black books as what you call "a frolic."
Banville: I had a television miniseries I had been commissioned to do—three hours. It wasn't going to get made, and I hate to waste anything. I thought, I'll turn it into a novel. I had just begun to read Georges Simenon. Simenon was a great revelation to me. When I saw what could be achieved with very scarce means, a very small vocabulary, direct speech, mainly dialogue-driven and plot-driven, I thought, I've got to try that. I was turning sixty. I thought, Here's an adventure to embark on.

Wiener: Simenon famously wrote fast. Does Benjamin Black write fast?
Banville: Yes. Poor old Banville takes three, four, five years to write a book.

Black does it in three or four months. Crime writers get very cross when I say this, as if the crime stuff I write is much inferior. But it's just different. It's an entirely different way of working. It's craft work.

Wiener: Benjamin Black's original character was Quirke, a criminal pathologist in Dublin in the 1950s. In Black's new book his protagonist is Philip Marlowe. Quirke's world is your world, the world of your childhood and youth. You know Quirke better than anybody. That's not true of you and Philip Marlowe.

Banville: I think I probably do know Marlowe as well as I know Quirke. I might know him a little better, because I'm not sure I know much about Quirke at all. He's a strange invention, very secretive, very dark and damaged. Marlowe is dark and damaged as well, but not so much as Quirke. And Marlowe, of course, is witty. He turns a nice phrase. Quirke is very dour, compared to him.

Wiener: Raymond Chandler wrote the Philip Marlowe books in the first person. Was it a challenge for you to get inside that character, this American from the 1940s?

Banville: Oh no. Writing in the first person, I find, is easier than writing in third person. Because you have a point of view. And you bring the reader on that journey from ignorance to some kind of clarity.

Wiener: When did you start reading Raymond Chandler, and what did it mean to you?

Banville: When I was in my early teens, my brother, who was older, introduced me to Chandler. This was a huge revelation. Here was crime fiction that wasn't just done like a crossword puzzle—which is sort of Agatha Christie's approach. You do end up wondering why you spent time reading those books—just to get to the end, to find out who did it. In the Chandler books, nobody cares about who did it. He said himself the only thing that will endure from this writing is the style. That was something I found very sympathetic.

Wiener: But Raymond Chandler was not the original inspiration for Benjamin Black.

Banville: It was Simenon—I had not read him until 2003, when a philosopher friend of mine recommended him. And I discovered this new world: a dark, acrid place, but very true to life. There are at least a dozen of Simenon's books, the ones he called his "hard novels," which I think are masterly—better than Camus, better than Sartre. They're the true existentialist fiction of the twentieth century.

Wiener: Your new book is written in Raymond Chandler's style, which is different from Simenon's.
Banville: Very different. It's poised; it's elegant; it's witty. It is very stylish. Chandler is something of a dandy when it comes to language. He's very much aware of his English education. He went to Dulwich College in London, where P. G. Wodehouse and C. S. Forester went to school. He brings that dandified English sensibility to writing crime fiction, set in Los Angeles. That's one of the things that makes it so rich and so interesting.

Wiener: Are there any tricks to writing in the Raymond Chandler style?
Banville: The one trick I discovered was that he never leaves a sentence alone. His sentences are almost always in two parts. He'd say, "I walked into the room—but I'd rather have been walking out." Really, he's an elegant writer, very poised, with a wonderful eye for eccentricities of human character. His minor characters are superb, wonderfully memorable. That's a great achievement.

Wiener: Place is an essential component of Raymond Chandler's writing. We're doing this interview in North Hollywood on Cahuenga Blvd. *The Black-Eyed Blonde* begins on the corner of Cahuenga Blvd. and Hollywood Blvd.—about a ten-minute drive from here. How important was it to you to get the landscape right?
Banville: I don't know how I had the effrontery to attempt it. Chandler himself is rather cavalier with the topography of Los Angeles. For reasons known only to himself, he changed Santa Monica into "Bay City." I felt I had the same license to push things around, especially since I was living in Dublin and had only been here a handful of times.

But we all imagine that we know Los Angeles very well indeed—from the movies of the 1940s and 1950s.

Wiener: Another essential component of the Raymond Chandler books is the sadness of Philip Marlowe.
Banville: The essence of Marlowe is his loneliness. He's a completely solitary creature: no family, no friends. No possessions. Lives in an anonymous rented house. All he seems to own is a chess set and a coffee pot. It is,

outwardly at least, a bleak life. But it's the life he has chosen for himself, because he values his freedom.

Wiener: Chandler's Marlowe can also be violent.
Banville: When Marlowe gets brutal, I think it's Chandler suddenly remembering he's writing crime fiction and he better get tough. I didn't feel I needed to do that.

Wiener: Do you ever imagine what it would have been like for you to live in LA in 1950 and be a writer of detective fiction then and there?
Banville: I'd love to have been one of those hack writers for the movies, living in a little cabin in the Hollywood Hills, hammering away at a typewriter, a glass of Scotch at my elbow, and a guy's coming in and saying, "You gotta have two scenes by four o'clock, and they better be good or you're off the picture!" I would have loved to work under that kind of pressure. And they made such marvelous movies.

Wiener: Which are your favorites of the Philip Marlowe movies?
Banville: Of course, *The Big Sleep*. It was unsurpassable. But Robert Mitchum and Charlotte Rampling made a wonderful version of *Farewell, My Lovely*. Mitchum was a different kind of Marlowe from Bogart's—he was lazy; he was tired. He was disenchanted in a way that Bogart couldn't be. And Charlotte Rampling is the perfect Chandler femme fatale.

Wiener: Both the Quirke and the Marlowe books are set in the 1950s—what drew you to that decade?
Banville: The '50s are a fascinating decade. People of my generation tried to forget about the '50s. In Ireland especially, the things we're discovering now about things that went on in the '50s makes it fascinating. We were always assured we were free and Eastern Europe was under the jackboot of atheistic communism. We didn't realize that we were in exactly the same position as Eastern Europe: they had the Communist Party dictating everybody's lives; we had the Catholic Church dictating everybody's lives. It was a mirror image, two sides of the same coin. In a way, our lives were more controlled than theirs under the Soviet regime. Ireland was a society run by power-hungry men who didn't have any allegiance to the state; their allegiance was to Rome, to the Vatican. It was a strange, dark time, full of secrets, with lots of cigarette smoke and fog, and clandestine sex; a perfect time to set a noir novel in.

Wiener: Of course, LA in the 1950s wasn't dominated by the Catholic Church the way Quirke's Dublin was. But we did have McCarthyism, which made for a different kind of dark time.

Banville: Oh yes, that was a terrifying time in America. It very nearly turned fascist at the end of the 1940s and beginning of the 1950s. It's a great tribute to your individuality and sense of freedom that you didn't allow that to happen. I'm a great admirer of America. I still believe America is the last great hope.

Wiener: Really?

Banville: Yes. Despite all your problems, you do amazing things. Who would have thought ten years ago that America would have a black president? Who was elected not once but twice? Who would have thought that a politician like Lyndon Johnson would have brought in civil rights legislation, would ram it down the throats of the politicians and a lot of the country as well? Where else could that happen?

Wiener: You were literary editor of the *Irish Times* and reviewed all sorts of books, fiction and nonfiction, and now you write for the *New York Review.* Where does reviewing fit into your life as a fiction writer?

Banville: That's a separate persona that I have. I think book reviewing is an honorable trade if it's done honestly. There's no point in doing it otherwise. It's not criticism. It's saying to the reader, "Here's a book that you will not have read yet; here's what I think of it. Take it or leave it." That's very important for the health of literature—people who will do a first tasting but have no pretensions of being critics. People say to me, "Will you bring out a collection of your criticism?" I say, "It's not criticism; it's book reviews. And I'm really not going to bring out a book of book reviews."

Wiener: You've been a novelist for several decades now—has your approach to writing fiction changed as you've gotten older?

Banville: I feel freer. I let my instincts run things far more than I did when I was younger. I've come to realize that writing fiction is much more like dreaming than anything else—a kind of controlled dreaming. Nietzsche said every man is an artist when he's asleep, which I think is true. Look at the fantastic creativity of your dreams: you lie down, you close your eyes, suddenly you're dealing with people you've never seen before, you're in places you've never been before, and you're developing an extraordinary and compelling world. It's that kind of deep power of the unconscious that novelists try to put discipline on.

Wiener: As a writer of fiction you've said, "A sentence can always be better."
Banville: That way lies what Henry James called "the madness of art." Artists live with failure because we aim constantly for perfection. We know we can't have it, but we keep striving toward it. All we can do, as Beckett says, is "fail again, fail better." Yes, a sentence can always be improved. You never finish a sentence. You just abandon it.

In Conversation with John Banville and Ed Victor

Claire Connolly and Jean Van Sinderen-Law / 2014

Reprinted by permission from Claire Connolly, professor of modern English, and Jean Van Sinderen-Law, associate vice president of development at University College Cork.

Claire Connolly: It really is a pleasure to welcome you back, John, to UCC. We feel very privileged to have you again, more or less within a week.

John Banville: Yes, I'm becoming addicted to Cork.

Connolly: We like the sound of that. When John was last here, he was being hosted by the School of Languages, Literatures, and Cultures, and I'm taking the place now that was taken then by my colleague in the Department of German, Dr. Rachel Magshamhrain. It was very striking listening to you talking to Rachel, John, the extent to which you were so comfortable and at home with a wide range of reference in terms of European literature. You're very comfortable talking about German literature, as you were with Rachel, and I suppose we would all think of you here, really, as our European novelist. Could you just say a little bit about what Europe means to you or has meant to you in your writing?

Banville: Last year, I was interviewed in Dublin by a Spanish journalist who had come to write a piece about the crash. He interviewed various people, including our minister for finance, Mr. Noonan. And at the end of the interview, Noonan said, "Who else are you speaking to?" and he said, "Well, I'll speak to Professor John Fitzgerald and an economist." Noonan said, "That's fine." And the journalist said, "And I'm speaking to John Banville." Noonan said, "Don't speak to him. He's only a tourist here." [laughter] So, it's nice to know what the government thinks of you.

I refuse to wear the green jersey. Do you know this phrase, Ed? If you're patriotic here, you have to wear the green jersey. Everything Irish has to be wonderful. I've always refused to do that, and I will continue to refuse to do that. There are other people who do it as well. They may not be as noisy about their refusal as I am. I went last year to Princeton for a weekend, ill-advisedly, because when I got there, I discovered it was Irish weekend, and they were all there clapping themselves on the backs. But I noticed Roddy Doyle, whom I hadn't really known before. Roddy was like me, had that sort of distaste, and he and I have since become friends. One has to be against things. One has to take an adversarial stance. This country has very little to be proud of, as we've discovered recently. We sold ourselves to the Church. We sold ourselves to devious and venal politicians for decades. So, this is all preliminary to saying I've always been a firm European and I will continue to be.

Connolly: And is it true to say that you think of Europe as offering some form of opposition to the ways in which Irish society and culture have been organized? Or do you think Europe is part of the problem now?

Banville: No, not at all. The Ireland that I grew up in didn't recognize Europe existed. There was only England. Beyond that there was just this blank map. We were absolutely obsessed with England in the fifties and the sixties. Then we joined what was then the EEC, and we got a new enemy, Brussels, which is good for us because suddenly we stopped worrying about England. We started saying, "It's Brussels that's doing it all to us!" or Strasbourg, or wherever. We never seemed to think that it's New York. Everything westward is fine; everything eastward is dreadful. I always felt that we should grow up. This is the thing that we refuse to do.

Connolly: But it would be true to say that your cosmopolitan sensibility— and it is remarkably such—is one that has flourished here on the island. You never thought of living elsewhere?

Banville: I remember years ago meeting Donna Tartt when she was about, I don't know, nine years old, and she'd been paid gazillions of money for her first book. She said to me, "John, have you got a place in New York?" I said, "Donna, I barely have a place in Ireland." I live here because, first of all, I can't do otherwise. I can't own a place in New York. I'd love to own a place in New York, and Paris, and maybe something down in the south as well. You listening, Ed? [laughter]

Connolly: Yes, Ed can work on this.

Ed Victor: It's coming.

Banville: But I like it here. I like the color. The climate is absolutely superb, not just for this weather we're having now, but I love the climate. I love those grey, those pearly days in November, December, January, February. I love them. It's an exquisite climate. It's absolutely perfect. It's never too hot, never too cold, just right. And the color of the light speaks to something in me that I need.

Connolly: Thinking about your work, perhaps here especially in Cork, situated as we are on the southwest edge of Europe, it's striking, the extent to which your work turns again and again to the sea, not just in the novel that has that title, but the extent to which you're drawn to coasts, to the light.

Banville: What's that statistic? You're never more than something like fifty-three miles from the sea wherever you are in Ireland. I remember spending some months in Iowa, and after three days, I noticed that, first of all, my hair was different because there was no salt.

Connolly: Was it better or worse?

Banville: Who am I to say? But then my skin went different as well because it didn't have salt in it. I remember one day, looking at this awful apartment I was in, and seeing a seagull, which had wandered down from the Great Lakes, wildly lost. A seagull! A seagull! And I realized how homesick I was. *Homesick* is the wrong word. I need this place in some peculiar way that I don't understand and that I don't want to understand.

Connolly: And the ways in which you might need or not need this place, I suppose those are refractors and reflectors in the fictions? You're a genius with first-person narratives. You've given us such a series of remarkable voices, not always likeable voices.

Banville: God, I should hope not.

Connolly: Yes, hardly ever. But voices that draw us in and make us think and ask questions. Could you say more about what draws you to the first-person voice in your novels?

Banville: I don't know any other way to do it. You may say I'm a genius with first-person. That's another way of saying I've no talent at all for third-person narrative. [laughter] It seems to me that one looks at the world from inside oneself. All I know about other people is their surfaces. I can't know what they're like inside. It seems to me the only way is to say, "This is my witness. I was here. This is what the world looked like to a person who was here for a very brief time on the surface of it, on the earth." The trouble with interviews like this is that I never know what I'm doing. All knowledge, certainly for an artist, is knowledge in hindsight. It's when we look back at work and say, "Oh, yes, that's what I was doing." When I'm doing it, I don't know at all.

Connolly: But to take a particular case of just that problem you have a narrator in *Ancient Light* who tells us story after story, the story of Billy Gray's mother and so on. You end up knowing a lot, but, of course, you realize quite startlingly at the end of that novel that you know very little at all, in fact. I was curious about the extent to which those things that are not said in the novel, which intrigue us and compel us and make us go back to your language again and again, are somehow things that are said somewhere in your brain. Or are they deeply unknown things that are never even said to yourself?

Banville: I suspect we all reach the end of our lives saying, "I knew nothing. I thought I did. I made little forays here and there into other people's lives, into other people's persons, into other people's heads, but I knew nothing. I was alone." This is one of the wonderful things about Beckett. At the end of all of his books, you come to that awful, bleak moment when it says, "You're alone. You're alone." I'd like to say otherwise. I'd like to say it's a wonderful community, and we're all in it together, but we're not. We're not.

Connolly: Perhaps this is something we'll come back to in relation to the role of the writer more generally.

Banville: Oh, let's not.

Connolly: Just in case the evening turns too gloomy. [laughter] But to explore a little bit more what you do with those words, could you tell us anymore about how you work with those voices?

Banville: I really can't. I don't know. They speak inside my head.

Connolly: Do you ever say them out loud?

Banville: Oh yes, all the time. I catch myself chanting these lines, and I don't know whose they are. And I don't know who *I* am. I always say that when I stand up from my desk, the person who wrote the books ceases to exist. Asking me about them is futile. I really don't know, and I don't want to know.

Connolly: And I suppose in the books one of the areas I want to encounter is that problem of unknowability, which draws us all to your work: how powerfully it expresses those limits and dilemmas, the way it often centers on the unknown or unknowable past, the childhood that we think we remember but has deceived us.

Banville: The past is fascinating in that the past was the present, and it was just as dull and boring as this present and tomorrow's present. But somehow the past becomes illuminated. It throbs with significance it didn't have when it was happening. Why do we confer this significance on the past? I don't know, but I know that, especially as I get older, there are moments of shivering communication with the past. And it sustains me. As a human being, but certainly as a writer, it does, but I don't understand it.

Connolly: And when you wrote those early novels, especially *Doctor Copernicus* and *Kepler*, and took us back into these particular periods in the past, I suppose it seemed, for a while, as if you might become a historical novelist or that you would be more interested in exploring particular places.

Banville: Oh, well, that was my European novelist of ideas phase. I was going to be a Thomas Mann or Hermann Broch. The Germans especially, you know I love them for their solidity and their lack of humor. I shouldn't say that. That's unjust. Thomas Mann is a very funny writer in his way. But yes, I had that notion myself, but I was young. I was in my twenties. I didn't know what I was doing. I certainly knew I didn't want to be an Irish writer. I didn't want to be labeled as "charming" and "garrulous" and "brothel boy." I didn't want any of that stuff. I wanted to be something else. Again, it was probably foolish, but one is very ambitious when one is foolish. When one is *young*. There's a nice slip. [laughter]

Connolly: And have you ever felt the pull of historical settings since, or is that something you've put behind?

Banville: No, no, no, no. That was mostly a waste of time. I wasted my time doing little bits of research and reading silly books I shouldn't have read, looking at pictures that were rather boring for the period detail. It was largely a waste of time. I should have trusted my imagination. I should have made it all up. Who's that good novelist who wrote *Being Dead*? Oh, God, how dreadful. My mind is going. Anyway, he [Jim Crace] wrote a wonderful novel about two corpses lying on a beach, a very good novel, and what happens to a body when it deteriorates and the names of all the things that eat you and so on. I said, "How did you do all of that research?" He said, "It's not research. I made it up." And another time, I was having lunch with Cormac McCarthy down in Santa Fe, years ago. Cormac had just published *All the Pretty Horses*. I said, "Cormac, you must have grown up with horses," and he said, "I don't know anything about horses." [laughter] Of course! You make it up.

Connolly: It's fiction.

Banville: That's what novelists do. It's fiction.

Connolly: There must be particular problems and limits when you try to make up things that you *do* know more intimately from your own past.

Banville: There are no limits. Look, being a novelist is like when you can sing scales in your mind, and you can sing a scale higher and higher and higher and higher and higher. You could do it forever. Being a novelist, you can make anything up, and people will believe it! And so they should because the imagination is a far more powerful implement than the capacity to absorb factual knowledge. When I was writing *Copernicus* and *Kepler*, my wife used to always say to me, "Stop being mesmerized by the facts. They're just facts. They're not necessarily the truth." The truth of art is something other than factual.

Connolly: I read someplace where you quoted Baudelaire's definition of genius as the ability to tap into one's *own* childhood, to realize the spirit of a moment or a place.

Banville: Yes, *genius* he meant in lowercase. He meant the old-fashioned sense. One's genius is the capacity to summon childhood at will. But, of course, I'm so far away from childhood now that it's *all* made up.

Connolly: Obviously in the novels you remind us all the time of those difficulties, the slips of memory, the things we think we see but don't actually see at all.

Banville: I find that almost everything I see in life turns out to be mistaken or misconceived. Sometimes wonderfully so. You fall in love and you think, "This being that I'm in love with is a goddess. This, a superhuman being." But after a few months, a few years, you discover it's just another person like me. In fact, what you were doing was holding a mirror in front of yourself and saying how wonderful *I* am, what a god *I* am. Those illusions are absolutely necessary, and they're beautiful. What's more enlivening, what's more intensifying than the sense of being alive and falling in love? But it's like starting a book: you *know* that it's going to fail. You know it's going to be just another bloody book. But one starts it in a spirit of "This is going to be the book that will set the world back on its heels. Generations from now they'll be speaking about me in tones of awe." But I know that it'll be just another bloody book.

Connolly: But you sustain it for a period in the same spirit to keep writing?

Banville: Yes, you start a book in great high spirits and frolic in this sense of "This is going to be wonderful." Then halfway through you're wading up to your armpits in mud, and you think, "But I'm stuck with this damn thing, and I have to get to the other side of this muddy river." And then you finish it and you think, "Get rid of that!" And you start a *new book*: "This is going to be a masterpiece! This is going to be superb!"

Connolly: If we go back to that question of love stories and how they all begin, you do seem to be more drawn recently to those kinds of dilemmas and relationships in your writing. Would that be fair to say?

Banville: Oh, God, I hope not.

Connolly: Would that be something that you would regard as unworthy of your time as a novelist?

Banville: Oh, nothing is unworthy of my time as a novelist. We only have life. Life is the only material we have. All novelists want to write, in fact, nothing. Flaubert and Joyce both stated that they wanted to write novels that would be about nothing. But you can't! Because all we have is life. It keeps coming back to its strangeness and its absurdity. Poor Anthony Burgess, almost forgotten now, but he was a wonderful novelist. And in one of his books, I can't remember which, he relates something, which is obviously his own experience. His character is in a hospital, dying, he thinks. In fact, he's not. But he's given up, and he says, "Okay, I'll die." And then in the corridor one day, he meets a little man. He says to the little man, "Why are you in hospital?" The little man says, "Well, I had this accident. You see, I'm a plumber and I got this nut caught on my private part." He asks, "Well why did you . . ." The little man says, "Well, I was using this nut, you know." And he's got his penis caught in this enormous nut, and the narrator says, "The world is so strange. I don't want to leave it. If I can have this kind of encounter in a hospital corridor, life is worth living." It's a wonderful moment.

Connolly: Affirmative, yeah.

Banville: It's affirmative in a sense, and it is so absurd and so silly and so ridiculous that why would you want to leave it? There's always going to be something more ridiculous coming tomorrow.

Jean van Sinderen-Law: Just as a transition, I heard you say at one point, John, that when you're writing a book, it's yours, and when a book is written, it's no longer yours. So, before we chat to Ed, can you talk about that? Because no doubt when the book is written, it goes into the hands of people like Ed.

Banville: There are no people like Ed. [laughter] He is unique. I had agents before Ed. When Ed became my agent, for about two years he'd phone me up and say, "Why have you done this stuff? You've said these things in public?" And I said, "But Ed, my other agents were never interested in this." He said, "Yeah, but I am interested." But, yes, of course, the book that one is doing is one's own. And when it's finished, almost in an air of disgust, one gives it out to the world. One of my favorite stories about Ed is that after receiving the first book he handled for me, my publisher told me, "Ed sent me this manuscript and he said, 'Here's John's new book. We want x amount of money and no fucking around.'" And my publisher said, "This was his first approach." [laughter] "How terrible was it going to get?"

Sinderen-Law: I'll ask Ed the question.

Ed Victor: Before you do this, I want to say that John is not the only author I've ever handled who, as you just said, when he finishes a book, he *finishes* it and moves on to the next. But I cannot send him a review. He refuses. Even a great review he doesn't want to see, and the only other author I handled all these years was Iris Murdoch, who when she finished a book, that was it. Goodbye, good luck, I'm on to the next thing. So, even good reviews he doesn't want to hear. Let alone bad ones.

Banville Especially the good reviews.

Sinderen-Law: So how did John Banville meet Ed Victor, or Ed Victor meet John Banville?

Victor: Well, this gets to be like *Rashomon*. [laughter] Because I will tell you my version of it.

Sinderen-Law: And we're amongst friends.

Victor: I was at a party in Wicklow at the home of Paul and Kathy McGuinness, who I think had a tradition going all the way back to the time they were at Trinity College, Dublin. They had no money then, so they served white Port, and they continued to serve white Port on New Year's Day. Although, they had a bit of money at this point. And John came up to me. We had met briefly earlier in that weekend. He said, "Could we get together in London and talk?" And I said, "Sure." And then we went out to lunch and began a conversation that led me taking over. But what I didn't realize was that, and you can correct me if I'm wrong, there was a gang consisting of Bono, Paul McGuinness, and Harry Crosby, and you said, "I'm sick and tired of being acclaimed for my literary novels and not making any money." And they said, "There's Ed Victor standing over there, *he'll* make you some money. Go over and talk to him." Was that correct?

Banville: Yes, it was, I'm told, as well. Paul is still annoyed that I don't give him enough credit for putting us together. The agents that I'd had weren't fun. Suddenly here was somebody who said, "Let's have fun. We'll make a bit of money, but we'll have fun." That was absolute music to my ears.

Victor: We had a lot of fun and made a lot of money, in no particular order.

Sinderen-Law: We were familiar with John as John Banville for many years, and then we got to know him as Benjamin Black. Were you involved in that, Ed?

Ed: I remember because John—and there's nothing shameful about this— said he wanted to make some more money. One day John came to my office, [to John] again you can comment on this, this is *Rashomon*. I said, "Do you like reading thrillers, John?" He said, "Why do you ask?" and I said, "Well, I represent the estate of Raymond Chandler and Fredrick Forsyth and Jack Higgins." He said, "Yes, I like certain thrillers. I like Simenon." Okay, the next thing that happens is he sends me a script he wrote called "Lost Innocence." He said, "I'm sending you this script. It's a television script. What do you think of it?" I read it and thought it was good, and he said, "Do you think it would make a novel?" I said, "Yes, I do." And he said, "Good, because I've written 30,000 words." [laughter]

Sinderen-Law: Right answer.

Victor: So, I said, "Send me these words." And I read these words, and, of course, John's laundry list would be wonderful. So, I asked John, "Do you have the right to make this into a novel?" He said, "Yes," and I said, "I'm going to ask you this again slowly. Do you have the right to make this into a novel?" He said, "I think so." He didn't, of course, because when you sign a contract for a script, they hoover up every possible right. So, I negotiated with the producers, got a quitclaim, and then offered the novel. We decided that John should set up a separate—and this is a well-known, well-worn thing—

Banville: Just before you go on, I should say that the contract for the script had been made by another agent, and when I sent Ed the contract, Ed phoned me up and said, "John, these people own you on Mars." [laughter]

Victor: They did, too, "throughout the universe," it said. So, we decided to create an alter ego, and I remember we were talking about what name it should be, and John said, "I have a character called Benjamin White in one of my earlier novels." I said, "No, it has to be Benjamin Black because you're writing thrillers, and also"—I know this is really venal of me—"*B* is earlier in the alphabet than *W*, and therefore, on the shelf, it comes earlier. You must think of these things."

Sinderen-Law: That's the agent talking.

Victor: That's the agent talking. And John took to this so wonderfully and was asked a lot of questions about how it was he could be Black and Banville, and the best answer of all the answers you gave was that he has become ambidextrous. He is doing with two different hands, but equally skillful, and the Black career has really flourished. And recently I combined two clients, John and the estate of Raymond Chandler, because I always thought that John should write a Philip Marlowe novel. I asked him to do that, and he just did it. There's a book called *The Black-Eyed Blonde* that he wrote, which is just an amazing book. I don't know how a man growing up in Wexford could channel Raymond Chandler, but this is a pure Philip Marlowe novel, a pure American novel.

Connolly: And we are talking today about your twenty-six letters made into words, and that's really what we're talking about: ideas, images, and whatever way we see them or read them.

Banville: It is an extraordinary thing. As I said, it is only because we have gotten used to it that we have lost sight of *how extraordinary* it is. We animals used to be tearing each other apart. We are still tearing each other apart. We were in the jungle. We have come out of the jungle, and we have made this extraordinary thing. As you said, twenty-six letters to express everything. Every possible conception. It's an amazing process.

Audience Member: Can I ask you, John, do you see a complete disconnect in your writing between John Banville and Benjamin Black, or do you see elements of Banville coming into the work of the Quirke novels?

Banville: As far as I'm concerned, these are two entirely separate ways of working. I think the result is entirely separate, as well. But I remember when I gave the first Benjamin Black book to my publisher. We were having a meeting with her, and she said, "Of course, this is not a crime book, this is a literary book," and I said, "Oh, Jesus, don't say that." That wasn't the point at all. I don't think they are literary. They certainly have no literary pretentions. With a Benjamin Black book what you see is what you get. They are simple and straightforward, and I'm proud of them. They are well crafted, but the Banville books are something else.

Victor: John once said to me, "I'm going to be late with the new John Banville novel because I realized that the last few chapters were written by Benjamin Black." [laughter]

Banville: Yes. I should be honest and say that the two of them do leak into each other. When I read over it, I see immediately that three o'clock on Tuesday afternoon I got lazy.

Audience Member: Even with a novel like *The Book of Evidence*, do you see some element of a kind of noir fiction, just a hint of Benjamin Black, even at that early stage of your writing?

Banville: Oh, yes, of course. When I say they're separate, I can't be two people. I am one sensibility, I think. If you look at something like *The Book of Evidence* or *The Untouchable*, you can see that there's a voice that is more superficial than the others. I used to have an editor who, when I gave him one of my books, would say, "Oh, this is an easy one. I know the next one is going to be impossible." I think I do, in some way, take a rest. Writing as Banville, I'm lost to myself. I don't know what I'm doing. I'm astray. But Black is always me. I always know what I'm doing.

Connolly: You made it sound earlier as if the decision to come to the alter ego was very easily made. Is that true?

Banville: Yes, it was an adventure. It was the early days with Ed, and Ed had provided this extraordinary notion that you can have fun with your agent. That it wouldn't be someone saying, "Oh, John, we won't even offer this one." I wrote a little book a few years ago called *The Newton Letter*, which was quite short. My agent in those days said, "Well, there's no point in offering this to publishers. It won't be published. Nobody publishes books this short." And then luckily Channel Four asked me to do a film script, and I did a script from the book, *The Newton Letter*, and I said to my agent, "I suppose I better, as a courtesy, send the book to my publisher, saying, 'There *is* this book.'" And, of course, they said, "There's no question that we'll publish it." Ed was, for me, a new kind of agent, both in terms of business, but also in terms of saying, "Let's have some fun here." One of my favorite things Ed said to me first—I think it was when we were having that first lunch. He said, "English publishers, you can't talk to them about money. You go out to a lunch like this, and you have the starter and the main course. And you talk about the latest best sellers; you talk about the weather; you talk about your golf handicap." Then with the coffee, the publisher goes, "Hmm, hmm. Sorry." And you know the money is coming. And Ed says, "I'm not sorry. This is *about* money." But there is, even still, this extraordinary notion in English publishing that it can't be about the money. No, that's too vulgar. And, of course, publishers used that for *many* decades—and I'm sure Ed would agree with this—in order to *not* pay authors anything. You go and see them in their tweed suits in their little offices in the top of narrow houses in SoHo. My first editor—I was like twenty-two or twenty-three—I'd see him at eleven in the morning, and he'd say, "Oh, that looks fine, we'll go with that." There'd be a mark on maybe page one, nothing else. Obviously, he hadn't read the rest of it. And he'd say, "Fancy a drink?" And he would pour me half a tumbler full of gin. Every time I saw him, I'd be drunk by midday. It was a *kind* of fun, but it wasn't the kind of fun that I should have been having. I remember he took me to lunch one day, Au Jardin des Gourmets in SoHo. I got a glimpse of the bill, and I said, "Jesus, David, next time could I just have the money instead of lunch." He said, "Yes, but I wouldn't get my lunch then, would I, old boy?" [laughter]

Sinderen-Law: John, do you ever not take the advice of your agent?

Victor: By the way, that was a perfect story of English publishing in the seventies. Perfect.

Banville: *Having* an agent is a point that should be emphasized. There has to be trust. I trust that Ed is looking out for my good. I have to disagree with him now and then, as he has to disagree with me. But we do trust each other. Because otherwise, it would be impossible. I have to tell this story. I'm terrified of air travel; I hate traveling. I hate going away, but I do it all the time. And Ed wrote to me one day after I asked him about going to Uzbekistan, the literary festival, or something. Ed said, "Remember what Nancy Reagan used to say about drugs? Just say no." And now I write to him and say, "Ed, they want me to come here." Ed writes and says, "Dear Ron, just say no. Love, Nancy."

Victor: There's a big Ron and Nancy correspondence between us. [laughter]

Banville: In a few weeks I'm going to a literary festival in Leicester. The reason I'm going is that the guy wrote to me, and I thought that he was a man in York whom I may know and whom I like. I got the names mixed up. I wrote and said, "Yes, of course, I'll come to Literary Leicester." And now I'm stuck going to Literary Leicester. On Ryan Air! On fucking Ryan Air! It's all my fault. [to Ed] I should have written to you. You would have said, "Dear Ron, just say no."

Victor: There was a wonderful song in the musical *Oklahoma*. Annie Oakley sings, "I'm jist a girl who cain't say no." [laughter]

Audience Member: As agent and author, you two seem to have a very good, trusting relationship. Is Ed ever tempted to give advice about the book's content, and is John ever prepared to listen?"

Victor: I don't really advise John about the content of books. But I tend to read them very early on, and I have occasional suggestions to make, which he either accepts or rejects. He is the author; I am not. And as for deal points, we discuss those together pretty carefully. John is an author unlike Iris Murdoch, who said, "Whatever you want, dear." We talk about the terms of contracts. We talk about where we're going to go for foreign publishers. When John wrote the Philip Marlowe novel, we could have taken it to the Benjamin Black publishers or the Raymond Chandler publishers. John said, "I want just the Benjamin Black publishers." That was a decision he took, and that's what I respected. I think we have a good collaborative conversation about all these things.

Banville: Yes, one would have to. It would be intolerable to be at loggerheads with one's agent, I think. Previous agents that I've had, and I've had many . . .

Victor: I'm his last. [laughter]

Banville: Yes, he's my last. They were, at worst, indifferent. I didn't fight with them. For the most part they couldn't remember who I was. But, yes, one would have to trust an agent. It would be intolerable otherwise because you know nobody trusts a publisher. Writers, we're so insecure. When I wrote *The Sea* and sent it to my publishers, I assumed that it would not be published. I assumed they would write to me and say, "John, this really isn't very good. Put it in the drawer, and we'll move on to the next one." So, one never knows, and it's very good for an agent to say, "Buck up there. Even if it's no good, we're going to sell it." And that is a good thing to be told because that removes the notion of "Oh, God, have I written a good book or a bad book?" It becomes the business of doing the business. It's therapeutic at the end of a book.

Victor: John was so insecure about *The Sea* that he called me. He had written a rather critical review of Ian McEwan's book, *Saturday*, in the *New York Review of Books*, and he said, "I have really done it now. I've written this review. Knowing the establishment, I'm not even going to make the long list." And I said, "You'll make the long list." And then he made the long list. And then he said, "I'm never going to make the short list." And he made the short list, and he said, "Well, I'm never going to win the Booker Prize. I've made a date the day after to go to Skidmore College in Saratoga Springs, New York." I said, "Was that wise?" And he said, "Yes, I'm never going to win it," and then he wins it. And then guess who had to call Skidmore to say, "He's not coming"?

Sinderen-Law: So he didn't take your advice?

Banville: Well, to be fair to me, my publishers had no notion that the book was going to win. It was a complete fluke. It was pushed by people who liked it, including Josephine Hart. These things are lotteries. But nobody had any notion that this would win, apart from Ed. It was wonderful. I had been offered to visit a creative writing class in Temple University in Philadelphia. And at the end of that, on the fifth day, Skidmore was offering me an honorary doctorate. It was the only honorary doctorate I've ever accepted. My son's a great fan of the Marx Brothers. He said, "Any college called Skidmore College has to be run by the Marx Brothers, so you have to go." [laughter] And that was actually going to be on the same night as the Booker dinner. And when the Booker short listed and the publishers phoned me and said, "This is wonderful. We'll see you in four weeks' time at the dinner." I said, "No, no. I'll be in Skidmore." And they said, "Oh, no, you won't." They said, "Whatever tiny chance you may have, if you don't go, you won't win." So the arrangement we made was that I got Skidmore to put the conferring of the doctorate off for one day, and I flew back to London from Philadelphia. I got in at six in the morning. I walked around London all day long. I went, and I won the bloody thing. Then Ed had to call them, and they said, "Well, we have a banquet for thirty people . . . and we . . ." But having won the thing you have to stay around.

Victor: Yes, you can't just leave the next day.

Audience Member: Which contemporary writers do you enjoy reading most, and what do you look for most in your own reading?

Banville: I read almost no fiction now. Richard Ford is a friend of mine, so I read his books. I think they're superb, and he's the best American writer. But I'm biased because he's a friend of mine. I read very little fiction. I read poetry; I read philosophy. I've started recently reading historians. I discovered Hugh Trevor-Roper a few years ago. One of the great prose stylists of *any* time, really. One of the great English stylists. And there are all kinds of things I haven't discovered yet; there's always a new book; there's always a new author waiting for me. But I read very little fiction. That's not a judgment on it; I think one gets to a certain age, that one doesn't need whatever it is that fiction does. That did for me when I was in my twenties, thirties, and forties and I read very little, but this is a regret to me when I don't seem to need fiction. I write more fiction now than I read, disgracefully.

Audience Member: You're reading less fiction now. Are you watching fewer films?

Banville: Oh no. I watch all the series on television because this really is a golden age of television, and it's writer-driven. Things like *The Sopranos*, *Breaking Bad*, all that; they're just superb. They're doing what the nineteenth-century novel used to do, and they're making the nineteenth-century aspect of the novel entirely redundant in our time. The problem is, of course, when you go back to watch them a second time around, you realize they're not as good, and it's entirely different with a book. You can go back and read quite a banal, mediocre book and still get something new out of it, but when you rewatch the series in television, you realize that what you've been seduced by is literally the spectacle. And there's also the fact that if you look at *The Sopranos*, and that's the first of the great series, what generates the excitement is that at some simmering level, you know that within at least ten minutes there'll be a piece of absolute violence that will surprise and shock you, horrify you. There'll be blood everywhere, and they'll be people's brains spattered around. And then he'll go back to see his psychiatrist, and he'll deal with his wife and so forth. But you always know the violence is coming. That is, in a peculiar way, despicable. Because in a way, it's the worst kind of abuse of the viewer or the reader or the listener because it's appealing both to a sense that you want the narrative, you want the subtlety, you want all that wonderful acting that's in this, but you also want the violence. You also want girls being cut up and raped, dumped in trucks. It appeals to the lowest in us, as well as the highest. The more I think about it, the more it gets immoral. There's a series on here called *Love/ Hate*. It's a wonderful series. It's about drug gangs and so on. Wonderfully done, wonderfully acted. But I watched the first episode last Sunday night, and I thought, I can't watch anymore of this because I'm being used here. I'm being manipulated here. Also, my eighteen-year-old daughter and her boyfriend settle down in front of this with a bag of popcorn, and it's *extraordinarily* violent. And, not only is it violent, but the world that these people live in is entirely amoral. The notion of there being morals to *break*, even, is ridiculous. There are no morals. Nobody's committing a crime. And I think we're being used. But I'd love to write one of them.

Connolly: Is it the conjunction of the stylish looks and the great writing and the violence that you find disturbing?

Banville: It's the convention that there is going to be extreme violence every ten to fifteen minutes. You just know this is going to happen. And that mad child in all of us that wants to see bloodshed and destruction is catered to by this.

Audience Member: John, you said you don't really feel the need to read as much fiction. Has that had an effect on the fiction you write?

Banville: Benjamin Black is a novelist. Banville is something else. I don't know what he does. He's not interested in plot, dialogue, character, or any of the things a novelist is supposed to be interested in, certainly not interested in society, politics, morals, or any of those things. Banville is trying to generate something else, so I never felt the mainstream fiction that I was reading had anything to do with what I was writing. That hasn't changed. The writers I still read are Henry James, Thomas Mann, Thackeray. I still think *Vanity Fair* is the greatest nineteenth-century novel because it has no illusions. It's about money, sex, and power, whilst the others are about girls falling for unsuitable men but discovering that they are suitable in the end. It seems to me childish stuff. There is a level at which we need to be told stories. There is a level in which I need to tell stories. Benjamin Black does that for me now. When I started writing the Benjamin Black books, it was great. I suddenly discovered play again. I could play with things; it was like playing with toy soldiers. I'd say, "What do I do with this character? I have this character right here, hasn't had any notice taken of him or her for a while. Let's bring him in and do something with him." There's great fun in that. But it's fun, and I've no notions that it's doing whatever it is Banville is trying to do, which is something else entirely. I always say about Banville that he's not interested in what people do, he's interested in what people *are*, so I don't care what my characters are doing. What I'm trying to do is strike through, near the stuff of life, to find something about existence itself. I know that sounds terribly pretentious, but I *am* pretentious.

Connolly: But you've said you're not interested in psychology, either.

Banville: Oh, I don't believe in psychology for a moment. What can I know? All I can know is what I see. I can't know how you are thinking. The people I've lived with and loved throughout my life, I still know nothing about them. They could still astonish me. I presume I can do the same for them. Makes life interesting. I also don't believe that there is a self. Psychiatry depends on there being a self that you're getting closer and closer to finding. But I don't believe there is such a self. There is only a series of selves that we invent, which is wonderful because that makes life infinitely interesting. We're remaking ourselves at every moment. So, with psychology, it simply doesn't work. It's a pastime for people, and I suppose it helps people in the way religion used to help people, to sustain their illusions about themselves and about others. And I have nothing against it for that reason. It's like religion, this poetic notion of what it is to be alive. But it's nowhere near actuality. Anyway, it's too late in the evening to start that kind of conversation.

Audience Member: This question is to Benjamin Black. John Banville said earlier that he's learned how to make things up. But when I've read some of the Benjamin Black books, as an old car enthusiast, I've noticed that the descriptions of cars are very convincing. It's as if Benjamin Black has an interest in cars and knows something about them.

Banville: Oh, no, that was just a joke. In one of the books I had him buy an Alvis. I had to look it up. My friend Harry Crosby actually gave me a whole book on the Alvis, and I was able to come up with all these spurious details. I knew nothing about it. I'm sorry. They look like beautiful things. I make it up. That is an important point. The made-up, the imagined, is infinitely more real than the real. This is how we bring the world into existence, by imagining it. We imagine ourselves into existence. This is what the process of growing up from infancy is. I have a five-year-old grandson and a granddaughter, and I watch them watching the world, thinking, They're assembling a self. They're assembling a version of a self.

Audience Member: Would you say something about creative writing programs?

Banville: I don't understand creative writing courses. They were before my time. They sort of flourished in the eighties. The only contact I've had with them was when I was escaping the Booker Prize and went to Temple. I had to deal with the students, all of whom were tremendously old. They were nearly thirty. One of the professors said to me, "Don't you realize, John, twenty-seven is the new seventeen?" And I wanted to say to all of them, "Why don't you get out and get a job? What are you doing here, spending your parents' money?" And, God forbid, that they should all succeed. The world would be thronged with novelists and poets and biographers and so on. It would be terrible. All vying with each other and all stabbing each other in the back and annoying people like Ed. I suppose you can teach the technique, but technique is the least of it. I can't think what else would be taught. I remember when I was in Iowa back in 1980, I was talking to a poet at a party one night, and she said, "I have to get back because I have to have a sestina written by eleven o'clock tomorrow." I said, "You just do it like that because you have to do it?" She said, "Yes." And I said, "What if you just felt the urge to write a poem?" And she looked at me and said, "I don't ever have the urge to write a poem. I write a poem because it's required for the course." That seemed to me an appalling thing. And she was quite a good poet. But my criterion, always, if I review a book or if I read a book, if I read a poem, is did this have to be written? Was this born out of compulsion? Out of an incapacity *not* to do it? And that, to me, is still the only criterion. And I can't see being required to write a sestina by eleven o'clock tomorrow morning is any kind of compulsion. But, look, I'm an old guy, and I'm biased. And I taught myself to do it. So, I'm not to be trusted.

Audience Member: John, do you have any thoughts on how your writing might have been informed by visual culture or the visual arts?

Banville: I grew up in the great days of the movies, in the fifties. In my day there were always two pictures: the main feature and the B movie. The ads came in the middle, and before that there were trailers. It was a long afternoon or evening in the cinema. And it was total immersion. And that's what still fascinates me about the cinema: the notion that you can get x-hundreds of people in. The Savoy was as big as a Roman amphitheater. There were probably thousands of people there watching this mad dream floating across the screen. That fascinated me, still fascinates me. And, yes, of course, all of fiction nowadays is influenced by the cinema, for good or ill.

Sinderen-Law: It's very clear from John and from Ed that there's a great relationship of trust between you, and no doubt a great friendship. I think you have mastered the art of the agent and the author so wonderfully.

Connolly: Tonight, we might think of it as making it up and making it work. Thank you.

"Glancing Encounters Are No Good"

Chris Morash / 2015

Reprinted by permission of Chris Morash, Seamus Heaney Professor of Irish Writing, Trinity College, Dublin.

On the evening of 2 December 2015, John Banville was interviewed in the Long Room Hub, Trinity College, Dublin, by Chris Morash, Seamus Heaney Professor of Irish Writing, Trinity College Dublin, before an audience of just over a hundred people, under the title "'Glancing Encounters Are No Good': Humanities Research and the Creative Process." The event was part of a year-long celebration of the Trinity College Dublin Library, which includes among its holdings the complete manuscript archives of John Banville's work, including the manuscript copy of what was, at the time of the interview, his most recent novel, *The Blue Guitar*. The manuscripts discussed in the interview are from this collection, and during the interview projected images of the manuscripts allowed the audience to see the handwritten pages that were being discussed. The original transcript of the interview was drafted by Zosia Kuczynska.

A podcast is available at: https://soundcloud.com/tlrhub/glancing -encounters-are-no-good-humanities-research-and-the-creative-process.

CM: Shall we begin at the beginning? This is the fiftieth anniversary of your first publication, a short story called 'The Party.'[1]
JB: Good lord . . .

CM: Do you remember when you started writing? Do you recall that impulse to see the world through "the mesh of language"?
JB: Well, in those days we all wrote short stories. Now everybody wants to be in the movies or to be a popstar. In those days our aims were modest; we just wanted to have a short story published in the *Kilkenny Magazine* or the *Dublin Magazine*; or, if you were really adventurous, the *Transatlantic*

Review in London. And then we would put together a book, which would be our first book, and our publishers would say, "Oh, we'll publish it, but you won't make any money out of it. We're only publishing it because we're waiting for your first novel." That was the way it worked in those days. I have been writing since I was very young; I can't remember, probably thirteen, fourteen. One had to just keep plugging away at it. Everything I wrote I knew was truly dreadful, but then I wrote that first story, the first story to be published. It's not a very good story, I don't think . . . I haven't read it for fifty years. But it was very important for me because it was the first one that drifted away from me, that was no longer part of me. And I knew then that perhaps I could be a writer, because it wasn't just about me, that I was going to make objects that would have a place in the world.

CM: So, you experienced a first sense of language having its own life, if you like, its own autonomy?

JB: No, that's a different thing. Language is always the angel that one wrestles with constantly. I mean that the finished object became something that was no longer mine. It became, as you say, a part of the world, and I was very glad that that was the first thing to be published. So yes, I knew then I could do something. But I'm still practicing.

CM: I want to focus this evening on that practice, on the process of writing. Do you have rituals in your writing? Perhaps rituals sounds a bit too grandiose or anthropological. How does John Banville's writing day start?

JB: Well, I worked for years in journalism and I worked in a daily newspaper, so I worked at night. I would work from five o'clock in the evening until one o'clock in the morning, sometimes 8:30 in the evening until four in the morning. So, my writing day was from ten o'clock or so until four or five in the afternoon. And I still pretty well keep to that, except that I work from about 9:30 to 6:00, five days a week in six days if I can, seven days if I'm *allowed*. I'd like nothing better than a weekend-less week. It keeps me out of trouble; it keeps me off the streets. It's a way of living—not much in the way of making a living, but it's a way of living, a way of being in the world. I can't imagine anymore *not* writing. I don't know what I'd do with my time. I'm sure it would fill up anyway. You know, I'd take up gardening or something. Or, as various people have warned me: don't take up politics and destroy the world. The writer's ego is a terrible thing, the artist's ego. That's not an angel, that's the devil one has to struggle with all the time: to suppress the ego, to suppress the personality from informing the work. That's what I spend most of my day doing: suppressing the personality, suppressing my Id.

CM: When you're writing, one of the things that struck me looking at the manuscripts of your novels, which are now held here in the Library of Trinity College, Dublin, is that you seem to have a very methodical way of writing. You write by hand. You write in hardbound notebooks. How did that practice develop, in this era where very few people write by hand?
JB: I always loved the paraphernalia of writing. I loved pencils, paper, fountain pens, ink. Typewriters, even, I love. The first typewriter I wrote on was my Aunt Sadie's Remington. It looked like a tractor. It made an extraordinary noise, and you really had to bash it to get it to work.

CM: And you hear that satisfying "ding" every time you return . . .
JB: Wonderful machine, very clever machines. I was talking to somebody the other day my own age, and you mention to anyone under thirty about carbon paper; they've never seen carbon paper. But I loved all that paraphernalia. And I always wrote by hand, and then I would transfer it onto the typewriter. Now I put it on word processors, which is so much easier. You know, the physical labor alone that it saves is marvelous. One of the problems about these new computers, the really good ones with the page that looks like a page on the screen, is that so often the thing looks as if it's written whereas it's merely typed. You have to resist that. It's also very, very fast. When I write my Banville books, I have to write in longhand because I need the resistance of the page to the nib. I was once having a fountain pen repaired, and the repair man said to me, "You do like a bit of friction, don't you?" We both decided to clear our throats and move on. So, I need that resistance. Handwriting is about the same pace at which I think. When I do the Benjamin Black books, I have to do them straight onto the computer because they need that speed, and they need that fluidity and spontaneity that a word processor gives.

CM: I get a sense looking at the manuscripts that the beginnings of the books go more fluidly than the middle sections.
JB: Oh yes, of course. You start off a novel full of hope, optimism, and then halfway through you wade up to your elbows through the mud or molasses or something hideous like that. There is nothing more difficult than the middle of a novel. Because you realize that all the things you did with such carefree abandon at the start of the book now have to be addressed. Frequently, they

can't be addressed if they're wrong. There's an awful grinding of gears. I'm sure from my workroom you can hear those gears crunching every day if I'm in the middle of the book, trying to get the direction back. Also, it's a matter of tone in and every writer knows this. If you can get the tone, then you've got the book. One of the books, (I think it was *Mefisto*),[2] I wrote the first paragraph over and over and over again, and I wrote the first few pages for about three months. I just kept rewriting, rewriting, rewriting. Sometimes it'll be the same thing, just writing the same thing out again, but that process is just necessary because one day suddenly it clicks. And you get the tone. I don't know how it happens. It can be anything. It can be changing the name of a character; it can be finding a particular fall of light, seeing somebody in the street. It can be anything. But that "click" comes, and you know that you've got the tone. It doesn't mean that it's easier after that—well, it doesn't mean it's *easy* after that, but it is *easier*. You can then get going with something like a sense of purpose and a sense of direction. But I need to get especially the first paragraph. I'll write the first paragraph over and over and over again, because apart from getting myself started, I want to say to the reader, "This is how you're going to have to read this book." In Tom McCarthy's latest book, *Satin Island*,[3] he starts talking about events, and in parentheses, he says, "Events? Events? If you're looking for that kind of thing you'd better go elsewhere." So, what I'm saying to the reader is you read this for the pleasure of style, the pleasure of language, the pleasure of language overcome, the pleasure of seeing language tamed; also, the pleasure of what language is capable of, the images it can summon, the ideas it can suggest. All that has to be indicated in the first paragraph. I remember Seamus Heaney phoning me up after *The Infinities*[4] came out, and he said, "When I read the first paragraph, I put the book away for days because," he said, "I didn't think anything else could come up to that standard." And probably it didn't. There is a kind of poetry that I try to distil in the first paragraph of the book that will tell the reader whether he or she wants to stay with this or not. It's remarkable how many decide not to.

CM: I suppose that tone is also associated with a narrator's voice. In those opening paragraphs, we're being introduced to a consciousness, a voice.

JB: Yes. I don't seem capable of . . . well, I don't seem *to want to* write in the third person. As Beckett used to say, in the last person. Yes, I like to write in the last person. There has to be a tone for me, but also the notion of the omniscient narrator has always seemed to me a con. I can't know anything except what I see. I can't know anything about other people except what

I see of them, hear of them, smell of them, taste of them, feel of them. I can't know what it's like to be them inside. I can imagine. And, in a way, we're not as complicated and/or diverse as we think we are. Beckett says, "Human souls, you should see how alike they are."[5] But I can't assume other people think alike. All I can do is present the evidence that I take in with my senses, with my singular senses. That seems to me the only—I was going to say the only *honest*—but it seems to me the only *authentic* way of working. Benjamin Black, of course, has no conscience or scruples or morals of any kind. He's quite happy to write in the third person.

CM: When I was looking through some of the manuscripts in the archive here in Trinity College Dublin, I was sometimes reminded of that phrase of Beckett's from around the time he was producing *Happy Days* for the first time, where he describes an effect that he's trying to achieve as "vaguening." For instance, in the first draft of *The Blue Guitar*, the first line initially is: "Call me Autolycus. Well, no, don't. Although I am, like *Will's* unfunny clown. . . . '"[6] And that gets changed to "like that unfunny clown."[7] So, people like me who go hunting after literary references would have pounced on "Will" as a reference to Shakespeare. However, in the final draft, that bit of scaffolding has been pulled away. Likewise, a little further down the page, the protagonist introduces himself: "Orme. That is my name. Oliver Orme. Oliver Orwell Orme, in fact. [. . .] The Orwell is not after George."[8] And then just to make sure there is no reference to George Orwell, in the published text, he becomes "Oliver Otway Orme," and the "Orwell" is gone.[9] Is there a process by which you consciously try to strip away specifics?
JB: No, I look on that "vaguening"—beautiful word effect—with a slight hint of suspicion. A friend of mine in Princeton—very good translator, a Kafka translator—he went back to the manuscript of *The Castle* and was astonished to find that it was quite straightforward. You knew who the land surveyor was, you knew what it was about, but Kafka took all that out, as he said himself, to make it a little bit *unheimlich*, a little bit uncanny, a little bit strange. I think I try the opposite. I try to make things as clear as I possibly can. I think that "vaguening" was a kind of modernist trope. I have to be very careful here; I mean, who am I to criticize Kafka or Beckett? I'm not criticizing them. I'm simply saying that I work in a different way. I try to be as clear as possible. I pride myself on the fact that a seven-year-old child can read my sentences and understand them—maybe not get all the nuances but understand them. There is nothing difficult in my work. There is nothing difficult in my work.

CM: One of the pleasures of reading fiction is arguably what we might call "world creation," in which the novel creates its own world . . .

JB: Oh yes. In *The Infinities* I created an alternative world in which motor cars run on sea water and so on. And that is the same world in which *The Blue Guitar* takes place. *That* is a process of "vaguening." Beckett and Kafka simplified things down to a bare landscape, a bowler hat, a bicycle, or a beetle. I can understand that, because I have no interest in writing about the world of cell phones and the internet. I'm trying to strike past the quotidian world to get at something essential, so you have to get rid of as much clutter as you possibly can. I always say I'm not interested in what people do, I'm interested in what people are. And that seems to me the only kind of novel that I'm interested in writing: one that tries to get the essentials of life.

CM: One of the things that struck me looking through some of the manuscripts for *The Blue Guitar* was that in the early drafts a lot of effort had gone into making this particular world, a strange Ireland where there was a highland German-speaking ruling class and where people used to have airplanes but now they had dirigibles. A lot of detail had gone into that world. But in the final, published text, only the tips of the icebergs are there, as it were. For example, in the first draft of *The Blue Guitar* there's one long passage where Oliver's talking about his father: "How my father hated the House of Hoheninarg. [. . .] He was a tartar, as folks around here would say, an old-fashioned republican. He could never forgive the Men of 1916 for [. . .] inviting in that gang, as he called them, who, having {against the odds} defeated one Empire went cap in hand to [. . .] [a] moribund empire;"[10] and so on. There's a whole alternative history taking shape in that passage, but only passing references remain in the published text.

JB: Well, yes, I suppose I had great fun at the beginning because in the GPO;[11] they did discuss bringing in a minor royal from one of the German principalities to be King of Ireland, because they couldn't conceive of an Ireland without a king. They gave up that idea—a pity, really; we'd all be bilingual, we'd be speaking German, and Angela Merkel would spend her holidays here. So, I had a lot of fun doing that, but it wasn't viable. I was having too much fun. But there are Germans still in the book, and there's a Germanic strain. Rather than "vaguening," I would say that I suppose what I want to do is to *make strange*. Don't they say that still about children, that they "make strange"? Wonderful term. And it's usually said about children when you can see they're looking into another world that we can no longer see. That's what I think art does: it "makes strange." It brings out the extraordinary in the ordinary. I mean, there's no such thing as the ordinary. Joyce always said he'd never met an ordinary man, and I think that's true. Human beings are infinitely, infinitely strange, and the world is infinitely strange. And I never get used to the world's strangeness. Maybe that's why I'm a writer, maybe that's where art springs from, that sense of being estranged. Wallace Stevens has wonderful lines in "Notes Towards a Supreme Fiction"; he says, "From this the poem springs: that we live in a place / That is not our own and, much more, not ourselves / And hard it is in spite of blazoned days."[12] That's wonderfully put, I think that *is* where a poem comes from: a place that's strange to us and to which we are strange. I don't think we really belong here. I think we were meant for somewhere else, and that's what I keep investigating. I should emphasize that I don't feel estranged from the world in a traumatic way. I think it's wonderful that this place is so strange, so odd. You never run out of curiosity about this odd place we've ended up in.

CM: I just want to go back to the process of writing. At one point, you talked about looking for a perfect sentence and knowing when a sentence was right. I would like to take another example from one of the manuscripts. This is the beginning of the first page of an early draft of *The Sea*: "There came the day of the strange tide."[13] I read that manuscript and I thought, What a great sentence, it has meter, it has . . .
JB: And then I ruined it . . . [laughing]

CM: . . . And then you changed it! I mean, how do you know a sentence is right? Maybe there's no answer to this question.
JB: Oh, you don't. You have to abandon it, but you have to get as near to perfection as you can. You have to get the music right; you have to get the rhythm right; you have to get the meaning right; you have to get the sense of the thing, as well as the sound of it. It's endlessly fascinating, the making of sentences. I never tire of it, and I never get it right. There's a wonderful little book by Robert Coover called *Spanking the Maid*[14]—I don't know if you've ever come across it. It's a novella about a man where every morning he gets up and he has to spank the maid, but he can never get it right. And she knows, and she's quite apologetic. And she does her best, but over and over again, he just spanks her every morning. And it's about the process of writing. That's what you do: you get up, you spank the maid, you change the bandages of the invalid in the wheelchair by the window, and you just do it over and over and over and over again, knowing you will never ever

get it right, that all you will ever do is get as close to it as you possibly can. It's like infinitesimal calculus that approaches closer and closer to infinity, but it never gets there. But it has its compensations along the way. I don't understand the power of certain phrases and sentences. I wrote a thing in *The Sea*, I think, where he says, "The past beats inside me like a second heart."[15] Scores of people have quoted that back to me. The other night—and that book was published ten years ago or more—somebody quoted it to me again and said, "That spoke to me." I've no idea why. It didn't seem to me a particularly remarkable sentence, but somehow it must be the cadence of it. It must be something it carries that speaks to people, but I don't know what it is. If I did, I'd keep doing it.

CM: It would seem that there is a relationship between the physical quality of the words and whatever it is that they mean. That sounds like a very simplistic way of putting it, but it seems as if the almost structural quality of the words, the rhythms, the sounds, are as important as meaning.

JB: Well, I think that in all literature you can see the terror of the writer who is constantly suppressing the realization that words don't actually mean anything at all. We all have that sensation where you're walking along, and you repeat a word over and over again—*horse, horse, horse*—and suddenly the signifier drifts away from the signified, and you realize it's just a noise. It's terrifying, absolutely terrifying. And that is the case with every word that you put down. You know, *horse* is not a horse. Joyce says a horse is a horse is another horse, but it's not. It's not; it's a noise that I make. Part of the excitement of literature is dancing elegantly on the edge of the abyss of meaninglessness.

CM: In that sense, are your narrators, or the novels themselves, in some ways, parables for writing? To put it another way, are they about attempts to find a shape that makes sense of this mess?

JB: I'm in no way a realistic writer. No painter could have that style; he would have had to spend his life not painting. So, from the start it's absurd. He would have to have no interest in realistic middlebrow fiction, none at all. This is one of the reasons I gave up reading reviews, because it's always the same old twaddle. Almost all reviews are reviews of the book that was not written, the book that the reviewer wants to have read and hasn't read, to his discontent. The novel is a sort of frosty old form; it's a vulgar form, and glorious for that. But people still expect all novels to be written in 1850, to have a clear story that will have interesting characters. They want Mr. Slope or whatever his name was in Anthony Trollope to get it in the neck; you want Becky Sharp[16] to succeed even though she's awful. That's been done. I shouldn't dismiss it entirely; I mean, all we have to work with is human beings, and human behavior is always strange and interesting and compelling, but what we're trying to do now, I think—some of us—is to poeticize the novel form. It began with Henry James. I've been reading acres of Henry James recently—he's the greatest novelist of all, I do believe, greater than Tolstoy and Proust. As a novelist, I think his achievement was the greatest, absolutely astonishing. But James thought of himself—certainly in his middle period—as a realist. I don't believe he was. I think that he was constantly shaping and polishing and burnishing the novel until it became more and more a poetic form. I think he recognized that in the last three or four novels. But it's his example that I follow. If I have any influences, it's Henry James.

CM: Can we pursue that idea of the poetic novel? Can we tie that in with some of what you were saying earlier, about the strangeness of the world? With your fiction, are we looking at what we might call a "secular transcendence" of the physical world through language?

JB: I wouldn't say the transcendence of the physical world; I would say the apotheosis of the physical world, the fixing of it. The work of art, if it's successful, gives you a heightened sense of what it is to be alive in the world. That's one of the reasons that we go to art. I came across again a lovely phrase of Henry James the other day, one of my favorites, where he says, "Art *makes* life, makes interest, makes importance."[17] And, of course, a lot of people rebel and say, "Oh, that's just typical ivory tower," but that wasn't what he meant. What he meant was that art doesn't put itself above life, doesn't see itself as more interesting or more important than life; it brings out the interest and the importance of life. By shaping incoherent experience into the finished object, the work of art, it gives us a more intense sense of what it is to be alive. I firmly believe that. And that's when the poetry comes in. I always quote John McGahern's nice distinction that "there's prose and there's verse and then there's poetry, and poetry can happen in either form." And being McGahern, he said, "It happens more often in the novel than in verse." But I think that that's true—poetry is something ineffable, something you cannot define. Like good art, you don't know what it is, but you know it when you see it.

CM: There are certain moments in the novels that are almost parables for the experience of writing. I'm thinking of some of the things you were talking about earlier when you were talking about writing. In *The Blue Guitar* there's a lovely passage where Oliver talks about one of the things he misses from his painting days is "a certain quality of silence": "As the working day progressed I sank steadily deeper into the depths of the painted surface, the world's prattle would retreat like an ebbing tide leaving me at the center of a great pall of stillness."[18] Is that something you've experienced when you've been writing: that sense of profound concentration?

JB: There is a wonderful essay by Blanchot . . . I think it's called "The Last Book" or "The End of the Book."[19] It's a wonderful parable about the time when the last book has been written, and after that, there arises a terrible babble and this noise has become so deafening it's unbearable. I see his point: that art does keep the babble down, it shapes and make sentences out of mere incoherent babble. Is that an answer to your question?

CM: Yes, that's a good answer. There are quite a few characters in your novels who have an intense involvement with the phenomenal world and who try to order the phenomenal world in some way, whether it's through painting, through mathematics, or whatever; and that, at the same time, as individuals they often have a distinct moral ambiguity. Is that something you're grappling with in your fiction?

JB: Well, you know, morals are a very tricky area. Do you want to venture into that? At its simplest but its most profound, I always think of Nietzsche, that wonderful aphorism. He says, "danger: the mother of morals."[20] You can think about that for a long time, and it gets deeper and deeper and deeper. He has a wonderful passage in (I think) it's *The Gay Science* when he talks about how the yellow eye of the tiger at the mouth of the cave became transformed into the notion of God, that there's always something watching us; there's always something trying to spring at us; there's always something about to rend us to pieces. We have to codify that fear into mythologies of the vengeful God. I think it is a beautiful passage, not to mention that it has the merit of being absolutely true. All our mythologies, all our religions, they're all based on primeval terrors. They spring from primeval terrors. So, morality is essential to the rules that we make. Somebody was telling me last night about—I'm sure you scholars here will know about it—"the Wicked Bible." It was published under James I. One of the commandments says: "Thou shalt commit adultery," instead of the "not." Imagine the mayhem that would cause. But I do agree with Oscar Wilde, who said that in art "the opposite of every truth is also true." I think that is the case. There are no morals in art. The art object itself may be a moral object, but that was no part of the intention of the artist; the artist simply wants to make something that is neither moral nor immoral. It's nothing to do with morals at all. It's just an object; it just exists in the way the world exists. I mean, the world has no morals. Animals, of which we are a rare species, have no morality; they have rules of behavior, but morality is something that we had to invent for ourselves because of consciousness and self-consciousness and because of the consciousness of death. Everything we do springs from primeval fears, and those primeval fears have their base in terror of death: terror of the mystery of death, the fact that we're here and one day, fairly soon, we won't be here. Again, I quote Beckett, this lovely thing he says, "The day of my death will be a day like any other only shorter."[21] I do think it's that terror of death, our incapacity to conceive the reality of our own deaths, and the deaths of our loved ones. These are the base of almost everything we do. I'm not a Freudian, but in late Freud, when he hit upon the death instinct, I think he was on the right track. But, again, I have to emphasize; this is a positive thing: death. I wrote a little radio play once about a meeting between Heidegger and Paul Celan.[22] Celan says to Heidegger, "Why did you throw your lot in with the Nazis?" and he says, "Because they gave death its due weight." He goes on to say death is the midwife; death stands by the elbow of the midwife and says, "Give me the child because I am the one who will give it life." And I believe that's true. I believe death gives us life. It gives us the sweetness of life, it gives us the sense of the weight and significance of life. I envy the animals. I watch my dog and all he wants to do is get out into the grass or jump into the sea after a ball I've thrown for him. It's an enviable life, but I like the one that we have with all its terrors and torments. I think we gain so much by gaining consciousness of death. It's a terrible weight. It torments us, it makes us sick, it fills us with trauma, but by God it makes the world interesting.

CM: Is the artwork then a protest against death?

JB: Well, I used to think when I was young—especially when I was coming to the end of a book—I could feel the presence of death almost like a dark force at my back, warning me, again wrestling with me, saying, "I'm not going to let you finish this." Now that death has become a distinct reality for me—it's just around the corner—I don't have that particular fear anymore. I suppose the work of art does affirm, and if it doesn't affirm it's not much good. Even a poisonous person like Céline in *Voyage to the End of the Night*[23] makes an affirming, wonderfully rich, exuberant work of art. It doesn't seem to matter how bad artists are, they can still make a beautiful object.

And as I say, an object which in itself has a moral force and a moral weight, but again I don't see that that's any part of the artist's task. If I set out to write something moral or political or social, I would fail, because the one thing that art absolutely insists on is absolute autonomy. You have a duty to reality, of course. The only material we have is human beings. What was it you said: prime living source material? Yes, that's all we have. But the work itself is autonomous.

CM: Can we bring Benjamin Black into the conversation at this point? His profession, perhaps, provides us with a continuity link from the topic of death.
JB: Sure.

CM: This is the opening page of something of a rarity: a handwritten Benjamin Black manuscript. In the middle of this first draft of *Christine Falls*, the first of the Benjamin Black novels' draft, there's a handwritten note to the effect that "the rest written direct to screen."
JB: Yes, it was too slow; it was too laborious. What I need in the Benjamin Black novels is spontaneity. If they haven't got spontaneity, they haven't got anything. They can't be labored over in the way the Banville books must be labored over. It's two entirely different ways of writing: writing the Benjamin Black books is infinitely boring; writing the John Banville books is infinitely tedious. There's a difference.

CM: Boring can be fast . . .
JB: Boring can be fast; tedium is slow.

CM: I think you said you sometimes write two-and-a-half thousand words a day on a Black book . . .
JB: Yes, if it's going well. I like to leave about three or four months. But I'm writing one at the moment which is giving me dreadful trouble because foolishly I wanted to get away from Quirke. I've set it in Prague in 1600.[24] I thought that would be easier, but it's not quite as easy as I thought it would be. And that is an interesting thing, because I've been going over the opening chapters of that again and again and again and again. This is one of the things about writing, even writing Benjamin Black books: you have to keep at it. You cannot settle for your own second-best. Even old Black has a standard that he has to reach. And if you don't, you're being dishonest, and the work will be dishonest. It will probably sell hundreds of thousands of copies, but

it wouldn't satisfy me. I would feel slightly grimy if I didn't go back again and again and try to get it right and get that maid spanked finally and definitively.

CM: The first sentence of the first Black novel in the original draft reads: "It was not the dead Quirke feared but the living."[25] In the published version, this becomes: "It was not the dead that seemed to Quirke uncanny, but the living."[26]

JB: All my sins are stored away here.

CM: They're all right here in the library.

JB: Well, I think the second sentence is truer and more interesting. The dead are not to be feared, but the living *are* slightly uncanny; I think the living are to be feared more than the dead.

CM: With the Black novels, there's an argument that they're perhaps more political than some of your other novels. Quirke is a product of that whole period of institutionalization in Ireland, and in that context he's a character who tries to act ethically.

JB: No, it's just a form of cannibalism. I use the material that's there. Our awful history has seventy or eighty years of child abuse and clerical wrongdoing, political criminality . . . rich material. I have no ambition to make any commentary on the state of the world, but I suppose inevitably these books can be read in a political way, because this is the world we came from. That world that I'm writing about is the world that made the one that we're in. In fact, the one that we are in is a reaction against that world. I can never forget when the story came out that Bishop Eamon Casey had an American mistress and a seventeen-year-old son by her and that he had *borrowed* £70,000 of parish funds to pay her off. When the floodgates opened, the real horrors came out, and we now look back on Bishop Eamon Casey with fondness and nostalgia. But I suppose it could be read as a commentary, but I certainly don't mean to make any exceptional political or moral points.

CM: Were you conscious when you started writing the Quirke novels of a crime wave in Irish writing at the time. We went from a point where there were very few people in Ireland writing crime fiction, and now there are a great many.

JB: Actually, my brother used to write very good crime fiction.[27] And it was he who showed me that it could be done, with style, with panache. I'd already seen that from people like Raymond Chandler and Richard Stark, and then I discovered Simenon. Simenon is Benjamin Black's father. That was where he came from.

CM: Although presumably you don't write the way he allegedly wrote, which was standing up, smoking a pipe, drinking coffee, writing for forty-eight hour stretches . . .

JB: Well, I don't know about that, but he certainly worked quickly. My God, he'd do a book in ten days. He would be violently sick every morning and every evening just from the sheer tension of it. But they're masterly books. He was always furious that they wouldn't give him the Nobel Prize, but they really should have. He was one of the few people of the twentieth century who deserved a Nobel Prize.

CM: With your novel *The Black-Eyed Blonde*,[28] Benjamin Black was channeling another writer, as it were, Raymond Chandler. How would you describe that experience?

JB: Oh, that was great fun. I found from the first day that I could do Chandler, that voice, and that was wonderful. The odd thing is that I have no memory of writing the book. None. I know that I spent the summer whenever it was, a few years ago, writing *The Black-Eyed Blonde*, but I can't remember doing it. Apparently, psychologists will tell you that it's possible when you have a task to do that is not immediately inspirational, that you put yourself into a sort of self-induced trance mode to get it done, and I suspect that's what I did. But I liked doing it.

CM: John, it's been a marvelous evening. Thank you.

Notes

1. John Banville, "The Party," *Kilkenny Magazine* 14 (Spring/Summer 1966): 75–82.
2. John Banville, *Mefisto* (1987).
3. Tom McCarthy, *Satin Island* (2015).
4. John Banville, *The Infinities* (2009).
5. Samuel Beckett, "The Expelled," originally published in *Stories and Texts for Nothing* (1955).
6. John Banville, *The Blue Guitar*, Banville Archive TCD Ms. 11517, p. 3.
7. John Banville, *The Blue Guitar* (2015), p. 3.
8. John Banville, *The Blue Guitar*, Banville Archive TCD Ms. 11517, p. 3.

9. John Banville, *The Blue Guitar* (2015), p. 3.

10. John Banville, *The Blue Guitar*, Banville Archive TCD Ms. 11517, pp. 25–26.

11. The GPO, or General Post Office in Dublin was one of the main sites of the 1916 Rising.

12. Wallace Stevens, *The Collected Poems of Wallace Stevens* (1954), p. 383. It is worth noting that the title of Banville's most recent novel at the time of the interview, *The Blue Guitar*, also takes its title from a Stevens poem, "The Man with the Blue Guitar."

13. John Banville, *The Sea*, Banville Archive TCD Ms. 11356/1/1, fol. 33, p. 38.

14. Robert Coover, *Spanking the Maid* (1981).

15. John Banville, *The Sea* (2005), p. 13.

16. Mr. Slope is a character in Anthony Trollope's *Barchester Towers* (1857); Becky Sharp is the heroine of W. M. Thackeray's *Vanity Fair* (1847–48).

17. Henry James, Letter to H. G. Wells, 10 July, *Henry James: Vol. IV: 1895–1916*, ed. Leon Edel (1984), p. 770.

18. John Banville, *The Blue Guitar* (2015), p. 204.

19. Maurice Blanchot, "The Absence of the Book" in *The Infinite Conversation* (1993).

20. Friedrich Nietzsche, *Beyond Good and Evil* (1886), § 262.

21. Samuel Beckett, *Malone Dies* (1951).

22. John Banville, *Conversation in the Mountains* (2006), scene XXI. Broadcast BBC Radio 4, 20 January 2006. The lines read:
Celan: "But why the Nazis? Why their system?"
Heidegger: "Because of their tragic affirmation of death!"

23. Louis-Ferdinand Céline, *Journey to the End of the Night* (1932).

24. Subsequently published as Benjamin Black, *Prague Nights* (2017).

25. Benjamin Black [John Banville], *Christine Falls* Banville Archive TCD Ms. 11356/1/4/, fol. 2, p. 1.

26. Benjamin Black, *Christine Falls* (London, 2006), p. 7.

27. Vincent Banville, *Death by Design* (1993); *Death the Pale Rider* (1995); *Sad Song* (1999); *Cannon Law* (2001); *An Accident Waiting to Happen* (2002). Vincent Banville's crime novels all feature the detective John Blaine.

28. Benjamin Black, *The Black-Eyed Blonde: A Philip Marlowe Novel* (London, 2014).

Finding a Jamesian Tone
and Digging Down

Hedwig Schwall / 2017

This interview was conducted in Dublin, 29 September 2017. The interview appeared in the *European English Messenger* 26.2 (2017): 82–98, and is reprinted here with the permission of Hedwig Schwall.

HS: Good to see you, and congratulations on your new novel. Over the years you have been saying you admired Henry James, and when I read *Mrs. Osmond*, I thought you do write on the same wavelength, even though the narrative is vintage Banville. Did you actually try to imitate James's style, or did you just let yourself sink into the Jamesian atmosphere?

JB: I didn't want to *imitate* James, but I did want to write in the spirit of *The Portrait of a Lady*. I couldn't have written this book in twenty-first-century English—it simply wouldn't have worked. I expected it to be a very difficult task, but it proved surprisingly . . . I won't say easy—writing fiction is never easy, but I did find a "tone," a Jamesian tone, very quickly. That was a surprise, and a delight.

HS: James's heroine seems to have imbibed a few Nietzschean values, like her hunger for life and her embracing of her fate; it is even in the quote from James that you chose as the motto for your own book: "Deep in her soul—deeper than any appetite for renunciation—was the sense that life would be her business for a long time to come."[1] The Nietzschean spirit must have helped you to feel at ease with James's Isabel.

JB: Well, Nietzsche is my philosopher—my poet. I can find few things in his work, and I've read most of it, that I disagree with. Except, of course, his attitude to women. But I wouldn't have thought of *Mrs. Osmond* as a Nietzschean work. Yet I suppose Isabel's determination to *affirm life* is a Nietzschean urge.

HS: That and his lack of humor at times—as in *Zarathustra*?

JB: I've never managed to get to the end of *Zarathustra*—it makes me giggle helplessly. This is a serious admission for a confirmed Nietzschean to make, but there it is. *The Genealogy of Morals*, *The Gaya Scienzia*, *Daybreak*, even that last one that his awful sister compiled—*The Will to Power*, is that it?— these are superb and astonishing works. Truly revolutionary. His writings are full of humor, but it's humor of a very dark, harsh variety. He didn't have enough experience of actual human beings—he had no friends to speak of, except Paul Rée, for a while, and the extraordinary Lou Andreas-Salomé, also for a while. One of the saddest things I read of him was a report by someone staying in the same *pensione* that he was in, in Genoa or Turin, I can't remember, who was going out to dinner and saw him playing the piano in the parlor, all alone—improvising, I imagine—and when the person came back from dinner, there he was, still playing, still alone. If he had found someone to love, it's possible we wouldn't have the philosophy. And what a loss that would be, not only to philosophy but to literature in general. He writes so beautifully: even in translation, Nietzsche's writing is so beautiful. But I doubt Henry James ever read a word he wrote.

HS: Both you and James often let Isabel use the word *happy* and *happiness* in a sense which does not necessarily mean "pleasant"; it can imply suffering, but only the kind which makes someone stronger, more resilient. Is this what you understand under *amor fati*?

JB: Yes, of course, Nietzsche is always in favor of life, messy, coarse, undecided life, against the naysayers. There's a wonderful poem by Constantine Cavafy, based on that passage in *Antony and Cleopatra*, when Antony hears the god—Dionysus?—abandoning him and his fallen fortunes. He hears in the street the departing music and revels as the god and his retinue leave, but the poet urges him to be strong, to be valorous, and not to feel sorry for himself. *"Say goodbye to her, to the Alexandria you are losing."* And, of course, in this instance, "Alexandria" represents all that has made Antony's life sweet up to now. Lawrence Durrell, of all people, put Cavafy as a character in his *Alexandria Quartet*. Cavafy is a wonderful poet, too little known. As to *amor fati*, that's what James was speaking of when he described Isabel as a young woman determined to "affront her fate."

HS: Usually your protagonists are very narcissistic men; now you pick a lady who James has fitted out with an intelligent and enterprising spirit, even with a lot of empathy, at times.

JB: James makes it very clear that she's not the high intellectual that she thinks she is. And he doesn't make her altruistic, really, though she has a "good heart." If you read her very closely in *Portrait*, she's selfish, self-willed, almost a monster of ego, though not at the level of Madame Merle or Gilbert Osmond, of course; being young, she just wishes to have her own way and sees no reason why she shouldn't. In her eager youthfulness, she reminds me of myself when I was young—she reminds me of *all* of us, when we were young. She knows her own mind, she knows what she wants and how to go about getting it—or imagines she does; but she learns the error of her ways, of her wishes, and of her will. Incidentally, it's one of the ironies of *Portrait* that many readers mistakenly believe James is writing about a young, untried American girl being set upon and maimed by nasty Europeans. But all the main players in *Portrait* are Americans. Madame Merle is American, born in Brooklyn; Gilbert Osmond is from Baltimore—Baltimore!—Caspar Goodwood is a New Englander; Henrietta Stackpole is quintessentially the "new" American female; and the Touchett family, who might be said to be the ones who initially set "in train" Isabel's disaster, they're American also. The only character of consequence who is European is Lord Warburton, but really he's not of *much* consequence, except to spin the plot along. I think the Isabel of *Portrait* is different to my Isabel. Mine is wiser and sadder, and older even, in a way—though she's not yet thirty, if my calculations are correct. I suspect that in the second half of *Portrait* James forgot just how young she still was and presents her as almost middle-aged, as *una grande signora*. I had to make her young again but toughened by all the horrors she has been through, very recently—in *Mrs. Osmond*, it's only a matter of weeks since she learned of how she was betrayed by Mme. Merle and her husband.

HS: Is Goodwood corrupted by Europe? In James he seems to be the perfect foil to Lord Warburton; the Lord practicing his charm in paneled rooms and oak-studded landscapes, while Goodwood is feverishly steaming back and forth over the ocean, crossing Europe in what seems a perfect train system, being the dynamic suitor. In your sequel, neither reappears on the stage, except in reflections.

JB: Goodwood is utterly incorruptible, which is one of the reasons Isabel finds him so boring. But then Warburton is hardly the firebrand he considers himself to be, and he too bores our heroine. I see Goodwood and Warburton as Tweedledum and Tweedledee, one in Boston, the other in the Home Counties. For Isabel it is easy to withstand Lord Warburton's blandishments: his grand title, his houses and castles, his thousands of acres. She just had to take one look at his sweet, mousy sisters—very minor characters with whom nevertheless James has splendid, subtle fun—to say to herself, *I'm not marrying into this.* But she knows she doesn't want Goodwood, either, his uprightness, his decency, his awkward ardor, his stiff New England values. All the same, it is he, at the very end of *Portrait*, who awakens Isabel to that Nietzschean sense of life and its possibilities—raw, coarse, *fleshly* life—when he seizes her in his arms in the twilit arbor at Gardencourt and kisses her as she has never been kissed before. If I were to criticize *Mrs. Osmond*—and God knows I have many critical things I could say of it, as of all my novels—I would deplore the fact that I didn't allow her to follow up on this erotic awakening. Perhaps someone else will do so—a woman?—in a sequel to my sequel. And so, *ad infinitum.*

HS: But in James she seems to genuinely like the Warburton sisters.
JB: She may like them, but she does not want that existence for herself. She says to herself, "Do I want to become like this–contained, trammeled, 'held down' by convention?" And that's what Warburton would have expected of her, and Goodwood too. Neither of them can offer her the freedom she so desires and considers her due. One of the things James understood very clearly was that men, when they are wooing women, say, "Oh, of course, you'll have your freedom." But when they marry, they say, "No, you'll have babies." Goodwood and Warburton would have set out just as determinedly as Gilbert Osmond did to break her spirit, even though their methods would have been softer and subtler.

HS: Your Isabel is, I think, the first feminist in your novels. Via the Misses Stackpole (who takes her time to get married) and Janeway, she finds her way (a distracted one) to contribute to the New Women's cause.
JB: She takes out the money as a gesture of liberation; she loses it because, subconsciously, she despises mere "filthy lucre." She has come to understand that all her troubles had their origin in money. When she's made the gesture of withdrawing a satchel of cash, what good is it to her? It's just money, and, inevitably, she mislays it. And then she thinks, I know what I'll do; I'll give it to "the cause"—even though she is not quite sure yet what the cause *is.* I like Miss Janeway, for all her coldness and calculation. I say of her at one point that she would lay waste of the world in order to further the cause. Janeway is a fanatic. And Isabel likes this. She has been taken in by people who behaved "nicely" and pretended to be civilized, but Miss Janeway doesn't

pretend to be anything other than ruthless. So, Isabel sees a way in which to take action, to "affront her fate," if only in terms of cash.

HS: Did you check on the legal rules of that period? Could she keep her own money?
JB: Of course not. This is fiction!

HS: When Isabel learns that Miss Janeway is dying and she decides to stay with the lady in her final struggle, she wonders, "Her end will mark, for me, a beginning . . . does that seem like my old selfishness asserting itself again?"[2] She is rather harsh on herself here.
JB: Isabel is self-willed, as we've observed. When Janeway's nephew tells her he wants to start up a newspaper, she's perfectly aware that she is being approached for money, yet again. And maybe she will give him the money—who knows?—but she will make sure that it is she who will run the newspaper. *She* will be the editor, not him. My original idea was that she was going to meet the nephew, they would fall in love—he would have been a more acceptable, a more malleable Caspar Goodwood, though not as handsome, which perhaps Isabel would have been glad of, handsome men being more persuasive. In that version, Myles Devenish would have said, *I want to see this "New World,"* and Isabel would suddenly have realized that was what she also wanted—to return home, and they would have gone off together; they would, like Huck Finn, have "lit out for the territory" . . . but then I thought better of it. The book had to end in ambiguity.

HS: James's *Portrait* ends with the sentence Isabel now knows her way will be straight back.[3] Your Isabel does not go straight home but passes by Paris, where she is invited to a palace full of Watteau-like rococo decorations out of which, suddenly, Madame Merle steps forth. In this episode your Isabel becomes one of your typical heroes who finds her usual perspective inverted: the world was not just a scene to watch, but she has been watched by the world. Is that what triggers her revenge?
JB: Isabel's not knowing how she was used, how she was "made a convenience of," as she says, must have had something in it of willful ignorance. Everybody else would have known what was going on, especially in a city like Rome, James's Rome, where there's nothing people don't know about. Yet Isabel is appalled when it occurs to her, in *Mrs. Osmond*, that her blindness was known to all. Equally, Mme. Merle is afraid of being exposed—it's one thing for people to know and keep quiet, but quite another that her

wickedness should be talked about openly in salons halfway across Europe and even in America. I think there is a question of gender here. I suspect women worry more about being disgraced in public than men do; women don't think of infidelity in graphic terms. A man would not so much care about people knowing; he would be more turned in on himself. The real torment for a man is *imagining the two of them together*. That is the absolute agony—think of Othello.

In my book Isabel is facing up to her mistakes. In her meeting with Miss Janeway, she begins slowly to realize how she might establish her freedom, and the first step in the process is to mislay the bag of money, which perhaps subconsciously she meant to do from the start. She has made her gesture to the cause—the freeing of womankind—and now she turns her mind to Mme. Merle and Osmond, and how she might exact from them a reckoning—not revenge; I don't see her as a vengeful character. There used to be an extraordinarily cruel method of execution, whereby a person was strapped face to face with a corpse and then thrown into a dungeon—imagine the fiendish mind that thought that up! It's a version of this punishment that Isabel wreaks upon Merle and Osmond: she has bound this man, who has never learned how to live, to this woman who had the misfortune, long ago, to meet and fall in love with him, and was thereby infected with the bacillus of his deathliness. They are a pair of corpses, and Isabel has lashed them together. Can you imagine them fighting over the palazzo?

HS: Sartre's *Huits clos* [*No Exit*] would be a bit like that: people stuck together who make each other face the mistakes of their past.
JB: I read that play when I was about fifteen. I remember thinking, Life can't be like this. But, of course, it can.

HS: You say Merle was "infected with . . . his deathliness"—could one say that Osmond is the death drive, *der Geist der stets verneint*?
JB: I'm not a Freudian, I never was a Freudian, and I never will be. I don't believe that all of our unconscious life is directed by sex. But I would agree that it is to a large extent directed by the death drive, or at least by our abiding consciousness of the fact of death. Paradoxically, however, I think it is this very knowledge that gives life its sweetness—the knowledge that all this, that's here for us, will end, makes it so painfully precious. But Gilbert Osmond is the very spirit of death-in-life. He is the spirit of negation. It was quite a feat of James to convince us that Isabel would be capable of marrying such a man—he's not even convincingly charming. He is a dried-out,

sterile dilettante, as Ralph Touchett assures Isabel; but what Ralph sees as desiccation of the spirit, Isabel takes for greatness. I've known people like this, people who would regard it vulgar to write a book or paint an original picture. One of the most wonderful scenes in *Portrait* is the one in which we see Osmond for the last time, when Isabel is leaving to go to Ralph Touchett, who is dying. What is Osmond doing? He is making a copy of a painting of a coin. He's not even painting the coin itself, *he's making a copy of a painting of a coin.* He is one of the living dead, like the ghost Peter Quint in *The Turn of the Screw.* James knew about these people, how they feed on other people's lives, how they take away people's freedom, which he considered a very great sin.

HS: You made it very clear in this book.
JB: Henry James makes it clear.

HS: But your Isabel suddenly realizes that it is purely her narcissism which makes her fall in love with Osmond: "it had not been Osmond she had fallen in love with, when she was young, but herself, through him," a recognition which she thinks has "a universal application."[4]
JB: Well, all my protagonists in all my books are mistaken about most things, and this is true also of Isabel in *Portrait.* James makes Isabel go through the fires of hell at the end of the novel—most of the action in his book takes place in the last thirty or forty pages, when she learns so many terrible things. But in my version, it is not the fires of hell she endures, but an alchemical fire. Isabel liked to be flattered, to be attended to, and Madame Merle was the perfect mirror for her. They went on a Grand Tour together, yet in all those months together Isabel never once saw the real Madame Merle. She saw what she wanted to see, and only later, after the crisis at the end of *Portrait,* she realizes she has been willfully ignorant. Love is always narcissistic. We all look into the eyes of the beloved, and we think, How wonderful I am, how beautiful I am, how altogether bewitching! We thrive, the ego thrives, when we look the beloved in the eyes and see ourselves reflected there. That's what love is for. It's not love for the other person; it's love for yourself. It doesn't last, of course, or last in an entirely different form. There should be a term for it, maybe something like "passionate friendship." That's the best we can hope for, and we should be glad of it.

HS: The theater metaphor is pretty basic in your work, it is omnipresent. Madame Merle fits the bill, she even fits in the Watteau-like scenes of Isabel's visit to Paris. Is she a nineteenth-century Madame de Merteuil [*Dangerous Liaisons*]?

JB: Certainly, though I'm not sure Mme. Merle is as clever or expertly manipulative as Mme. de Merteuil. But Merle is the perfect actress, the expert in the theater of life. Osmond is not, he is too egotistical to be a good actor, but he can keep up pretenses when he needs to. Both Merle and Osmond are poor, and poverty is destructive of the spirit. A friend and I once agreed that money is the root of all happiness. And the lack of it, Henry James and I would add, is the root of much unhappiness and ruthlessness and cruelty.

HS: But what about Ralph's role in this theater? He is rich and uses his money for an experiment. He tweaks things a bit and then sits back—yet, in your version, not quite, as "the intensest living Ralph had done he had done through her, by way of a passionate vicariousness, watching in smiling wonderment from his seat at the ringside."⁵

JB: There is an argument to be made that he is the one who inadvertently almost destroyed Isabel's life by arranging secretly for her to have half of his inheritance. Ralph has manipulated her life in just the same way that Madame Merle did. Or maybe not exactly the same way; he does it for amusement, because he's dying, and is desperate to see Isabel live as fully as he's incapable of doing. Madame Merle too is desperate, but desperate for life, and the things of life that money can bring—for instance, a dowry for Pansy. All these people act out of desperation in one form or another. Gilbert Osmond is not young anymore, he has no money, he has an expensive daughter who's getting bigger all the time, and he has to buy new clothes for her. What's he going to do? He's desperate. And then comes Madame Merle to say to him, *Look! I've found an heiress for you.*

What I love about *Portrait* is the intricacy of it, and the relentlessness; it digs down and down, and then down deeper again, and there are still more intricacies. What was the motive of this person, what was the motive of that person? James was a Freud before Freud; he was a greater psychologist than Freud.

HS: He certainly is more literary. Coming back to the cast of characters in this book, you definitely give Pansy a twist.

JB: I never believed in Henry James's portrait of Pansy. Her father is Gilbert Osmond, her mother is Madame Merle, but she is this little angel? No! At the end of *Mrs. Osmond*, Isabel comes into a room and sees her from behind and thinks at first it is Madame Merle. And when Pansy is leaving, she looks at Isabel through half-closed eyes, just as Osmond does. For the first time, it strikes her that Pansy is the daughter of a pair of monsters. You could write a novel about Pansy's future life, but it wouldn't be a very pleasant novel. And the Countess Gemini, of course, is a wonderful character, one of the best and most entertaining in the novel.

HS: I had a good laugh when her "comely calf" has been appreciated "in more than one bedchamber."[6] You really pick up on the comic aspect, especially in Warburton, "he of the half-dozen castles and the myriads of acres,"[7] presented together with Goodwood "not as a comic duo in a slapstick show, but like the mechanical figures in a medieval clock tower."[8] Where the comic aspect remains somehow subdued in James, you seem to revel in it.

JB: Yes, I suppose there is some humor there. But James is funny, too, in his sly fashion. We have to read him in our time, but if we were reading him in *his* time, we would see the humor much more plainly than we see it now, because we live in a time in which there is nothing you cannot say. No words are banned anymore, whereas in James's day, novelists had to resort to euphemism. Though James does have the odd bit of indecent fun—recall Mrs. Condrip in *The Ambassadors*, and in the same novel the grossly named Mamie Pocock. Oh yes, James wasn't as pure of mind as he pretended.

HS: Talking about names: in your book, Isabel's servant, Staines, not only gets a name but a vital role as well. And Staines has always understood Pansy, better than her mother.

JB: Servants know everything; they watch everything; they see everything. When their employers and their guests are at table, they are standing behind them, listening to everything that is being said. James, in his lordly fashion, never took any notice of the servants. Do you know Henry Green's novel *Loving*? It's about the lives of servants in a big house in Ireland in 1941, during the war; it's beautiful, a kind of *Midsummer Night's Dream*. Green's people seem simple, but of course they aren't at all—they're every bit as complicated as their "betters." I like Staines; she's comic, but endearing, and, I hope, *real*.

HS: She reminds me a bit of Billie Stryker in *Ancient Light*, who gets on well with Lydia, Alex's wife. Likewise, Staines gets on well with Lydia Touchett.

JB: As people do. My aristocratic friend Beatrice von Rezzori, who lives in Tuscany, gets on with the servants: it's the middle class that she disdains.

Beatrice and the servants speak the same language. They are, Beatrice included, primitive. In the same way, it's not surprising that Staines and Mrs. Touchett get along well. Mrs. Touchett seems another monster, but as we learn in *Mrs. Osmond*, she has had a hard life. She, too, was once betrayed.

HS: And suddenly, in Banvillean fashion, there's a half-brother.
JB: But doesn't it explain the mystery of the marriage between her and the "wonderful" Daniel Touchett? As my wife Janet would say, the wonderful man turned out to be *just a man.*

HS: I understand you wrote *Mrs. Osmond* on Janet's suggestion?
JB: Yes, it was Janet who urged me, years ago, to "complete" *The Portrait of a Lady*. At the time, I didn't think I could do it.

HS: Your Lydia Touchett reveals a few things, but so does Staines. Why does Staines speak up so late?
JB: She didn't reveal the things she knows earlier because it's not the place of servants to speak up; and besides, it just would have been too hurtful to Isabel to know the truth, and Staines loves Isabel and tries to keep her from harm and pain. It's when she comes to understand that Isabel is in danger of being betrayed again, of getting into the clutches of Madame Merle again, that she decides it's time to "tell all." I imagine you've known marriages in which the husband or wife was having an affair; did you go straight away to one or the other and say, "You know what . . . ?" That's another of James's great themes: do not interfere in other people's lives. Let them make their mistakes.

HS: There is the scene in the beginning and the ending of your book about the man in Paddington Station who is visibly in despair. He is the opposite of Merle's smoothness. Why is this scene so important to you, that it marks the start and end of your book?
JB: Because I saw him one day, a red-haired man on a street corner weeping helplessly, and the image stayed with me so vividly that I knew I had to use it. He seemed to me the perfect "objective correlative" for Isabel's inner agony, this man suffering helplessly in public. She feels for him, and with him. As she says, "Why don't we *all* stand on street corners weeping?" And in the end, the great test of the shallow young man Myles Devenish is for Isabel to ask him, "What would *you* have done?" Isabel still feels *she* should have done something; the weeping man seemed to offer her a task, and she shirked it. And so, with his bland reply to her question, Devenish fails the

test. So, Isabel, I assume, is going to turn down the offer—of love?—that he seems to be tentatively offering her. She won't fall for another Gilbert Osmond, even one as pleasant and attractive as Devenish, but will find a way actually to *do* things, to take action.

HS: It must have been great fun for you to write this book, with a complicated heroine who travels all over Europe towards your favorite country—Italy—to find there one of your favorite dark characters, Osmond.

JB: Italy is the country where people know how to live. They have figured out the food, the wine, the weather, the passion. Life is exquisite there. Italy is the most beautiful country in the world. The first time I visited Rome, when I was eighteen, I arrived at night, and in the morning, I stepped out of the *pensione* and opened a map. And two men—they *both* looked like Federico Fellini—were passing by, and one of them, seeing me with the map, stopped and with a sweeping gesture said, *"Issa Roma!"* I knew nothing about the world, but Rome, Italy, set about teaching me. In a bar I stood at a very small marble table—I can see it still—and all I had was a glass of Frascati and a piece of Parmesan cheese, and I thought, *This* is the world, while Ireland was diminishing to a tiny green spot way off in the distance.

HS: This brings us back to the Europe-America thing. Whereas James merely says his Isabel is a great reader, you specify that she reads Emerson, Hegel, and Maistre . . .

JB: She reads Emerson because she is from the same part of the world, and, of course, everybody was reading Emerson in those days: he was the Sage of Concord. Yet one of the big moral problems for American intellectuals in those days was, what to do about the wilderness? Out there, in the "territory," was slavery and the slaughter of the American Indians. Emerson never once mentioned, to my memory, the aboriginal American people. He says a few things about black people, but not to much effect. His kind of intellectual just wasn't interested; their gaze was still turned eastwards, towards Europe. Emerson's great essay "The American Scholar" is the second American Constitution. In it he declares to his fellow Americans, "We no longer owe anything to Europe; we are a new thing; we are a new phenomenon." Anybody who wants to understand America has to read "The American Scholar" and its sister piece, "Self-Reliance." So, Isabel is a product of that intellectual world, and when we meet her first, in *Portrait*, there she is, diligently reading philosophy—but in translation, as James slyly informs us.

HS: You are a very European writer—with Kleist as one of your major heroes. I loved the passage in *The Infinities* where someone says, "it was the poet Goethe—entirely forgotten now but in his time there were those who would have ranked him above the sublime Kleist !"[9]

JB: I have the highest admiration for Kleist, and I pay due homage to him in *The Infinities*, the book of mine that displeases me least. In it, lightness and weight are evenly balanced, as always in Kleist. There is far more of him in that book than there is of *The Tempest* or of *A Midsummer Night's Dream*.

HS: In *Mrs. Osmond*, too, Shakespeare pops up but in a negative way, as Isabel feels she cannot present Merle as Lady Macbeth, "thrusting incarnadined hands towards a cold heaven," as life is more complicated than a play.

JB: One of my favorite lines, that, though it borrows shamelessly not only from *Macbeth* but also from Yeats's poem "The Cold Heaven." But my favorite little joke, or perhaps it's more a knowing nudge, occurs when Isabel confronts Madame Merle with the full extent of her and Osmond's deceit, and I write of Merle's gaze being "fixed upon a mote in the middle distance." As I'm sure you know, Max Beerbohm wrote a famous parody of Henry James called "The Mote in the Middle Distance."

HS: I also liked the joke where Isabel, at the start of your novel, finds herself in London being watched by a man who feels her eye on him, while she feels "held . . . in the unblinking beam of those preternaturally wide-open . . . organs," feeling "reassessed" by "the portraitist . . . looking to see how his composition had weathered with the years, and what time had done to the quality of the pigment."

JB: Yes, I thought it only right that old HJ should make a fleeting appearance, like Hitchcock in his films.

HS: Yeats, too, seems an undercurrent in your writing, in this novel and others. I think of the opening of *Mefisto*[10] where there are overtones of "Leda and the Swan."

JB: He is one of my great influences! Nobody ever picks up on that, for some reason. He is a wonderful poet, the greatest of the twentieth century, without doubt. Of course, like all poets he writes lines that sound splendid but mean nothing.

HS: To write as poetically as you do, with structures rather than plots, it sounds like a novel for you is like a painting, a composition?

JB: When I go to my room and start work, more often than not, I have no idea what is going to appear on the page. I act out of sheer desperation. And every morning it is the same: I don't know how I managed to write yesterday, how I will write today. It all seems an utter impossibility. Then another version of me takes over, and I'm off. Writing is done in the dark, and one must never leave the darkness out. The writer must follow instincts, even into the deepest blackness. Those are the moments that are most worthwhile, when you lose yourself, when you trust the medium itself. And gradually you see patterns emerging, and they fall into place, and you hone them. Art is a thing of beauty but made from a mess.

HS: The rag and bone shop of the heart?
JB: Yes. Old W. B. again.

HS: I was hoping that some painters would find their way into this novel. James himself mentions a Bonington that Isabel is paying attention to; in your version this painter becomes part of the next scheme to "sell" Pansy off, but he is also paired with Turner. What do you like about them?
JB: Bonington is a wonderful painter; he is not a great painter, but a wonderful miniaturist. Turner I admire, but I wouldn't go further than that. I mean, he's not great as Piero della Francesca is, as Bonnard is, as Velasquez is. The world of painting is so wide—let's not venture into it; we'd get lost.

HS: A last question maybe? James writes psychological novels; yours seem more mythological: instead of explaining people, you describe atmospheric shifts, ascribing them to fauns or other funny divine forms—metaphors for poetry, as in *The Infinities*? In *Mrs. Osmond* I found only few and slight mythological presences. Does that mean you want to move more into psychology?[11]
JB: Mrs. Osmond is a "one-off," not to be repeated. I wanted to see if I could write a "psychological" novel, just for the interest of it. As I said earlier, I was writing in the spirit of HJ, not of JB. The latter writes of a nonexistent world, where the gods still rule, which is a parallel to ours. I've said it before, and it's true: I'm not interested in what people do, only in what they are. You know that wonderful, seemingly enigmatic but, to me, entirely congenial outburst of Kafka's in the so-called *Zürau Aphorisms*? "Never again psychology!" he cries. I'm going to have that carved in marble and fixed to the wall above my desk.

HS: To then translate the mud you mentioned earlier into marble? There's alchemical fire for you. Many thanks, indeed, for your generous sharing of time and ideas.

Notes

1. John Banville, *Mrs. Osmond*. New York: Alfred A. Knopf,: 2017; epigraph.

2. *Mrs. Osmond*, Chapter 36, 367.

3. "She had not known where to turn; but she knew now. There was a very straight path." Henry James, *Portrait of a Lady*, New York: Barnes & Noble Classics, 2004; Chapter 55, 612.

4. Chapter 28, 274.

5. Chapter 1, 5.

6. For the full passage: "she was gracefully endowed in her lower extremities, being possessed in particular of a comely calf, as she had been gallantly assured on more than one occasion, and in more than one bedchamber" (Chapter 20, 202).

7. Chapter 16, 154.

8. Chapter 9, 94.

9. *The Infinities*, New York: Vintage, 147.

10. . . . surging in frantic ardour towards the burning town, the white room and Castor dead. (John Banville. *Mefisto*. Jaffrey New Hampshire: David R. Godine, 1999, 3).

11. In this last question I am referring to passages such as "with the garden all around them, two wild things, nymph and faun, struggling in the midst of subdued nature, like an old master's illustration of a moment out of Ovid" (John Banville, *Eclipse*, New York: Vintage, 2002, 162):

"There is a multi-colored patch in my memory of the moment, a shimmer of variegated brightness where her hands hover. Let me linger here with her a little while, before Rose appears, and Myles and Chloe return from wherever they are, and her goatish husband comes clattering on to the scene; she will be displaced soon enough from the throbbing centre of my attentions" (John Banville. *The Sea*. London: Picador, 2005; 86); in *The Infinities* one of my favorite sentences is when Helen, actress who has to impersonate Alcmene in *Amphitryon*, "walks from the room . . . and what she takes to be Roddy's eyes on her is in fact my dad [Hermes's father, Zeus] shambling eagerly in her warm wake." (John Banville, *The Infinities*. New York: Vintage, 2011; 175)

"In the course of these somewhat aimless animadversions, an observer of the pair of friends as they circumambulated the dusty perimeter of the little pleasure garden might have been forgiven for thinking that one of them, namely Miss Stackpole, had herself drifted into that very state of unappreciated potential upon which Isabel had just been musing. However, such an assumption, on the part of a speculative faun, say, peeping out from his hiding place among the verdure skirting the path, would have been mistaken" (*Mrs. Osmond*, Chapter 13, 126).

Dermot Bolger and John Banville

Dermot Bolger / 2017

Reprinted by permission of Dermot Bolger, Irish poet, novelist, and playwright who conducted this interview during the 2017 Red Line Book Festival in Dublin.

Dermot Bolger: In your new memoir, *Time Pieces*, you mention with praise Tony Cronin's *Dead as Doornails*. At the end of Cronin's memoir, he meets Patrick Kavanagh, who says, "You're off to America. There'll be no more conversation until you're back." Last year we were meant to hold this public conversation, but you needed to go to America. So we had no more conversation for a year, but now you are back and I am delighted to have you here. I was fascinated by your memoir, *Time Pieces*. I loved it for all kinds of reasons. I loved the little cameos. Julie [Parsons] was talking earlier about people not actually having a house but having a floor of a house or having a flat of a house. And by sheer fluke, the flat that you wind up sharing with your aunt has the daughter of William Butler Yeats downstairs.

Banville: Yes. I moved to Dublin from Wexford when I was seventeen or eighteen. I was lucky enough to share a flat with my aunt in upper Mount Street, which I think is one of the most beautiful, well, is *the* most beautiful street that I know, in any of the cities I've visited, really. Of course, I'm biased because it was my street. If you stand at the government buildings and look up, that vista through Merrion Square up to the Pepper Cannister at the end of Mount Street, I think, is absolutely exquisite. Even as a callow teenager, I realized that this was a lovely place to live. The house that we lived in, of course, was falling down. It was owned by Green Properties, which was one of Fianna Fáil's scams at the time. The rent was about three pounds a week, which was quite high for those days. It was decrepit. It had a gas geyser. I don't believe you're old enough to remember a gas geyser. You put money into it and put a match to it, and you hoped that it didn't explode. In fact, one day, it did explode, and I ended up without eyebrows for a while. But it was a wonderful place to live. The Dolmen Press was directly opposite us, so Paddy Kavanagh would come and sit on the steps at the front of the house and *glare* across at the Dolmen Press, which didn't publish him. I'm not going to romanticize Dublin in the rare old times. It *wasn't* Dublin in the rare old times. It was an ugly time to live in. But I was lucky enough to live in a beautiful place in this ugly time. After eight o'clock in the evening, the street was crowded with prostitutes. Most of them teenagers, fifteen-, sixteen-year-old girls. Maybe I should've written about their lives.

Bolger: There's one very vivid moment where you actually talk to one of them, and you ask, "Does your father know you're out here?" And she says very vividly, "My father does know I'm out here."

Banville: Oh, yes, and she said it in that way, "Oh, yeah, he knows I'm here." He was probably her pimp. We're starting on a high note. We'll get cheerier as we go along.

Bolger: Although you don't romanticize Dublin, which is very, very wise, because it was a grim sort of city in many ways at that time. But your mother had this very romantic notion of Dublin because you were born on the Feast of the Immaculate Conception, which was a day when country people descended upon Dublin to do their shopping and to marvel at the Christmas lights. So, as a child your first sense of Dublin was quite romantic because you always went there on your birthday.

Banville: Yes, of course, having a birthday that late in the year is always a bit of a cheat because you get combined birthday and Christmas presents. But it was magical to come from Wexford. We would get the train at around 7:30 in the morning when it was still dark. I think dawn used to start coming up around Arklow and those pink, frosted fields. I can still see them. And then we would arrive in Dublin in a drizzle; it was always drizzling in Dublin. The pavements outside Westland Row were always greasy with drizzle. But it didn't matter. To me it was Paris; it was Moscow; it was the center of the world. It was fabulously romantic. I would be taken to the—I get the name wrong; I call it the Palm Grove, or a similar name—I'd be taken there to have a Knickerbocker Glory or a banana split, both of which were equally hideous. But to me they seemed the height of sophistication. It was lovely. I would be taken to Clery's Store to be bought a ten-and-sixpenny watch, which would stop working very quickly. They would last about two months and then stop. It's always very difficult to talk about the past because all we retain from the past are the good times, if you had a good life, or the horrible times, if you had a bad life. I was lucky enough, or, as a writer, unfortunate enough, to have a happy childhood. So, I remember the good times. But, as we began by saying, it was a bleak time in this country. I would not have wanted to be a woman. I would not have wanted to be an orphan. And, to be fair, I would not have wanted to be a Christian Brother or a priest either because their lives were hideous as well. We won't even *talk* about the nuns.

Bolger: Their lives were ruled by snobbery, because all these social hierarchies existed within the Church that dictated your status and what exact order of nuns or priests you could aspire to join. But this is a book about Dublin, and it's a memoir. And it's also a book of photographs where the only two photographs of you, if I'm correct, are of the back of your head because you drift in and you drift out of the story. But is it also a book about Wexford? Is it a book about somebody having a perception of their native place that makes them feel they have to leave? And maybe that perception changes over time. There is a feeling in the book that Wexford was thought of as a more oppressive, backward place than it actually was, and that your perception of Wexford has changed over the years.

Banville: Yes, I didn't recognize it at the time, but Wexford was a fascinating place. But it was very primitive. When I look back to Wexford now, it's like looking in a Bruegel painting from the 1500s. We had the "village idiot." We had all sorts of unfortunates that people used to follow and throw stones at and make fun of. I *hope* that doesn't happen now. So, it was a primitive time, and I wanted to get away from there. But it was just *small*. For a teenager with high ambitions, this was the worst aspect of it, that it was small. I wanted to get away, and Dublin was big. I didn't realize how small Dublin was until I got there. I realized when I started writing the memoir how foolish I was to embark on this strange adventure. It was fascinating to me to look back and to see how much I could dredge up from my memories of Dublin in those days: fishing for minnows in the canal, and all one ever caught, really, were dead dogs. I was talking to a friend of mine recently, and I was very indignantly saying that the Fianna Fáil government of the '60s had a plan to cover *in* the canals and make a big road that would lead out of the city and so on. And underneath, instead of the canals, they were going to put sewers. The friend of mine said, "Yes, but what would they have done with all of the dead dogs if they'd covered in the canals?" [laughter] One of the extraordinary things that I find about Dublin is that all that little area that I wrote about is still there. Mount Street was luckily preserved.

Bolger: And that was the extraordinary thing because if you read, say, Dave Dickson's huge history of Dublin [*Dublin: The Making of a Capital City*], you realize that the remarkable thing isn't that parts of Georgian Dublin were destroyed. The remarkable thing was how much of it survived. There was a plan to build a Catholic cathedral in Merrion Square and to knock down all of Merrion Square and all of that area, eventually. It didn't happen because the idea eventually ran out of steam. But there was a sense among the government and the Church that Georgian Dublin was essentially part of a foreign occupier's culture and not really a valued part of Ireland's heritage.

Banville: That would have happened. That was one of [Archbishop] John Charles McQuaid's grandiloquent ideas. He was going to build a huge cathedral in Merrion Square and knock down all the buildings. You can imagine what that would have looked like. But, you see, you have to remember, too, there was still this lingering resentment that we were living in a city, a very beautiful city, which was not built by *us*. I remember a friend of mine saying that when she was in the Arts Council, there was some Irish-Georgian silver that was being sold in Sotheby's and she went to Charlie Haughey and said, "Look, it's not going to cost much. We should keep this for the state, for Ireland." And he said, "Ah, let the Brits have their own stuff." But this was completely ridiculous because we should've accepted that. All right, we had all this oppression and all this stuff, but we had this very, very beautiful city. And, as you say, it is remarkable that so much of it has been preserved.

Bolger: Was it strange to go back in time and remember it? Because you say in the book, "Memory walks in inscrutable fashion and seizes on and tucks away for safekeeping the most negligible trifles, clinging to them through years." It seems that we remember these very random things and we forget major things. As you began to go back and write a memoir, were you amazed at the things you could remember and at the gaps that were there, and at the quite trivial things that were stuck in your mind forever?

Banville: Yes. I'm not sure that we remember. I think that we invent. I think we imagine the past into existence. Neurologists now are coming to agree with me at last that we don't register what we see. What we do is we make a model of what we see, and this is implanted in our memories. And, of course, models decay over time. This explains why we go back to a house we haven't been to for thirty years, and the window is in the wrong place; the door is in the wrong place, and everything is slightly askew. It's because the model of it that you've kept in your head has decayed. I like the notion of the decaying past that we summon up.

Bolger: Yeats has the line, "O chestnut tree, great rooted blossomer, Are you the leaf, the blossom or the bole" ["Among School Children"]. Are you still the John Banville who at eighteen years of age lived with his aunt in that flat? Do we change so much in our lives that memoir is impossible because we simply are not the people that we're writing about?

Banville: Of course not. What I wrote in that little book is a man who's now in his seventies looking back on himself when he was in his teens. And, of course, I am that person, but also I'm not. It's very hard for us to conceive of the fact that the mewling baby at its mother's breast is us now. It's a mystery. It is a very strange thing what time does to us. We feel that we should be able to go back and *be* that person, but we can't. All we can do is imagine it from now. But the world imagined is infinitely more real than the real world.

Bolger: You didn't go into *exile*, a posh word for *emigrate*, as Joyce and Beckett had before you. You worked as a clerk at Aer Lingus and you worked as a subeditor in the *Irish Press*. There's a sense of your almost creating your own space. Joyce's novel *Ulysses* had colonized Dublin so much that you felt that there wasn't the imaginative space for you to write about Dublin until, in some ways, you invented the persona of Benjamin Black, years later and began to revisit that world.

Banville: You have to keep in mind that Joyce went away, and people in Dublin have great sentimental love for Joyce. You know, "our Jimmy Joyce." Most of them haven't read him for a start, and most of them don't realize that he *hated* the place. He came back *once*, after he left, with the plan of opening a cinema, and never again. The Dublin that he knew was the second city to the British Empire, pre-1916, pre-1922. It was an entirely different world. He couldn't have written about the Dublin of his time. That wouldn't have worked at all. He invented the place. In a way, that is what all writers do. We invent a world that by some peculiar magic looks like the world that we live in, that we move around in. This is a very strange thing about fiction. It looks like, it smells like, it feels like, it tastes like life. But it's nothing like life, at all. A novel is nothing like life. It is a stylization of life that by, as I say, some peculiar magic, looks and feels like life. This is the mystery of fiction. Joyce left because the place was stultifying. He had met a woman who was going to be the love of his life, in many ways a simple Galway girl.

But they went off on this wonderful adventure. Joyce knew from very early on what he could do, what he was going to do. The rest of us didn't have that kind of confidence. Beckett went because he just didn't like Ireland. He wanted to be Parisian, although I remember John Montague's saying that he was at a party in Beckett's apartment in Paris and that Beckett was saying that he had no interest in Ireland. He didn't care anything about it. But Montague noticed that Jackie Yeats was on the wall; they were drinking Jameson. Everything about the place was Irish. So, we carry with us, even if we live here, we carry with us a version of the past, of the place that we grew up in, the place we lived in, the place we were happy or unhappy in. But it is a version of it; it is not the place itself.

Bolger: I enjoyed your recent novel, *The Blue Guitar*, enormously. I enjoyed its wondrousness and its factualism. At certain times I would say, "I am actually in Wexford town," and then it would totally distort like a spoon in a glass, and you are suddenly looking at the whole world. It is as if you were revisiting some moments of the past, but you create a very fantastical world and deliberately change it and distort it. The Benjamin Black novels are very much rooted in a version of this very real world that you describe in this book. Why do you think you were able to explore *that* Dublin as a crime writer more than as a novelist, or rather a different *type* of novelist.

Banville: Benjamin Black is a craftsman. The imagined Dublin that he writes about is not Joyce's Dublin. If *I* were to write about Dublin it *would* be Joyce's Dublin. If I were to mention Nelson's Pillar, everybody would say, "Ah, yes, the two old ladies with the plums going up," and if I mention, down around Busáras, they'd say, "Ah, it's night time." He used up the place, so I had to invent a new world. My friend Harry Crosbie says to me, "You're bringing out another novel. Is it going to be about Wexford again?" I say, "It's not about Wexford." He says, "Yes, they're all about Wexford." And we do, I think, return to the place where we were born, but it's not the place where we were born; it's invented, imagined. We take real places, and we pass them through the furnace fire of the imagination, the alchemical fire of the imagination. It comes out the other side being something new, something rich and strange. That's how *I* work. My friend Billy Roche, the playwright, writes plays about the real Wexford, and I admire him for it. I wish I could do it, but I can't. If he were here, he'd probably say, "Oh, no, it's not the real Wexford." My old friend John McGahern, whose books are very autobiographical, would say, "Nope. It's all made up." And he's right. Even if you write as realistically as you can about a place that you remember, it's still going to be invented. It has to be. That's what art does. Art transmutes the mere real into something new and strange that, yet, in an odd way, reflects and is very like the mere real.

Bolger: If I had to pick, fifteen years ago, two writers who would never write memoirs, I would've said John Banville and John McGahern. They're very, very different memoirs. I know John knew that the end of his life was approaching. Were you surprised that he wrote a memoir?

Banville: I was, yes, I was. In a way I thought it was superfluous since all of his novels are memoirs, really. [laughs] I remember when *Amongst Women* was published, we were at a launch and Tom Kilroy leaned over to me and said, "What's he going to do now that he's fixed the old fellow?" And he did skewer his father in that book. But, again, it wasn't his father; it was a version of his father. John was right. It is all made up. The more we try to write about the real world that we live in and that we grew up in, the more it has to be imagined. It's like the infinitesimal in calculus. The closer we get to reality, the more it has to be imagined.

Bolger: When people from abroad ask me about John McGahern and should they read the memoir, I say, "No, if you want the truth, read the novels." He's very truthful in the memoir, but the story shines more when it is shone through the reflection of his imagination in *The Barracks* and in *The Dark* and all those books. What you do with the memoir is totally different. You drift in and out of the book. You also have a lot of fun with it because you also go on excursions to Dublin with Harry Crosbie, under an assumed name, and one gets the sense of visiting places and being shown around, and that adds a great sense of fun to the book.

Banville: Yes, I realized that as a small-town boy I had come to Dublin, and I had made a small town in Dublin around Baggot Street, Merrion Square, that area. That was my little Wexford. And Harry was able to say to me, "Well, there's a place up by the Mater Hospital that I bet you haven't seen," or "There's a house in Henrietta Street you haven't seen." This was absolutely a thrill for me to see this new Dublin. I had this wonderful experience, for those of you who haven't read it. In the early parts of the book, I talk about how my father used to leave his work, in Wexford, and have one pint in his brother's pub across the way before he went home for his tea. On the very last day that Harry and I were going about Dublin we said, "Let's go down and have a glass in Mulligan's down in Townsend Street or wherever it is.

We were sitting there, and my son came in to have a pint on his way home from work. Nobody believes it, but it was absolutely true. This wonderful circle that I wrote about was closed: My father going for a pint when he was finished work at the end of the day, and at the end of Harry and my travels around Dublin, my son came in for a pint on the way home. Life is so banal. It does repeat itself. But I was delighted. My son was astonished. We were astonished. It was a perfect closure for the book.

Bolger: Although I think you say in the book that there's no such thing as coincidence.

Banville: Well, no, there isn't. You'd have to believe in fairies and heaven and hell and all that if you believe in coincidence.

Bolger: I think that writers are instinctively lazy people. I occasionally write book reviews, and I always do it on a Sunday night at around eleven o'clock because that's when I did my homework as a schoolboy and you always avoid things until the last minute. So, if I have a book review to write, I always wind up doing it on a Sunday night. Unless there's a deadline, you don't do it. Do you think that if you hadn't been working on this book that you would never have explored those paths of Dublin with Harry Crosbie? You would never have got to Henrietta St. or the Blessington Basin or any of these places?

Banville: Oh, no. It's much more prosaic. It's much more banal. I sleepwalked into writing this book because an acquaintance of mine, Paul Joyce, a photographer, wrote to me out of the blue, and said, "We haven't met for a long time, but I have these photographs I took in the 1970s in Dublin. How about we collaborate on a book?" And I said, "Yes." Then I discovered that he hadn't dated the photographs. He hadn't identified where they were. By that stage I decided to write the book, so we had to bring him over to take new photographs of the old places. I was rather desperate because I realized that I didn't know Dublin. I didn't really know very much about it. I had a brilliant idea one day. I thought, I'll get Harry to come and help me. Harry knows Dublin like the back of his hand and knows wonderful places. One of my favorite memories is of standing with him in number 3 Henrietta Street, a tumbledown house. He was saying, "Look how beautiful this must have been." I think it's being renovated now, but then it was a complete wreck. But we found this little patch of wallpaper that was the original wallpaper from the mid-1700s, maybe

1760. He said, "Do you realize that wallpaper has been there since 1760?" And we stared at this. I think that was the moment that I discovered a Dublin that I hadn't known. I shouldn't say "discovered." I felt that I was in touch with a Dublin that I hadn't known. Also, traveling around with Harry is always fun.

Bolger: That comes across in the book. It would be remiss of me not to ask you to read something.

Banville: Oh, no, nobody wants to hear.

Bolger: Would people like John to read if we twisted his arm very gently?

Banville: I don't know about you, but I hate readings.

Bolger: You could read from the new novel, or you can read from the memoir.

Banville: I'll read from the memoir. I'm sure you've all heard Marie Heaney's wonderful formulation. She said—Flann O'Brien has said, "There's no such thing as a large whiskey." Mary says there's no such thing as a short reading. [laughter] I'll just read a bit, a couple of paragraphs for those of you who haven't read it to hear what it sounds like.

[Reads from the opening pages of *Time Pieces*]

Bolger: We have a few moments left, and I would love any questions for John.

Audience Member: Do you feel that your work has successfully represented the epochs and the zeitgeists of the periods that it deals with?

Banville: *That's* a nice simple question. I can't possibly say what my work has achieved. That's for other people to say.

Bolger: The first time I read your work was in a Wexford publication called *The Gorey Detail*. It was an extract from an early novel-in-progress about a mathematician, and those early books, *The Newton Letter*, for example, deliberately didn't set out to chart contemporary time. They set out to explore a far, far wider question. So, was there a sense of not setting your work in Ireland early on, of setting your work in history?

Banville: I didn't want to try to be Joyce. I didn't want to be Seán Ó Faoláin, Benedict Kiely, those Irish writers, *wonderful* Irish writers. I wanted to be something else. We all did. Neil Jordan went into the movies. Other people did other things. We had to find a way out from under the weight of tradition, the great, delightful, golden weight of tradition. But it was a burden on us, and we had to find new ways of doing things. The last thing I wanted to be was an "Irish writer," quote-unquote, whom people in New York would come up to, shake my hand and say, "Wonderful to see somebody from the old country," and all that awful stuff. I didn't want that at all. I wanted to be something else, probably mistakenly, but one does what one does.

Bolger: I only met Brian Moore once. I don't know if you ever knew Brian Moore, a writer who was very, very successful in a long succession of novels who's now almost totally forgotten even though he's not long dead. He said to me that Joyce got a whole life out of Dublin, but he hated Belfast. And he got two novels out of Belfast. And then he was on his own, left to his own imagination, which is why his books were all set in different places and that there was a sense of moving away from his own experience. But how much of yourself is in all your novels?

Banville: Everything. I'm the only material I have to work with, so it's me. But to attempt to answer this man's question, I don't think it's the business of the artist to represent the epoch that he or she lives in. It's the duty of an artist to make a work of art that will live past its time and that will inform even the time *before* the time in which it was written. It has to be timeless. Representing your epoch is for journalists and sociologists.

Audience Member: You say you're in all your books, but Philip Marlowe has been in Benjamin Black and Henry James is very much in *Mrs. Osmond*, not just because of the subject matter. I'm reading it at the moment but because of the way it's written—the syntax and prose seem to follow the writing of Henry James quite closely. Are you just imbued with James, his methods and way of writing, because you read him so much, or was it a conscious attempt to copy the style of the original book? And for that matter, why did you feel the need to continue the story of Isabel Archer?

Banville: I don't know. My wife suggested to me years ago that I should write the second half of *The Portrait of a Lady*, which Henry James himself recognized wasn't finished. And I thought at the time, No, I didn't want to do it. It would be like feeding on the carcass of a lion. But, then, obviously I needed to take a new direction, and I did it. The problem about answering a question like yours, which is a very good and pertinent question, is that I don't know the answer to it. I don't know why I do things. God forbid that I should. Art is a mysterious business. We find ourselves embarked on things, and we stop halfway through or a quarter way through and say, "Why am I doing this?" You say, "Don't ask; just keep going." You make a thing to put it into the world, a thing that wasn't there before. That's the only reason for making a work of art, really. So, I didn't have any intention of parroting Henry James or Raymond Chandler. I wanted to write in the spirit in which they'd written, and I suppose I wanted to make an homage to writers that I admired immensely.

Audience Member: John, you introduced me to Simenon and Richard Stark. Do you consider the [Detective Jules] Maigret novels works of art?

Banville: No, the Maigret novels I don't. They're work-a-day. They're very good. I think they're wonderful. My God, the imagination that went into making these endless stories. He could write them in about ten days. But they're craft work. They're entertainment. But his *romans durs*, his hard novels, which usually have a crime in them, but they are not crime novels. They have no policemen in them. I think there are at least half a dozen that I've read that are up there with the best of literature of the twentieth century. He was looked down upon by the French establishment because he didn't go along with the fads of the day. He didn't go along with the existentialists. He didn't drink wine in the Café de Flore with Sartre and de Beauvoir and so on. He just lived and wrote. He was a true artist, I think, and those books are superb. They were written very quickly, as well. If you haven't read them, I recommend them to you, books like *Dirty Snow*, *The Man Who Watched Trains Go By*, *Monsieur Monde Vanishes*. These are just superb, superb works. And Richard Stark—Donald Westlake, his pseudonym was Richard Stark—wrote a series of Parker novels. John Boorman made that wonderful film *Point Blank* from the first one. Again, a superb, superb writer. A lot of the *best* literature of the twentieth century was written in the crime genre.

Bolger: Let me just move to the last question for you, John. You were very generous with your time. You mentioned Benjamin Black as being more of a craftsman. Is there a difference in the way you write those crime novels and the way you write your other novels? The crime novels have a certain continuity to them in terms of style. Whereas, although you know within two or three paragraphs that you're in a John Banville novel, you don't know where that novel is going to take you because they are each a reinvention of your material. Whereas the crime novels are working within a genre; they're subverting a genre. Is one easier to write than the other, or is it the same difficult task?

Banville: It's nothing to do with being easier; it's just an entirely different way of working. I write Benjamin Black novels very quickly, very spontaneously. You have to keep going. It's sort of like falling down a hill. Remember when we were kids, we used to roll down hills? Writing a Benjamin Black novel is like that. You mustn't stop; you mustn't try to pause. Whereas the Banville books I have to give years to them. I have to write them very slowly, write them with a fountain pen on paper. The Black books I write directly onto the screen. It's just two entirely different ways of doing it, and I hope the results are entirely different as well.

Bolger: Is one more liberating than the other? Did you find that suddenly by having this Benjamin Black persona, it freed up the other paths of your imagination because you didn't have to be writing a John Banville novel all the time? It allows you to take that mental space.

Banville: Again, I can't answer that. I don't know. I can't read these books. I did them. I made them. They usurp you. Everybody else can read their work, but you can't. You're the only person in the world that can't read your own work. I wouldn't want to. But even if I were compelled to, I couldn't read my own work because I would bring to it all the baggage that went into the making of the book. Maybe there are writers who can go back and read their own work and enjoy it. If I went back and I read one of my books, I'd be spotting failures and flaws and moments of cowardice, moments of weariness on every page. It would be just an awful experience.

Bolger: Well, that's the way with writers, often you just remember the quirks, John. But the thing is that they read beautifully, and they have been an enlightenment in my life for a very, very long time, ever since reading *The Gorey Detail* and then going off and finding the novel when it was published. And it's been a pleasure to see each of those books arrive in print. You've enriched the lives of readers in Ireland and around the world for a very long time, constantly reinventing and constantly surprising us. Thank you for coming out to Tallaght, John. Thank you all for taking part in "Readers Day."

Banville: Thank you. It's been a pleasure.

Bolger: John Banville and Benjamin Black!

Banville: And thank you, Dermot, for your generosity and good spirit.

"To Make the World Blush in the Awareness of Itself"

Earl G. Ingersoll and John Cusatis / 2018

This interview was conducted on 10 November 2018.

Earl G. Ingersoll: In an early interview with Hedwig Schwall, you speak of your older brother's sending you a copy of *Dubliners* and its large effect upon you as a very young writer. As a mature writer, you have found Joyce wanting and much prefer Samuel Beckett, even though *Ulysses* topped most of the lists of the most important twentieth-century novel. Has your judgment of those two Irish writers changed?

John Banville: I don't think I would—I don't think I *could*—say that I find an incomparable writer such as Joyce "wanting." It's simply that it seemed, when I was starting out as a writer, that for me there were two available paths to follow, the Joycean and the Beckettian, and that I must choose between the two. Looking back, I now see that was a foolish notion. One follows one's own path, with the help of signposts left by others. Joyce and Beckett are entirely dissimilar but equally great.

EGI: In your conversation with Laura Izarra, you spoke of hating a novel just before it appears because you want to go back and overhaul it, but of course it's too late. As you probably know, Virginia Woolf often had a "nervous breakdown" awaiting the publication of her novels. And after Colum McCann published a novel, he would have nightmares he'd never be able to write the next one. Is it disappointment with your "failure" in a novel about to appear that impels you to begin writing the next one before the present one appears? Does that stratagem sometimes not work as a method of dealing with the novel about to be published?

JB: I find all my novels, unlike Joyce's, "wanting," in that I set out on each one with the aim of achieving perfection. This is, of course, an impossible endeavor. Each novel is a failure, in the perhaps special sense that it is not and cannot be perfect—indeed, what would a perfect work of art *be*? What counts is the quality of the failure. And I comfort myself with the thought that all works of art, no matter how great, inevitably fail. Iris Murdoch, asked why she wrote so many novels, said she thought each new one might exonerate her for having written all the others. My sentiments, exactly. Of course, the truly great, unique, and incontrovertible masterpiece is . . . the next one, as yet unwritten.

EGI: In your expression of anxiety about your and our "performances" and "masks" with Laura Izarra in 2002, you "threaten" to write a simple book about your childhood. Is *Time Pieces* in part the fulfilment of that "threat"?

JB: Did I say that to Laura? One really shouldn't give such hostages to the future. *Time Pieces* was a *jeu d'esprit*. I might do another book in the same vein, and I hope it would be undertaken in the same light-hearted spirit. But neither the written nor the projected book should be considered part of the fulfilment of an artistic plan. I have no such plan—and a good thing too. Every time I begin to write a book, I embark on an enchanting new venture. By the time it has come to the point of no return—usually about 35,000 words in—the enchantment has entirely faded, of course, and what was begun on the wings of Ariel is now a burden on Caliban's back.

EGI: One of the elements readers find in your conversations, especially those conducted before an audience, is your signature openness. Speaking of Nietzsche's *Also Sprach Zarathustra*, you confess that you've never been able to read this work without "giggling," an admission few would make to a large audience. Also, you have more than once admitted to being "arrogant." What are readers to make of these "true confessions"?

JB: I don't think they're true confessions; rather, I would hope such remarks are, as you say, a sign of frankness, which is a different matter—one can be frank without stepping into the confessional. I see no point in speaking in public unless one is prepared to say what is truly on one's mind—insofar as one can know what is on, or in, one's mind. By now I regret that at the beginning I didn't take Beckett's example, and avoid public utterances altogether—though Beckett himself gave far more interviews, especially in his younger years, than he cared to acknowledge. Though I treasure his response to someone who asked him, late in his life, why he didn't do interviews: "Because I have no views to inter."

EGI: Many years ago, in the *Paris Review* conversation with Belinda McKeon, you admitted that you are a "graphomaniac" who "cannot not write." Has that mania abated as you become a gentleman of a certain age?

JB: Have I become a gentleman of a certain age? What a sobering thought. I feel I'm just as youthfully foolish as I always was. But of course, I am still addicted to writing. No, it's more than an addiction: for me, to give up writing would be tantamount to giving up breathing. It is said that when Henry James was on his deathbed and in a coma, his hand was still moving across the bedsheet, grasping a phantom pen, still writing his phantom fictions. I hope it will be the same with me, when the awful time comes.

EGI: You seem to have had a lover's quarrel with the country of your birth and residence. Has your great success as a writer reduced that quarrel?

JB: My great success as a writer? Hmm. And I know of no lover's quarrel with Ireland. I have lived there all my life, except for a couple of stints in America and London. It's the place where my children were born, and where my books were conceived and written. Of course, the country has its faults, like any other, but I must say, as I look about the world at the moment—it's the autumn of 2018—I think the land of my birth is doing rather well. Why, Ireland may again become a moral light in a darkened Europe, as it is said to have been in the Middle Ages!

EGI: In your conversation with Jon Wiener, you refer to film more positively than many novelists might—given that film has "usurped" the power of storytelling. At one point, for example, you comically imagine having been "one of those hack writers for the movies, living in a little cabin in the Hollywood hills, hammering away at a typewriter, a glass of Scotch at my elbow, and a guy's coming in and saying, 'You gotta have two scenes by four o'clock, and they better be good or you're off the picture!'" How would you feel if approached by a producer who wanted to buy the film rights to, say, *The Infinities*, the novel you hate the least?

JB: I would be thrilled beyond words—which, you'll agree, would be a novel state in which to find myself. But I would hope they would ask me to write the screenplay. What a wonderful challenge! Film is public poetry—the poetry of the people, if you like—or used to be, in the great days of the vast picture-palaces, when a couple of thousand people would crowd into a cinema on a rainy night to watch some silly, erotic, transporting dream flash and float across the screen, and lose themselves to romance.

EGI: At another point, you tell Wiener: "I am an admirer of America. I still believe that America is the last great hope." Has the current occupier of the White House had any effect on your belief?

JB: As I write, in November 2018, I am in America, and another election has just been decided, in a way that affords a little hope. This poor country is in a bad state at the moment, but then, it has been in a bad state before. One has only to cast one's mind back to the much-celebrated 1960s, and the horrors of that decade in the "Age of Aquarius." America has great powers of recuperation, and I refuse to give up my faith in its essential decency. Keep in mind, the American Constitution was framed with the intention of *protecting* the country from democracy, as distinct from liberal democracy. But what do I know, mere scribbler that I am? As well ask your plumber, or your brain surgeon, as ask me about politics.

EGI: I was fascinated by your response to Chris Morash's question about how you and Benjamin Black actually get words "down on paper," or the computer screen. Do you ever get the illusion that all the works you want are somewhere in the computer and your job is to unearth them?

JB: No, I regard the computer merely as a machine, with no ghost in it. Someone once remarked to Igor Oistrakh on the wonderful tone of his violin. He put his ear to the instrument and shook it, saying: "I hear no tone." *He* was the maker of the tone. I need the quickness and dash of the keyboard and screen when I am concocting one of BB's capers, whereas JB requires the resistance of the page to the pen to set his pace.

EGI: In your conversation with Chris Morash you quote Wallace Stevens's "Notes Towards a Supreme Fiction": "From this the poem springs: that we live in a place / That is not our own and, much more, not ourselves / And hard it is in spite of blazoned days." Do you think the poetry of your novels might spring from your estrangement from the country you've lived in all your life?

JB: No. First of all, I am not estranged from Ireland—where does this notion come from? Secondly, one lives in the world, not in a country. At the moment, I happen to be in South Bend, Indiana, and find I am no different here than I would be were I in Ireland. One carries it all with one, as a snail does its shell. That said, I have to add that, of course, as a human being I am necessarily estranged in a world into which, as Heidegger would say, I have been thrown. And as an artist I feel, living in this world, unhoused— like, indeed, a snail extracted from its shell, and sprinkled with salt, for good, that is, bad, measure. You see the contradictions. What would life be without them?

EGI: I'm curious about the impact of Benjamin Black's fiction on yours, JB. I recently reread *The Sea*, which I hadn't read since it appeared in 2005, and was surprised to see some of the thriller narrative in its last pages, and even more so in *Mrs. Osmond*. As you doubtless know, less sophisticated interviewers often ask beginning novelists who influenced them. Have you been conscious of Black's influence?

JB: No, I don't think there's much in common between JB and BB—but who am I to say?—except that they both work within the novel form, which, though very tired, is not exhausted. The *story*, alas, still exerts a powerful force, and humankind has a deep need of it. And don't forget, the greatest ones have cleaved to the suspenseful aspect of the form. Consider Beckett's *coup de théâtre* when the Boy appears in *Godot* or when Moran writes at the end of *Molloy*, "It was not midnight. It was not raining," or when the narrator of *How It Is* admits at the end that he has been alone all along. And indeed, Moran is himself a private detective—Beckett was a keen reader of French *série noire* crime fiction. The novel form, even at its most aesthetically attenuated, cannot deny its roots in the vulgar—thank goodness. Recall in *Ulysses* the toe-curlingly saccharine appearance of little Rudi, Leopold and Molly's lost child. Joyce would say he intended the schmaltz; really?

EGI: When Hedwig Schwall in her recent interview notes the echoes of W. B. Yeats in the opening of *The Infinities*, you respond that Yeats "is one of my great influences! Nobody ever picks up on that, for some reason. He is a wonderful poet, the greatest of the twentieth century, without doubt." I concur but find many younger academics who would not agree because Yeats was right of center, like other modernists—Eliot, Pound, et al.—in the cultural politics of his time. Should poets be ignored because of their politics?

JB: This question hardly merits a response. I wonder where Sophocles stood on the question of democracy, or Goethe on women's rights. To misquote

Eliot, the man who suffers and the artist who creates are entirely separate beings. Philip Larkin, by all accounts a repellent person—I'm not so sure of it: he loved to hide his true self inside his jokes—is the poet who, in "Cut Grass," wrote one of the most nearly perfect lyrics in the language. The many younger academics you speak of should bethink themselves.

John Cusatis: While reading Emerson's essay on Goethe, the title character of *Mrs. Osmond* is distracted by a menacing thought: "What might have been had her aunt not lighted upon her that day and on the spot proposed to carry her off to Europe and to a new and infinitely richer life than she could ever have realized in Albany?" Another time she muses, "Had she refused Aunt Lydia's handsome invitation . . . and stayed in Albany, what would have become of her?" Can you recall any such pivotal moments in your own early life in which you either embraced or rejected an opportunity that later caused you to ask, "What might have been?" or "What would have become of me?"

JB: I don't mean to be either evasive or facetious when I say that I face such moments a myriad times a day. This holds not only in my life, but in my work, or especially in my work. As Martin Amis wisely observed—I hope I am quoting him accurately—any page of prose is the result of a thousand wrong decisions, though for my part I suspect a thousand is a rather a conservative figure. Like Kafka, I write in "deepest darkness"; I am a Kafkaesque old mole, endlessly shoring up the crumbling walls of my lair and sending the odd report of underground matters up into the light, with the greatest trepidation.

JC: In interviews, you have expressed your bitterness regarding the oppression, hypocrisy, and corruption within the Roman Catholic Church. Are there, however, ways in which your Catholic upbringing influenced you in positive ways that may continue to inform your fiction? For example, the garden seems to be a recurring symbol, weighted with biblical significance, and an intense reverence for natural creation pervades many of your novels. Can these or other tendencies be rooted in your religious upbringing?

JB: Yes, of course, Catholicism had a profound influence on me. If nothing else, it gave me an acute awareness of the tragic aspect of life and of the importance of ritual. I do not make, or try not to make, the mistake of confusing religion with the Church. As Nietzsche remarked, there was only one Christian, and he died on the cross. But there is no doubt that the Church was a blight on Ireland for decades, wielding absolute power, and for the most part abusing it. I cannot forgive the Church authorities for its sins, or the secular powers which allowed it to wreak so much havoc in so many lives. Yet I am at one with my friend the philosopher John Gray, who abjures the fundamentalist atheists and suggest that religion is a poetic interpretation of life and to be valued as such.

JC: In his memoir *Chronicles*, the singer-songwriter Bob Dylan recalls his early days in New York City when he began a regimen of self-education in his quest for self-definition, reading voraciously, visiting libraries and museums, and reveling in the discovery of new artists and thinkers, whose ideas and aesthetics eventually found their way into his songs. Your work reveals the extensive depth and breadth of your own reading and your erudition in so many fields. As an autodidact yourself, can you describe your early educational journey, and were there any artists or thinkers whose work was particularly significant in helping to pave the way?

JB: That would be a very large undertaking—I have no intention of writing a chronicle of my life. Of course, I read voraciously—by the way, have you noticed that reading seems to be the only thing these days that is referred to as being done "voraciously"?—went to galleries, to the theatre and concerts, etcetera. All the things an autodidact does. I read the other day that critics often make the point that I pack my work with erudite references as a way of making up for the fact that I didn't go to university. I wonder if the same critics have ever looked at the work of Beckett, the greatest scholar among the moderns? And what about Stephen Dedalus's walk along Sandymount strand in *Ulysses*—has there ever been a more shameless parade of erudition? As you see, I am sensitive on this point. The sensitivity is due not to the fact that I lack a university education—a thing I regret, flickeringly— but to the assumption that I, therefore, have no right to ground my work in the great tradition of European culture. The fact is, I have a voracious curiosity about the world and ideas. Indeed, my infection by the bug of ideation is probably one of the things that damages my work—certainly *Doctor Copernicus* and *Kepler* suffer from the bacillus of the idea . . .

JC: Critics consistently praise the poetic beauty of your prose: A chapter in *Mrs. Osmond* opens, "The day had indeed cooled somewhat. The sunlit mist in the valley had softened from glitter to glow, and even the crickets seemed less desperate in the flinging out of their nets of scraped and numbingly vibrant song." Your rhythmic arrangement of words, enhanced by internal rhyme, assonance, consonance, and alliteration, could easily be set in stanzas. What poets have helped you, consciously or unconsciously, to craft sentences with such measured poetic precision and musicality, and, for you, what are the touchstones of great poetry?

JB: I began with Keats, perhaps inadvisedly, then went on to Yeats, Rilke, Bradstreet, Wallace Stevens, Elizabeth Bishop . . . The list is very long. John McGahern used to say that there is verse and there is prose, and then there is poetry, which can be manifest in either medium. Poetry is an intensification of feeling and of concentration, to the point that the object considered by the poet achieves a state of transcendent self-awareness. To be in touch with poetry is to be intensely aware of what it is to be alive on this earth and of the life of the earth itself.

JC: Your novel *Mrs. Osmond* offers, to borrow a phrase from an old Miller Lite commercial, "everything you ever wanted" in a Henry James novel, "and less." Without overly assimilating James's sometimes cumbersome syntax and lofty diction, you capture his style in a way that allows your novel to pick up seamlessly where his leaves off. You adopt some of his more salient traits, such as setting off sentences between hyphens, and some of his subtler techniques, such as attention to detail, yet you never manage to sound as if you are parodying James. Was this a risk you consciously avoided?

JB: One stumbles into these things, hoping for the best, expecting the second-best. Looking back, I feel I had no real doubts that I could write the book, although I probably underestimated the labor it would require. It will seem odd when I say it, but I don't feel that *I* wrote the book—but now that I think of it, I don't feel that *I* wrote any of my books. When I finish work for the day and stand up from my desk, "John Banville" ceases to exist, and John Banville takes over. It's an odd business, this state of not-being-there-ness out of which art is made.

JC: *The Book of Evidence* calls to mind Albert Camus's *The Stranger*, and the plan Isabel Osmond arranges for "two condemned souls," her husband and his mistress, Madame Merle, to be reunited and "torment each other" in a kind of hell, as her sister-in-law describes it, parallels the situation of Jean-Paul Sartre's

No Exit. In addition, several of your characters marvel at the strangeness of what Heidegger called *dasein*, "being there," or as Freddie Montgomery contemplates, the "oddness" of being *anywhere*. Freddie also comments on mankind's tendency to be directed by others: "the puppet show twitching that passes for consciousness." What have you gleaned from the existentialists?

JB: Frankly, as far as my own life and thinking are concerned, I was there before the existentialists. As a child I felt acutely the strangeness of mere existence and found the world always baffling, terrifying, and inexhaustibly beautiful. To read Kierkegaard, Heidegger, Sartre, etcetera, was to encounter the familiar. Then I discovered Nietzsche, and everything I had ever thought and felt was confirmed. Mind you, when it comes to women, which it so frequently does, or used to do, I am no Nietzschean.

JC: In *Birchwood*, you write, "The exotic, once experienced, becomes commonplace, that is a great drawback in this world. One touches the gold and it turns to dross." Forty years later, you write in *Time Pieces*, "The process of growing up is, sadly, a process of turning the mysterious into the mundane. We cease to be amazed by things." How have you managed to remain amazed and to what extent is art an antidote to man's blindness to mystery? Do you often find yourself saying, like Freddie Montgomery, "What a surprise the familiar always is"?

JB: Yes, the familiar is always unfamiliar, the ordinary extraordinary. Thank God that, as a writer, I've never lost the childish sense of wonderment before the spectacle of the mundane world. I look outside just now and see that it's raining—rain!—swift, silvery, life-giving water, falling out of the sky! It's one of the world's wonders, though all we ever do is complain about it. And the prolixity of the whole thing, the mad abundance: clouds and worms, and all the rest in between! Oh dear, it's a sad pass when an interviewee resorts to exclamation marks.

JC: On a related note, Isabel Osmond, you write, is "hardly conscious of what she is about." Many of your characters are unclear regarding why they are doing things. How great an influence do you feel the unconscious mind plays in both art and daily life? Do you believe, as Nietzsche writes in *Human, All Too Human*, that "Our destiny commands us, even when we do not know what it is; it is the future which gives the rule to our present"?

JB: More and more I believe it's out of the things we *don't* know that we make art. And although I hesitate to offer the faintest protest against Nietzsche, I think it's the past, rather than the future, that compels us. All decisions are decisions made in retrospect: when they were made, they weren't decisions, but merely aspects of the drift which is life. The past is the golden mountain, ever growing higher, on which we perch, looking all about in wonderment.

JC: Your work often embodies the oppositions that inform it in closely related characters, often siblings, sometimes twins. *Doctor Copernicus*, for example, since we are talking about Nietzsche, captures the dichotomy, which that philosopher introduces in *The Birth of Tragedy*, between the Dionysian and the Apollonian, suggested by Andreas and Nicolas Copernicus, respectively. Nietzsche proposes that these two opposing aspects are necessary to produce great art. How have you managed to balance the Dionysian and the Apollonian sides of yourself to continue to produce such vital, abiding works of art?

JB: Yes, I believe it's the mark of Nietzsche's greatness to have fixed on that opposition between, and frequent mingling of, those two forces as the essence of human life and action. I think all artists, in work no less than in life, are faced with the task of balancing between the rational and the instinctive. I used, when young, to think it was all a matter of the mind, but now I know it's the imagination that is the true driving force.

JC: You have a strong affinity for nineteenth-century artists. You offer explicit and implicit nods to the Transcendentalists, Emerson and Thoreau, in your work. The narrator of *The Sea* seems to speak for many of your characters when he understatedly utters in response to discerning the extraordinary in the ordinary: "Honestly, this world." What can the twenty-first century learn from the voices of the nineteenth?

JB: Emerson and Thoreau are remarkably apposite to the times we are living through. The former's celebration of America and its potential—which endures even still—to be a shining city on the hill, and the latter's emphasis on the importance for human life of the natural world, should be attended to very carefully. Of course, the world is always cruel, always violent. I dwell frequently these days on those lovely, melancholy lines from one of Shakespeare's sonnets:

How with this rage shall beauty hold a plea,
Whose action is no stronger than a flower?

JC: In *Time Pieces* you cite Wordsworth's paradoxical line, "The Child is father of the Man." Looking back on your life thus far, what aspects of your childhood seem particularly prophetic regarding the man—and the artist— you have become?

JB: Everything is there in childhood, and remains there, perfectly preserved, the food for future art. Didn't Baudelaire say something to the effect that genius consists in the ability to summon childhood at will? Of course, genius here is used in its old form, as meaning one's spirit, one's daemon. As a boy I had a keen eye for what used to be called Nature—in those days often still spelled, rhapsodically, with a capital *N*—and now is known as the environment. I never felt, as Wordsworth sighed, that the world is too much with us; I couldn't get enough of it. There was a certain tree, standing in the center of a field near where I lived then, as a boy, a chestnut tree, solitary, ruminative, a hummer in summer and a groaner in wintertime. I recall it as I would recall a loved one lost. Does this make me seem embarrassingly Keatsian? Well, so be it: as Christopher Ricks has ingeniously pointed out, embarrassment is a key component of Keats's poetry. I would go further and say it's the aim of all art. The artist brings such an intensity of concentration to bear on the objects of his scrutiny that the poor objects, which never expected to be thus singled out, become self-conscious to the point of embarrassment. They blush. And this, I contend, is the artist's task: to make the world blush in the awareness of itself. This I have known since childhood, that childhood the second instalment of which I shall be embarking upon any day now.

Index

Aer Lingus, 40, 75, 186
Allied Irish Banks Prize, 8
Allingham, Margery, 48
Amis, Martin, 200
Auden, W. H., 30, 38, 55, 73, 116, 117
Austen, Jane, 9, 105

Bach, Johann Sebastian, 56
Bakhtin, Mikhail, 29
Banville, Agnes (mother), 31, 36, 38, 40,
    183
Banville, Janet (wife), 28, 42, 58, 60, 71,
    72, 139, 177, 191–92
Banville, John: admiration for America,
    131, 198, 204; aging, 30, 54, 119,
    137; aims as an artist, iv, 5, 18, 22,
    24, 32, 38, 43, 55, 59, 60–61,
    64–65, 66–68, 78–79, 83, 84–85,
    99, 102, 121, 158–59, 161, 162–64,
    187–88, 191, 192, 205; allure of
    violence on television, 149;
    ancient Greeks, 56, 78, 93; anxiety
    before publication, 35, 110,
    195–96; anxiety in between
    novels, 4, 30, 195–96; arrogance,
    xii, 40, 47, 50, 196; art as celebra-
    tion, 60–61, 67, 83, 84, 121, 161; art
    as validation of reality, 26, 38–39,
    70–71, 153; aspiring for artistic
    perfection, ix, 118, 132, 159–60,
    195–96; attachment to Ireland, xi,
    7, 27, 28, 67, 77, 102–3, 104–5,
    134–35, 187, 197, 198; autodidacti-
    cism, 40, 152, 201; avant-garde,
101; avoidance of moral, political,
    and social commentary in his
    fiction, 30, 50, 65, 105, 150,
    162–64; avoidance of psychology
    in his fiction, 14, 43, 78, 150, 180;
    avoidance of solemnity in his
    fiction, 67, 81; beauty offsetting
    horror in the world, 18, 60–61,
    121, 173, 199, 204–5; beginnings
    and early years as a writer, 26,
    37–40, 43, 84, 109, 137–38, 153–54,
    195; benefits of technology to
    writers, 51–53, 124, 155, 164, 193,
    198; best two reviews he ever
    received, 58; *Birchwood* as Irish
    novel, 27, 28, 41; book jacket
    blurbs, 111; candid nature of
    fiction writing, 110; childhood and
    adolescence, 26, 31, 38, 120–21,
    123, 182–83, 184, 186, 188, 205; the
    cinema, 152, 197–98; clarity in his
    fiction, 101, 157; comic nature of
    his fiction, 13, 18, 42, 62, 64, 77,
    80–82, 92–96; connection
    between art and science, 5, 32, 83;
    consciousness, x, 82, 86, 102, 163;
    consciousness of death, 62,
    67–68, 82, 126, 163, 173; continuity
    among his novels, 109, 193;
    cosmic alienation, 18, 31, 60,
    67–68, 121, 136, 159, 198–99;
    creative writing programs, 151;
    cultural stagnation, 57; difficulty
    of the creative process, 13, 39, 42,

About the Editors

Photo credit Meghan Finnerty

Earl G. Ingersoll is a Distinguished Professor emeritus at the State University of New York, Brockport. Although he completed his PhD in English at the University of Wisconsin, Madison, where his training was in British and American modernism, his interests have spread into more recent literature as well as Irish and Canadian writers such as John Banville and Margaret Atwood in the twentieth century.

Photo credit Harold Senn

John Cusatis earned a PhD in English from the University of South Carolina in 2003. He is the author of *Understanding Colum McCann*, the first critical study of the Irish-born National Book Award winner, and the editor of *Post War Literature, 1945–1970* and three volumes of the *Dictionary of Literary Biography*. He teaches at the School of the Arts in Charleston, South Carolina. About the Editors

Printed in the United States
By Bookmasters